CONSTRUCTING ANTICHRIST

CONSTRUCTING ANTICHRIST

Paul, Biblical Commentary, and the

Development of Doctrine in the

Early Middle Ages

KEVIN L. HUGHES

The Catholic University of America Press
Washington, D.C.

The paper used in this publication meets the minimum requirements of American National Standards for Information Science—Permanence of Paper for Printed Library materials,
ANSI Z39.48–1984.

∞

LIBRARY OF CONGRESS CATALOGING-IN-PUBLICATION DATA
Hughes, Kevin L.
Constructing antichrist : Paul, biblical commentary, and the development
of doctrine in the early middle ages / Kevin L. Hughes.
p. cm.
Includes bibliographical references and index.
ISBN 0-8132-1415-7 (cloth : alk. paper)
1. Antichrist—History of doctrines. 2. Bible. N.T. Thessalonians, 2nd—
Commentaries—History. I. Title.
BT985.H84 2005
236—dc22
2004004192

CONTENTS

SERIES ABBREVIATIONS

CCSL   *Corpus Christianorum, Series Latina.* Turnhout: Brepols.

CCCM   *Corpus Christianorum, Continuatio Medievalis.* Turnhout: Brepols.

CSEL   *Corpus Scriptorum Ecclesiasticorum Latinorum.* Vienna:
        Hoelder-Pichler-Tempsky.

MGH   *Monumenta Germaniae Historica.* Hanover and Berlin;
        Impensis Bibliopolii Hahniani, 1826–

PL   *Patrologia Latina.* Paris: Migne.

ACKNOWLEDGMENTS

As one nears the end of a long project, especially a project about the end of the world, it is hard to resist the sense that the time to settle accounts has come. Many debts have accrued. I have been thinking about Paul and Antichrist for ten years, in one way or another, and so many people have left an impression upon some part or another of this work that I cannot imagine calling all of them to mind to thank them properly. So I will offer thanks to those to whom I owe the most obvious debts, sure that my memory has failed and some have been left out. Thanks to my colleagues at the Institute for the Advanced Study of Religion, now reborn as the Martin Marty Center, at the University of Chicago Divinity School, where I was a junior fellow for the 1995–96 academic year and wrote a substantial portion of the dissertation that was the seed of this book. Thanks, too, to my Chicago friends and colleagues, now scattered around the country, who made graduate school (of all things!) such a delightful time of life; Robert Wilson Black, Patricia Beckman, Gordon Rudy, Charles Mathewes, Sam Portaro, Richard Rosengarten, Dante Scala, and Susan Schreiner all had a hand in this project in some way or another, and I am deeply grateful.

At Villanova University, I have had the support and guidance of John Doody, Arthur Chappell, and Bernard Prusak, and I have depended upon the friendship of Thomas W. Smith, Martin Laird, William Werpehowski, and Anthony Godzieba. Thanks are due to Gregory LaNave at The Catholic University of America Press for helping me navigate the publishing world and to my copy editor, Carol Kennedy, for bringing some consistency and harmony to the book. Special thanks to Kevin Madigan, who read the entire manuscript, and to E. Ann Matter, who, in addition to reading the entire manuscript, has helped me with this project in so many ways over the years.

My deepest thanks are for my parents, Gerry and Leo, who taught me to love learning, and for my wife, Bridget. When we were just getting to know each other, Bridget inspired me to re-read the Letters of Paul, so without her inspiration, this project would never have come. But even this is petty change compared to the way she inspires me as a human being with her uncanny wisdom and keen insight. Together we are raising three daughters, Rachel, Sarah, and Elizabeth, and all together, these women in my life have kept me rooted through all the aerial flights of academe, reminding me every day that there is much more in heaven and earth than I have dreamt in my theologies. Or my histories.

In some ways, this is a book about a tradition of learning, and so I am dedicating it to my teachers, John C. Cavadini and Bernard McGinn. John was my first teacher in college theology, my perpetual scholarly resource through graduate school, a reader of my dissertation, and my constant inspiration for more than fifteen years. Bernie's mentoring has given me whatever scholarly virtues I may have, and I hope to continue learning from him to add whatever I have missed along the way.

Portions of Chapters 3, 4, and 6 have appeared as "Augustine and the Adversary: Strategies of Synthesis in Early Medieval Exegesis," *Augustinian Studies* 30:2 (1999): 221–33, and in the introduction to *Second Thessalonians: Two Early Medieval Apocalyptic Commentaries, Haimo of Auxerre, Exposition in Epistolam II ad Thessalonicneses; Thietland of Einsiedeln, In Epistolam II ad Thessalonicenses*, Steven R. Cartwright and Kevin L. Hughes, eds. TEAMS Commentary Series (Kalamazoo: Medieval Institute Press, 2001). The author gratefully acknowledges permission to reprint revised versions of these works.

THE VULGATE TEXT OF
2 THESSALONIANS

The Second Letter to the Thessalonians

Biblia sacra iuxta vulgatam versionem, 4th revised edition, edited by
Roger Gryson (Stuttgart: Deutsches Bibelgesellschaft, 1969, 1994).
Used by permission

Chapter 1

1. Paulus et Silvanus et Timotheus ecclesiae Thessalonicensium in Deo
   Patre nostro et Domino Iesu Christo
2. gratia vobis et pax a Deo Patre nostro et Domino Iesu Christo
3. gratias agere debemus Deo semper pro vobis fratres ita ut dignum
   est, quoniam supercrescit fides vestra, et abundat caritas unius-
   cuiusque omnium vestrum in invicem
4. ita ut et nos ipsi in vobis gloriemur in ecclesiis Dei, pro patientia vestra et fide in omnibus persecutionibus vestris et tribulationibus quas
   sustinetis
5. in exemplum iusti iudicii Dei, ut digni habeamini regno Dei pro quo
   et patimini
6. si tamen iustum est apud Deum retribuere tribulationem his qui vos
   tribulant
7. et vobis qui tribulamini requiem nobiscum in revelatione Domini
   Iesu de caelo cum angelis virtutis eius,
8. in flamma ignis dantis vindictam his qui non noverunt Deum et qui
   non oboediunt evangelio Domini nostri Iesu

THE VULGATE TEXT OF
2 THESSALONIANS

The Second Letter to the Thessalonians

Translated from the Latin Vulgate Text by Kevin L. Hughes

Chapter 1

1. Paul, Silvanus, and Timothy, to the Church of the Thessalonians, in God our Father and in the Lord Jesus Christ,

2. grace and peace to you from God our Father and from the Lord Jesus Christ.

3. We ought to give thanks to God at all times for you, brothers, as is fitting, since your faith grows and the love of all of you for one another abounds,

4. such that we ourselves boast in the churches of God about your patience and faith in all your persecutions and all the tribulations you have endured

5. as an example of the just judgment of God, that you may be worthy of the kingdom of God for which you suffer.

6. Since it is just with God to return suffering to those who make you suffer

7. and to return to you who are suffering peace with us at the revelation of the Lord Jesus, coming from heaven with the angels of his power.

8. He will bring judgment on those who do not know God and who are not obedient to the gospel of our Lord Jesus.

9. qui poenas dabunt in interitu aeternas a facie Domini et a gloria virtutis eius

10. cum venerit glorificari in sanctis suis, et admirabilis fieri in omnibus qui crediderunt quia creditum est testimonium nostrum super vos in die illo.

11. in quo etiam oramus semper pro vobis, ut dignetur vos vocatione sua Deus, et impleat omnem voluntatem bonitatis et opus fidei in virtute

12. ut clarificetur nomen Domini nostri Iesu Christi in vobis, et vos in illo secundum gratiam Dei nostri et Domini Iesu Christi

Chapter 2

1. Rogamus autem vos fratres, per adventum Domini nostri Iesu Christi et nostrae congregationis in ipsum

2. ut non cito moveamini a sensu, neque terreamini neque per spiritum, neque per sermonem, neque per epistulam tamquam per nos, quasi instet dies Domini

3. ne quis vos seducat ullo modo, quoniam nisi venerit discessio primum, et revelatus fuerit homo peccati, filius perditionis

4. qui adversatur et extollitur supra omne quod dicitur Deus aut quod colitur ita ut in templo Dei sedeat, ostendens se quia sit Deus

5. non retinetis quod cum adhuc essem apud vos haec dicebam vobis

6. et nunc quid detineat scitis, ut revelatur in suo tempore

7. nam mysterium iam operatur iniquitatis, tantum ut qui tenet nunc teneat[1] donec de medio fiat

---

1. Variant text, found in at least six Vulgate MSS (ARKC7M). See note 2 below.

9. They will give satisfaction in eternal destruction, away from the face of God and from the glory of his power.

10. When he will have come to be glorified in his saints and to be honored among all those who have believed. Since our testimony to you was believed on that day,

11. for this reason we always pray for you, that God may find you worthy of his calling and complete in power every good resolve and work of faith,

12. that the Name of our Lord Jesus Christ may shine brightly in you, and you in him by the grace of our God and the Lord Jesus Christ.

Chapter 2

1. And so we implore you, brothers, as to the coming of our Lord Jesus Christ and of our gathering into him,

2. that you be not easily moved from your senses nor be frightened, either by spirit or by word or letter as if from us, as if the Day of the Lord approaches.

3. Let no one persuade you in any way, unless the desertion will have come first and the Man of Sin, the Son of Perdition will have been revealed,

4. the one who is opposed to and exalted above everything which is called God or which is worshipped, so that he may sit in the temple of God, displaying himself as if he were God.

5. Do you not remember that I told you these things while I was still there with you?

6. So now you know what holds him, that he may be revealed in his own time.

7. For now the mystery of iniquity is already at work, such that the one who holds now may hold until he be taken from the midst.[2]

---

2. The 1969 Stuttgart Edition of the Vulgate reads, *"tantum ut qui tenet nunc donec de medio fiat,"* or *"*such that until the one who now holds is taken from the midst." I have chosen to translate the verse as it appears in **D** (see p. xx) and in six Vulgate manuscripts: *"tantum ut qui nunc tenet teneat donec de medio fiat."* This is the version found in most of the commentaries on 2 Thessalonians.

8. et tunc revelabitur ille iniquus, quem Dominus Iesus interficiet spiritu oris sui et destruet inlustratione adventus sui,

9. eum cuius adventus secundum operationem Satanae in omni virtute et signis et prodigiis mendacibus

10. et in omni seductione iniquitatis his qui pereunt, eo quod caritatem veritatis non receperunt ut salvi fierunt

11. ideo mittit illis Deus operationem erroris, ut credant mendacio

12. ut iudicentur omnes qui non crediderunt veritati, sed consenserunt iniquitati

13. nos autem debemus gratias agere Deo semper pro vobis fratres dilecti a Deo, quod elegerit nos Deus primitias in salutem, in sanctificatione Spiritus et fide veritatis

14. ad quod et vocavit vos per evangelium nostrum in adquisitionem gloriae Domini nostri Iesu Christi

15. itaque fratres state et teneti traditiones quas didicistis, sive per sermonem, sive per epistulam nostram

16. ipse autem Dominus noster Iesus Christus et Deus et Pater noster, qui dilexit nos et dedit consolationem aeternam et spem bonam in gratia

17. exhortetur corda vestra et confirmet in omni opere et sermone bono

Chapter 3

1. De cetero fratres orate pro nobis, ut sermo Domini currat et clarificetur siceut et apud vos

2. et ut liberemur ab inportunis et malis hominibus, non enim omnium est fides

3. fidelis autem Dominus est, qui confirmabit vos et custodiet a malo

4. confidimus autem de vobis in Domino, quoniam quae praecipimus et facitis et facietis

5. Dominus autem dirigat corda vestra in caritate Dei et patientia Christi

6. denuntiamus autem vobis fratres in nomine Domini Iesu Christi, ut subtrahatis vos ab omni fratre ambulante inordinate, et non secundum traditionem quam acceperunt a nobis

7. ipsi enim scitis quemadmodum oporteat imitari nos, quoniam non inquieti fuimus inter vos

8. Then that iniquitous one will be revealed, whom the Lord Jesus will kill with the breath of his mouth. With the brilliance of his coming, he will destroy

9. him whose coming is by the work of Satan, in all power and with lying signs and prodigies,

10. and with every seduction of iniquity for those who are perishing because they have not accepted the love of truth that they may be saved.

11. So God sent them a work of error that they may believe in the lie

12. such that all those who have not believed in the truth but have consented to iniquity may be judged.

13. But we are bound always to give thanks for you, brothers beloved by God, because God will have chosen us, the first-fruits, for salvation in the sanctification of the Spirit and by faith in the truth.

14. He has called you by our Gospel to acquire the glory of our Lord Jesus Christ.

15. Therefore, brothers, stand fast and grasp firmly the traditions we have taught, whether by the word of our mouths or by our letter.

16. May our Lord Jesus Christ himself and our God and Father, who has loved us and has given us eternal consolation and good hope in grace,

17. stir and strengthen your hearts in every good word and work.

Chapter 3

1. As for the rest, brothers, pray for us, that the word of the Lord may spread and be glorified just as it is among you,

2. and that we may be freed from cruel and evil people, for not all have faith.

3. But God is faithful. He will strengthen you and protect you from evil.

4. We have confidence in the Lord concerning you, since you are doing and will continue to do what we command.

5. May the Lord direct your hearts in the love of God and in the patience of Christ.

6. We direct you, brothers, in the name of our Lord Jesus Christ, to remove yourselves from every brother walking on the wrong path and not according to the tradition that they have received from us.

7. You yourselves know how it is proper that we be imitated, since we were not restless among you,

8. neque gratis panem manducavimus ab aliquo, sed in labore et fatigatione nocte et die operantes ne quem vestrum gravaremus

9. non quasi non habuerimus potestatem, sed ut nosmet ipsos formam daremus vobis ad imitandum nos

10. nam et cum essemus apud vos hoc denuntiabamus vobis, quoniam si quies non vult operari nec manducet

11. audimus enim inter vos quosdam ambulare inquiete nihil operantes sed curiose agentes

12. his autem qui eiusmodi sunt denuntiamus et obsecramus in Domino Iesu Christo, ut cum silentio operantes suum panem manducent

13. vos autem fratres nolite deficere benefacientes

14. quod si quis non oboedit verbo nostro per epistulam hunc notate et non commisceamini cum illo ut confundatur

15. et nolite quasi inimicum existimare, sed corripite ut fratrem

16. ipse autem Dominus pacis det vobis pacem sempiternam in omni loco Dominus cum omnibus vobis

17. salutatio mea manu Pauli, quod est signum in omni epistula ita scribo

18. gratia Domini nostri Iesu Christi cum omnibus vobis amen

8. nor did we eat anyone's bread for free, but working day and night in labor and toil, lest we burden any of you.

9. Not as if we do not have the power, but that we may give ourselves as a model for you to imitate.

10. For when we were with you, we instructed you that if someone does not want to work, he should not eat.

11. But we hear that there are some among you who walk around restlessly, doing nothing but acting in mischief.

12. To these people we instruct and command you, in our Lord Jesus Christ to do your work in silence and earn your own bread.

13. Brothers, never tire of doing good.

14. If someone does not obey our word in this letter, make a note of it and do not associate with him, that he may be ashamed.

15. But do not treat him as an enemy, but correct him as a brother.

16. May the Lord of Peace himself give you peace all the time in every place. The Lord be with all of you.

17. This greeting is in my hand, the hand of Paul, which is the seal on every letter I write.

18. The grace of our Lord Jesus Christ be with all of you. Amen.

Comments on the Text

Since my work is focused upon exegesis in the Late Antique and Medieval Latin West, I have given and translated the Latin Vulgate edition, the "standard edition" upon which many post-Carolingian commentaries rely. Of course, the Stuttgart edition of the Vulgate shows that even this "standard" can only be said to be a compendium of "vulgates" from the Medieval period, and Hermann Josef Frede's research in the Beuron *Vetus Latina* project points to even more diversity in non-Vulgate versions that are copied and distributed at least until the ninth century.

Scholars have attempted to trace evidence of the earliest "urtext" of a Latin translation of Paul, and they believe it to date from the second century, probably in Italy. Frede's *Vetus Latina* edition identifies five major subsequent textual traditions: **X, K, D, I,** and **V** (Vulgate), several of which may be revisions of this initial translation.

X is the "senior text" of the Pauline corpus, not in evidence as a complete manuscript but found in the works of Tertullian and Victorinus of Pettau. This translation of 2 Thessalonians is the most at odds with the later Vulgate and does not have much of a history in the medieval commentary tradition.

K is a text of North African provenance, appearing in the works of Cyprian and African pseudo-Cyprianic literature, which seems to date from ca. 250 to the end of the third century, with a later Italian version appearing in the fourth or fifth century. In a few of the fourth-century manuscripts (e.g., pseudo-Cyprian), this text is mixed and "europeanized," but not enough to create a subtype. We have very few citations of 2 Thessalonians from this text, although its version of 1 and 2 Timothy is quite influential.

D is found in bilingual editions of the Pauline corpus in manuscripts from the fifth and ninth centuries, but its Latin-only edition spread more widely throughout the West. The 2 Thessalonians text appears in the works of Tyconius, and, through him, in Augustine. For example, it is Tyconius who uses the term "Refuga" in 2 Th 2:3, which Augustine picks up in *City of God* 20.19. Variations on 2 Th 2:17 include "quod detinet," not "qui tenet"; "facinoris," not "iniquitatis"; "nunc tenet teneat."

I is the Latin text of Ambrosiaster, but it may be dated earlier to the time of Novatian, Cyprian's European contemporary in the third century. It has three subtypes, **J, A,** and **M.** Its vocabulary and style are superior to **K** and **D.** Its subtype **J** is found in Ambrose, Jerome, Rufinus, Pelagius, Augustine, and Cassiodorus, and Tyconius as well, and its subtype **A** is used by Hesychius in his letter to Augustine. Its variants include both "Defectio" and "Apostasia" for 2 Th 2:3, "in templum" for "in templo" in 2 Th 2:4, "quoadusque" in 2 Th 2:7. Jerome's Letter 121 uses this version, while most of his other incidental citations come from **V.**

V is a revision of an Old Latin text based upon the Greek from the latter part of the fourth century. The Greek revisions are based upon an Alexandrian Greek text. The text is rarely found "pure," and still carries bits and pieces of other translations. It often contains admixtures of **D** and **I.** One such mixed text is distinctive enough to claim its own subtype, **S,** of Spanish provenance. It uses what becomes the standard term, "Discessio," for 2 Th 2:3.

According to Frede's research, the verse most often cited or alluded to in patristic literature (including Bede and Isidore) is 2 Th 2:3, discussing the nature of the "falling away" or "rebellion." Fittingly enough, this also seems to be one of the greatest variants in the text. As the reader will note, the choices made on this verse often affect the interpretation of the basic sense of the letter. For example, Tyconius and Augustine's use of the **D** text at this point, with *refuga* as opposed to *apostasia* or *defectio* (**I, J, A**), or *discessio* (**V**), allows them to apply the verse to Antichrist and not to some event that precedes Antichrist (see Chapter Three). Similarly, Tyconius's and Augustine's use of **I**'s accusative *(in templum)* instead of ablative of place where *(in templo,* **V**) in 2 Th 2:4 is important to the spiritual reading of the temple as the social body of Antichrist. These variants show that there was no single authoritative Latin text of 2 Thessalonians throughout the patristic era, and the variants themselves facilitate the development of a spiritual reading of the text. This is not to say that spiritual or alternative readings of the text are "mistakes" or even that they are accidental. Augustine, for example, invokes the **I** text of 2:4 precisely *as an alternative reading.* In this case, the openness of the text permitted the openness of interpretation.

CONSTRUCTING ANTICHRIST

CHAPTER I

INTRODUCTION

Constructing Antichrist

According to the grace of God given to me, like a wise master

builder I laid the foundation, and another is building upon it.

1 Corinthians 3:10

History makes strange bedfellows. This book suggests that two figures—one historical and one mythical, one who stands at the beginning of Christianity and the other who stands at its imagined end—are intimately related in the history of theology. It assumes, rather than argues, that Antichrist has a history, that the figure of Antichrist does not spring fully formed from the pages of Scripture. Rather, he is a figure whose profile and significance took shape over nearly a millennium of reflection on a variety of hints and clues scattered throughout the Scriptures and traditions of Christian faith. Some clues are more significant than others; in this case, the portrait of Antichrist is tied in a particularly vital way to the man medieval Christians knew simply as "the Apostle"—St. Paul of Tarsus.

What does Paul have to do with Antichrist? In the study that follows, I argue that the western medieval doctrines of Antichrist and the Last Days cannot be understood rightly apart from the development of Latin traditions of New Testament exegesis. 2 Thessaloni-

1

ans—a brief but important Pauline text in New Testament apocalyptic literature—was a center of speculation and debate about matters apocalyptic in the early Church. Thus, the way one decides to interpret Paul shapes the way one understands Antichrist. Will the fall of Rome signal the End of Time? Is Antichrist to be a single individual in the future, or is it better to understand it in the spiritual sense, "the Body of Antichrist" (evil people) within the "Body of Christ" (the Church) right now? Medieval Christians wrestled with these questions by grappling both with 2 Thessalonians itself and with the traditions of interpretation that preceded them. By the twelfth century, the tradition of reflection distilled from the many and various early interpretations a synthetic understanding of Antichrist and the End as both present and to come, both historical and spiritual. In this book, I follow the process of distillation as it occurs through the formal genre of commentary. Using the tools of scriptural commentary, medieval scholars aimed to correlate the questions they brought to the text with the many possible senses of the text and the words of the fathers *on* the text and synthesize them into one intelligible whole. Commentaries on 2 Thessalonians, then, provided the "architecture" for the developing doctrine of Antichrist.

The Context and the Sense of Apocalyptic Thought

But who and what is Antichrist? This mythical figure emerges out of the matrix of thought we call *apocalyptic eschatology*, which Ernst Käsemann famously called the "mother of all Christian theology." Antichrist is "the Adversary," the greatest Christian antihero, the final opponent of Christ, doomed, before he even begins, to failure at the apocalyptic judgment seat. But he is only one figure in a host of adversaries imagined in apocalyptic literature. To get a sense for who he is particularly, we will have to explore the matrix of thought from which he emerges.

There is considerable "terminological anarchy" when it comes to modern scholarly use of *eschatology, apocalypticism, millennialism,* and *chiliasm,* so I shall clarify how I use these terms. (See Figure 1 below.) *Eschatology* is a general term referring to theological reflection upon history or time in light of its end.[1] By definition, then, all Christian (or at least ancient and medieval Christian) reflections on history are eschatological in some sense, whether they emphasize the imminence of the end and the events leading up to it or not. *Apocalyptic* eschatology is a subtype of that theological reflection, which has emerged from a genre of texts in biblical and apocryphal literature called "apocalypses."

TERMS. *The terms move from general to specific, left to right, and are not exclusive of other subtypes under each heading.*

The apocalypse as a genre appears in Hellenistic Judaism after ca. 250 B.C.E. and carries over into Christian thought. John Collins, together with other biblical scholars, has defined the genre as follows:

Apocalypse is a genre of revelatory literature with a narrative framework in which revelation is mediated by an otherworldly being to a human recipient, disclosing a transcendent reality which is both *temporal,* insofar as it envisages eschatological salvation, and *spatial* insofar as it involves another, supernatural world.[2]

Within the apocalypse genre, we can discern two general types. One type emphasizes the "spatial" dimension over the "temporal," often portraying an "otherworldly journey" into heaven. This type will not

1. Note that eschatological reflection may address the history or life of the individual person in light of his or her end, and thus be a reflection on death and "the afterlife." The concerns addressed by 2 Thessalonians, and indeed, most examples of apocalyptic eschatology, are more social, political, and historical, and so these elements will be emphasized throughout my discussion.

2. John J. Collins, *The Apocalyptic Imagination* (New York: Crossroad, 1989), 4.

4 / CONSTRUCTING ANTICHRIST

concern us here. The other type emphasizes the "temporal," or historical, aspect more than the "spatial." This historical type generally portrays a fixed course of events determined by God in time. These events generally fit a threefold pattern of "Crisis-Judgment-Reward," and their imminent approach can usually be discerned in the historical, political, and cosmological events of the present through the revealed wisdom offered in a "sacred book." *Apocalyptic eschatology* is the set of ideas, including determinism, Crisis-Judgment-Reward, and the like, generated within and out of the "temporal" type of apocalypse. *Apocalypticism* refers more generally to a culture or worldview influenced significantly by an apocalyptic eschatology.

Apocalyptic eschatology's deterministic view of history aims to construe a present situation as either good or evil in light of the final Judgment. This moral interpretation of the present is always a component of apocalyptic texts, and often takes the shape of a call to believers to reaffirm their commitment to God's will.[3] Thus, although the course of history is radically determined, the reader/hearer is free to choose in the present between Good and Evil, between God and God's enemies. Her choice is made all the more urgent by the sense of imminence conveyed in the text. For some apocalypses, the imminence of the end is literal, perhaps predicted to the day and year and heralded by clear signs. Other apocalyptic writings warn explicitly against prediction—"Keep awake, therefore, for you do not know on what day your Lord is coming" (Mt 24:42). But even without this "literal" imminence, apocalyptic eschatology possesses what Bernard McGinn has called "psychological imminence," the sense that present decisions have ultimate significance—hence, "Keep awake!" The reader's choices are perceived always in the light of coming judgment.[4] In fact, refusing to predict the end can serve to heighten or sustain apocalyptic eschatology, since one does not

3. Bernard McGinn, "John's Apocalypse and the Apocalyptic Mentality," in *The Apocalypse in the Middle Ages,* ed. Richard K. Emmerson and Bernard McGinn (Ithaca, N.Y.: Cornell University Press, 1992), 8ff.

4. McGinn, "John's Apocalypse," 13.

know the day or the hour. It is precisely this sort of non-predictive apocalypticism that is a consistent constitutive element of the medieval imagination.[5]

Millennialism, millenarianism, and chiliasm all refer to a particular subtype of apocalyptic eschatology, based for Christian texts in a reading Revelations 21, which asserts that time and history will be consummated in a terrestrial "1,000-year reign" of Christ or his representatives. Very often, this millennium is believed to be imminent, as in the famous case of the Spiritual Franciscans in the fourteenth century,[6] but a significant medieval millennialist tradition is not.[7] Many Christian intellectuals rejected millennialism because of its earthy description of millennial bliss, believing that God's rewards are richer and deeper than earthly abundance. But some of these retained an essentially apocalyptic eschatology, as we will see in the case of Jerome. None of these terms—*millennialism, millenarianism, chiliasm, apocalypticism*—communicates in itself a sense of temporally imminent expectation; rather they all refer only to the formal structure of the doctrine or narrative. *Imminence* is best used adjectivally—*imminent apocalypticism*, or *imminent millennialism*—since there are numerous non-imminent cases that still share in the basic structural and symbolic elements of apocalyptic eschatology.[8]

Apocalyptic eschatology overflows with imaginative images of

5. McGinn, "The End of the World and the Beginning of Christendom," in *Apocalypse Theory and the Ends of the World,* ed. Malcolm Bull (London: Blackwell Publishers, 1995), passim.

6. Bernard McGinn, *Apocalyptic Spirituality* (Mahwah: Paulist Press, 1979), 149–82; David Burr, *Olivi's Peaceable Kingdom: A Reading of the Apocalypse Commentary* (Philadelphia: University of Pennsylvania Press, 1993).

7. See Robert E. Lerner, "The Refreshment of the Saints: The Time after Antichrist as a Station for Earthly Progress in Medieval Thought," *Traditio* 32 (1976): 97–144, and "Millennialism," in *Encyclopedia of Apocalypticism,* vol. 2, ed. John J. Collins, Bernard McGinn, and Stephen J. Stein (New York: Continuum Press, 1998), 326–60. See also my discussion of Adso in Chapter 4, pp. 167–77.

8. Many scholars use *apocalyptic* or *apocalypticism* to denote texts or ideas that bear a sense of historical imminence (see the influential essay of Richard A. Landes, "Lest the Millennium Be Fulfilled: Apocalyptic Expectations and the Pattern

cosmological cataclysms and violent combat between supernatural characters. Some of these characters are "hyperreal" beasts that stretch the imagination beyond visual composition. (It is difficult to picture, for example, a "flying eagle" with "six wings" and "full of eyes all around and inside" [Rv 4:7–8].) Other characters, however, are anthropomorphic and, indeed, "human, all too human." Antichrist, Christ's final Adversary, is usually portrayed in this way.[9] Indeed, it is Antichrist's human identity that makes him theologically interesting and existentially compelling. Although he possesses supernatural powers and conspires with the Satan (supernatural Evil itself), Antichrist represents the consummation of all *human* evil. The development of the tradition is careful to preserve his humanity from the blasphemous notion that he is the incarnation of the Devil. He is the personification of human resistance to the work and person of Christ. To understand him is to understand the mystery of human evil itself.[10]

Of course, this study begins from the assumption that Antichrist is not so easily understood, and neither is human evil. Antichrist is a symbol that "gives rise to thought"[11] along several different vectors, and his meaning therefore is not exhausted in any one interpreta-

---

of Western Chronography, 100–800 CE," in *The Use and Abuse of Eschatology in the Middle Ages,* Medievalia Lovaniensia, Series 1, Studia 15, ed. Werner Verbeke, Daniel Verhelst, and Andries Welkenhuysen (Leuven: Leuven University Press, 1988), 137–211; and Paula Fredriksen, "Apocalypse and Redemption: From John of Patmos to Augustine of Hippo," *Vigiliae Christianae* 45:2 (1991): 151–83.) Others have followed the more structural definition emerging out of current biblical research (McGinn, *Apocalyptic Spirituality;* Collins, *Apocalyptic Imagination;* Richard K. Emmerson, *Antichrist in the Middle Ages* (Seattle: University of Washington Press, 1981).

9. See Bernard McGinn, *Antichrist: Two Thousand Years of the Human Fascination with Evil,* 2nd ed. (New York: Columbia University Press, 1999), 68–70, 72–73, 103–7, for discussion of images and physical descriptions of Antichrist in the patristic and medieval periods.

10. For a more developed discussion of Antichrist's humanity and why it is theologically significant, see the introduction of McGinn, *Antichrist,* 1–7.

11. Paul Ricoeur, *The Symbolism of Evil,* trans. Emerson Buchanan (Boston: Beacon Press, 1969), 348.

tion. He emerges from the development of reflection on several very different canonical and noncanonical sources, of which 2 Thessalonians is only one. The history of Antichrist is an index to the broad variety of Christian readings of the mystery of evil. Bernard McGinn has traced this development around two "polarities," an "external-internal" field and a "dread-deception" field.[12] The first polarity occurs as the believer reflects on his/her relationship to evil. Evil comes either *from without,* as in persecution or an external attack from an "evil empire," or *from within,* as for example in the case of heresy or rebellion from among the elect, or even from within the believer's own heart. Few in the Christian tradition would ever decide clearly for one option to the exclusion of the other; however, most emphasize one polarity more. Myths and legends of a coming evil empire that will oppose the righteous abound in the history of Christianity, and perhaps even our experience in the twentieth and twenty-first centuries can give us pause before we discount the possibility that evil does in fact come from without. And yet many of the greatest Christian thinkers in the medieval period and beyond have asserted with equal conviction that the true mystery of evil is found within our hearts.

The second polarity ponders the nature of Antichrist's evil work. In the tradition of thought about the "Man of Sin," people have conceived of him as a persecuting tyrant, often thought to be the culmination of tyrannical rule modeled in great persecuting emperors of Rome such as Nero. As the purveyor of *dread,* Antichrist is the evil emperor who will try to destroy true religion among the faithful. Like Milton's great antihero Satan, Antichrist in this strain of tradition is the great rebel warrior leading an attack on the ranks of God's army of faith.

But Antichrist is not only the rebel tyrant. From the earliest layers of tradition (and in 2 Thessalonians itself), he also is a "false Christ," a *deceiver* whose signs and wonders lure the faithful away.

12. Bernard McGinn, *Antichrist,* 4ff.

He "displays himself as if he were God" (2 Th 2:4), and even tries to
ascend into heaven from the Mount of Olives, as Christ did. The
theme of deception is present across the spectrum of the first polarity: While the legendary accounts of an external type of "false
prophet" abound, the deception theme can also be internalized.
Since Augustine, Western Christian thought has remained convinced that one of the surest proofs of human sin is our capacity to
deceive ourselves. Indeed, McGinn takes Augustine's own comment
on Antichrist, that "everyone must question his conscience whether
he be such,"[13] to be the "real meaning of the Antichrist."[14] It is this
self-critical reflection that keeps the Antichrist symbol from consign-
ment to the dusty archives of "medievalisms."

I contend that the meaning of Antichrist lies in this internal reflection and beyond. Any sufficient understanding of the power of
this daunting symbol must be able to encompass in some fashion all
four polar points on the map of human sin. Human evil is both external and internal, both in the force exerted by one over another
(dread) and in persuasion and temptation (deception). From antiquity to the twentieth-first century, actions we judge by near consensus
to be truly evil can be drawn in all their complexity upon this four-
point map. For example, the "banality of evil" described by Hannah
Arendt in *Eichmann in Jerusalem* depends on the complexity of guilt,
where the finger can be pointed at no specific point of origin, but no
"cog in the machine" like Eichmann is thereby exonerated. Is totali-
tarian evil internal or external? Is its power rooted in dread or deception? To either question, one cannot help but answer, "Both." The
history of Antichrist reflects this complexity. While strains of the
tradition of Antichrist have often supported more romantic notions
of evil, a more comprehensive understanding of the whole tradition
cannot but testify to the depth *and* the breadth, the force *and* the illu-

13. Augustine, *Homilies on I John*, 3.4, PL 34.1999. I have used John Burnaby's
translation in *Augustine: Later Works*, Library of Christian Classics (Philadelphia:
Westminster Press, 1954), 280.
14. McGinn, *Antichrist*, 5.

sion, of human evil. And thought about Antichrist has embraced all of these.

Even more, I suggest a third, temporal polarity, in which Antichrist is understood to be "present" or "to come," or to be "immanent" and "imminent." Augustine's comment quoted above suggests an understanding of Antichrist as spiritually present now in the Church and in the hearts of believers. This interior sense of presence finds great support and amplification in the thought of Gregory the Great, and thus carries great authority in the tradition. But it is chastened in both Augustine and Gregory by a living sense that the Man of Sin is still "to come." Even these two most spiritual of Antichrist's interpreters never understand his diffuse presence in the Church to exclude his future advent. While most modern interpreters of Antichrist (e.g., D. H. Lawrence, Bernard McGinn) seem to conclude that the real meaning of Antichrist is in his immanence, I would argue that an important facet of Antichrist's power in the tradition emerges from the temporal dimension of the apocalyptic perspective. It is the sense of dreaded anticipation, even in the absence of a literal or predictive imminence, that fires the believer's desire to "keep awake." It is this "sense of an ending,"[15] the awareness that "time was growing short," that gave early-medieval apocalyptic symbols their persuasive power, and this is the reason for their enduring vitality in Christian self-understanding. If Antichrist suggests a tradition of understanding human evil, it is always an evil that is "in process" and suspended in time. Evil is always already at work now, but it also threatens from the future.

The symbol of Antichrist is necessarily three-dimensional. Most early medieval thinkers would agree that Antichrist's threat is *both* internal and external, *both* of dread and of deception, and *both* immanent and imminent. Differing portraits of Antichrist derive from

15. I take the term from Frank Kermode's short but provocative book, *The Sense of an Ending: Studies in the Theory of Fiction* (New York: Oxford University Press, 1966), which gives a modern perspective on the temporal dimension in apocalyptic thought from the literary-critical perspective.

answering questions of degree along these three axes. My purpose in this study is to take a broad view of the whole map, at least inasmuch as it derives from the exegesis of 2 Thessalonians. To understand the tradition of exegesis, it will be helpful to examine first the structure and argument of the letter itself, and second the ways in which medieval thinkers read and commented upon the Bible in general and this text in particular.

2 Thessalonians: Pauline "Antichristology"

2 Thessalonians is an essential theological source for the development of the doctrine of Antichrist in the Latin West.[16] But the letter poses something of a mystery to scholars of the New Testament. 1 Thessalonians is generally considered to be the earliest of Paul's authentic letters, but contemporary scholars can't seem to come to consensus over the authenticity of 2 Thessalonians. Wilhelm Wrede offered the classic critique of its Pauline authenticity in 1903.[17] Wrede argued that the literary dependence of the second letter on the first is unmatched anywhere in the Pauline corpus, and thus not terribly characteristic of Paul. In addition, he pointed to the apparent differences in apocalyptic outlook between 1 Thessalonians 5:1–11 (with an apparent emphasis on the nearness and unpredictability of the "day of the Lord") and 2 Thessalonians 2:1–13 (with its orientation toward clear signs of the future coming) and argued that they could not credibly be maintained to have emerged from the same pen. Many contemporary Pauline scholars remain persuaded at least by Wrede's first argument.[18] When I first began

16. Horst-Dieter Rauh, *Das Bild des Antichrist im Mittelalter: Von Tyconius zum Deutschen Symbolismus* (Münster: Verlag Aschendorff, 1973), 55.

17. Wilhelm Wrede, *Die Echtheit der zweiten Thessalonischer-briefs untersucht,* Texte und Untersuchungen zur Geschichte der altchristlichen Literatur, neue Folge 9/2 (Leipzig: Hinrichs, 1903).

18. Nevertheless, scholars who side with Wrede struggle to present a plausible alternative scenario for forgery. Noteworthy among recent attempts, Frank Witt Hughes has argued that 2 Thessalonians is evidence of conflict between two later

research on 2 Thessalonians a decade ago, it was difficult to find any mainstream scholar who would support its authenticity.[19]

Recently, however, Abraham Malherbe's commentary on the Thessalonian correspondence for the Anchor Bible commentary series may indicate a turning of the scholarly tide.[20] The authorship issue is controversial enough that Malherbe offers a substantial chapter on each hypothesis, carefully constructing possible scenarios for either case. However, having laid out each side carefully, he concludes that the arguments for inauthenticity are improbable. For Malherbe, 2 Thessalonians' careful echoing of the structure and language of the first letter is more likely due to Paul's desire, explicit in the letter, to correct misinterpretations of his first letter and develop his teachings as the situation in Thessalonica deteriorated. Persecution of new converts had continued, erroneous eschatological teaching had taken some hold in the Thessalonian community, and some members refused to work for their own living. 2 Thessalonians is a pastoral letter written by Paul to address these several problems. Indeed, 2 Thessalonians 3:17 explicitly invites the community to verify the letter's authority by comparing its signature to the first—a fact for which Wrede and his followers had to construct a

---

Pauline schools ("Early Christian Rhetoric and 2 Thessalonians," *Journal for the Study of the New Testament,* Supp. Series 30 [1989]). 2 Thessalonians, according to Hughes, is written by the more apocalyptic of the two to refute the more realized eschatology of Ephesians and Colossians. But the letter's close attention to what appears to be a particular situation in Thessalonica seems to question that claim.

19. Robert Jewett was perhaps the most intriguing exception. Using traditional historical criticism, rhetorical analysis, and social-model theory, Jewett tried to construct a plausible millenarian setting in Thessalonica in which Paul's first evangelical strategy backfired, forcing him to use more caution and speak more explicitly of the deferred end. Jewett's combination of methods build a most interesting mousetrap that might answer Wrede's argument about eschatological consistency. Robert Jewett, *The Thessalonian Correspondence: Pauline Rhetoric and Millenarian Piety* (Philadelphia: Fortress Press, 1986).

20. Abraham J. Malherbe, *The Letters to the Thessalonians: A New Translation with Introduction and Commentary,* Anchor Bible 32B (New York: Doubleday, 2000), 347–463.

rather elaborate counter-story. The apparent difference between the letters' eschatological teachings in this light represents a correction, not a contradiction, balancing 1 Thessalonians' "already" or present eschatology (1 Th 5:5, "For all of you are children of the light and of the day") with a deeper sense of the "not yet."[21] This tension makes the letters complementary and consistent with the broader scope of Pauline eschatology that asserts both the "already" and the "not yet." Perhaps at the turn of the second millennium we may find ourselves, surprisingly, to be of one mind with medieval commentators, all of whom assumed that Paul was the author of 2 Thessalonians. However this issue may eventually be resolved, I will follow Malherbe and the medieval commentators and refer to the author as "Paul."

Although the exegetical history of the letter, and thus my study, focuses upon the figure of Antichrist, this "Son of Perdition" is clearly not the center of Paul's discussion. As Malherbe points out, 2 Thessalonians seems as concerned with persecution (2 Th 1) and the refusal to work (2 Th 3) as it does with eschatology, and this figure of the "Man of Sin, the Son of Perdition" is just one element of an eschatolgical scenario that defers the "coming of the Lord" until after certain signs—the *apostasia,* the "restraining power" and its/his removal, and the coming of the "lawless one" and all his acts. The scenario of the last events selects and condenses images from the Hellenistic Jewish apocalyptic tradition, and it has remarkable similarities to the so-called "little apocalypse" of the synoptic Gospels of the Christian New Testament (Mk 13; Mt 24; Lk 21).

But while the two accounts have similar elements, Paul's version

---

21. Malherbe, 368–69. See also Karl Donfried and I. Howard Marshall, *The Theology of the Shorter Pauline Letters* (Cambridge: Cambridge University Press, 1993), 96, 102, for this argument in greater detail, although Donfried is willing to attribute authorship to Paul's companion Timothy. For discussion of the Pauline tension between "already" and "not yet," see Oscar Cullmann, *Christ and Time: The Primitive Christian Conception of Time and History* (Philadelphia: Westminster Press, 1964).

has a distinctive theological signature that the "little apocalypse" lacks. Glen Holland has noticed in 2 Thessalonians a threefold symbolic progression from general references to specific personal ones. Paul's apocalyptic vision is one in which hidden "forces" presently at work are unified and personified in a crisis of the eschatological future. First, the "rebellion" *(apostasia)* is followed by the "man of lawlessness" *(ho anthropos tes anomias)*. Second, the "restraining power" *(to katechon)* is followed by the "restrainer" *(ho katechon)*. Finally, the "mystery of lawlessness" *(to mysterion tes anomias)* is followed by the "lawless one" *(ho anomias)*. This seems related to a positive-pole progression of the Church into "the Body of Christ," or "our being gathered together to him" (2 Th 2:1)—evidence of a possible convergence motif in Paul's eschatological thought.[22] Though Paul's opaque references make the picture fuzzy, he portrays an Antichrist whose threat is more external than internal and who is more a deceiver than a tyrant. Note, too, that this symbolic progression points to an Antichrist that is both *present,* though in a mysterious, impersonal form, and *future,* as the "Man of Sin." 2 Thessalonians' apocalyptic vision sees the gradual solidification of those who believe in the gospel and those who oppose it into polar forces that finally clash when Christ will slay Antichrist "with the breath of his mouth."

Thus the Man of Sin is but one element in an eschatological pattern of convergence. This eschatological pattern points in turn toward a broader Pauline "pattern of redemption."[23] Paul Ricoeur has pointed to the centrality of the figure of Adam in Paul's thought. While the Hebrews tradition was far more interested in Noah and Abraham than in Adam, Paul found in the "first man" a symbolic key to understanding the work of Christ. "It was St. Paul who

22. Glen Holland, *The Tradition that You Received from Us: 2 Thessalonians in the Pauline Tradition,* Hermeneutische Untersuchungen zur Theologie (Tübingen: J. C. B. Mohr/Paul Siebeck, 1988), 112.

23. I steal this term from the title of Edward T. Oakes, *Pattern of Redemption: The Theology of Hans Urs von Balthasar* (New York: Continuum Press, 1994).

roused the Adamic theme from its lethargy; by means of the contrast between the 'old man' and the 'new man,' he set up the figure
of Adam as the inverse of that of Christ, called the second Adam.
. . . [It] was Christology that consolidated Adamology."[24] Bernard
McGinn has suggested that Ricoeur's bipolar symbolic development
might be expanded. Pauline Christology certainly gives new life to
"Adamology" in the archetypal origin; perhaps it also gives rise to
the equally personal, equally significant symbolic antitype of the eschatological future, the final human Adversary, Antichrist. If the second Adam consolidates the first, then perhaps, too, the Son of Man
consolidates the Man of Sin, the Son of Perdition.

After the Apostle: The Shape of the
2 Thessalonians Tradition

If this reconstruction of Pauline salvation history is plausible,
then 2 Thessalonians has effectively given a Pauline theological
stamp to the Hellenistic Jewish and even early Christian apocalyptic
scenario. A mysterious personification of human evil has entered
the apocalyptic scenario and, in effect, initiated a new strand in the
tradition of apocalyptic thought. Consequently, ancient and medieval commentaries upon the text of 2 Thessalonians are the work-
shops in which the doctrine of Antichrist is shaped. Theories about
the "rebellion" of 2 Thessalonians 2:3, the personal nature of Antichrist, the relationship between Antichrist and Satan, and other
doctrines are accepted, rejected, corrected, or adapted by scholars in
the process of their commentary upon the text. This argument suspended through time forms a *tradition* that is continually constructed and reconstructed through the ever-developing practice of medieval commentary.[25]

24. Ricoeur, 238.
25. Paul J. Griffiths, *Religious Reading: The Place of Reading in the Practice of Religion* (New York: Oxford University Press, 1999). Griffiths gives helpful formal cri-
teria for defining what is properly a commentary: (1) there must be a direct rela-

Tradition and Innovation in Medieval Commentary

Grappling with the formation of a commentary tradition such as this requires the historian of exegesis to avoid two vices: the fallacies of "hermeneuticism" and "historicism."[26] The former temptation is to think of meaning as constituted simply between the text and the interpreter, yielding the sort of decontextualized "history of ideas" that one finds in Arthur O. Lovejoy's *Great Chain of Being*.[27] An exegete is always shaped and conditioned by the cultural and social air he breaths. The historian ignores these, *both* the formal constraints and possibilities of historically situated methods and practices *and* the social constraints of the world in which the exegesis is done, to his peril. But the temptation to *historicism* is equally seductive: "to see the commentary *primarily* in its facing toward the events or circumstances of its time, and to view its response to and representation of those events as being only slightly veiled by the formal guise of the scriptural exegesis in which it is wrapped."[28] One must avoid conceiving biblical commentary as a pretext for political argument, or even primarily as a lens through which to view the exegete's world. Both the scriptural text and its traditional interpretations form "worlds" unto themselves that demand the interpreter's attention. The meaning of a text is discovered in the negotiated transactions between text, earlier commentaries, and the exegete, creating a "socially-situated discursive universe"[29] that is not limited

---

tion to some other work, making the commentary a "metawork"; (2) the signs of the other work must predominate, either qualitatively or quantitatively; (3) the structure and order of the metawork must come largely from the other work (85). He also identifies six uses to which commentaries are put: explanation, application, justification, refutation, absorption, and the fulfillment of extratextual needs. (89)

26. Steven Fraade, *From Tradition to Commentary: Torah and Its Interpretation in the Midrash Sifre to Deuteronomy* (Albany: SUNY Press, 1991), 14ff.

27. Arthur O. Lovejoy, *The Great Chain of Being: A Study in the History of an Idea* (Cambridge, Mass.: Harvard University Press, 1950).

28. Fraade, 14. (italics mine)   29. Fraade, 14.

to, but does not exclude, the exegete's particular social and political circumstances. Karlfried Froehlich offers an instructive example: he discovered that formal commentaries on Matthew 16:18 ("You are Peter, and on this rock . . .") in the high Middle Ages continued to insist with Augustine that the "rock" refers to Christ, long after sermons and canonical documents confidently asserted to the contrary.[30] The "signs of the times" in the ascendancy of papal monarchy failed to be reflected in the tradition of commentary, since the weight of patristic authority had trumped them in the discursive universe of the gospel commentary tradition.

This is particularly instructive in the case of 2 Thessalonians in the Middle Ages. Much work has been done in recent years by Richard Landes, Johannes Fried, and others to recover traces of apocalyptic crisis throughout the Middle Ages. While often accused of returning to a Romantic vision of the "terrors of the year 1000,"[31] this school of thought aims to recover something deeper and more pervasive than one occasion or several occasions of mass hysteria. They argue the more persuasive point that millennial expectation is a constant in medieval culture that has a tendency to intensify around certain key dates or events.[32] These moments of intensity, when their hopes for the end are disappointed, are read out of the historical record by historians who now know better.[33] Johannes Fried has identified "peaks" of millennialism around the years 100,

30. Froehlich, "Saint Peter, Papal Primacy, and the Exegetical Tradition, 1150–1300," in *The Religious Role of the Papacy: Ideals and Realities 1150–1300*, ed. Christopher J. Ryan, Papers in Medieval Studies 8 (Toronto: Pontifical Institute of Medieval Studies, 1989), 3–44.

31. Usually attributed to the nineteenth-century French historian Jules Michelet, *Histoire de France*, rev. ed., vol. 2 (Paris: C Marpon and E. Flammarion, 1879–84), 132.

32. My argument in this book shares the conviction that some form of apocalyptic expectation is a constant in medieval culture. My differences with this argument have more to do with the particular nature and shape of that medieval apocalypticism.

33. Richard A. Landes, "The Fear of an Apocalyptic Year 1000: Augustinian Historiography, Medieval and Modern," *Speculum* 75:1 (January 2000): 97–145,

400, 800, 1000, and 1250.[34] Richard Landes has argued that the tradition of western chronography, if read against the grain, is in fact a "conspiracy" among ecclesial officials to quell millennial expectations by postponing the eschaton to a safe distance from the present.[35] With this in mind as one takes up a topic such as Antichrist in 2 Thessalonians, one might expect to find numerous possible connections and links to the political ideology of the time. One might hypothesize, for example, that interest in the Roman empire and its "translation" to the Carolingian world might crop up significantly in commentaries written in the ninth century within the empire's borders. Frankly, such were my expectations when I began this project. But such expectations tread dangerously close to the historicist fallacy, and mine had to be abandoned or at least modified as this study progressed.

In fact, the insight was precisely that—that what I was tracing in these texts was a *literary* tradition within a specific genre, one in which the weight of the past did not burden later interpreters so much as it gave the tradition of commentary considerable momentum along several trajectories. Often speculations as to whether the Frankish kings would survive to the next generation or whether the Muslims would overrun the known world were less significant to the mainline tradition of commentary on 2 Thessalonians, though these very questions are at the heart of other contemporary apocalyptic traditions.[36] Instead, the commentaries struggle to articulate a

---

and ibid., *"Millenarismus absconditus:* L'historiographie augustinienne et le millenarisme du Haut Moyen Age jusqu'en l'an Mil," *Le Moyen Age* 98:3–4 (1992): 355–77; 99:1 (1993): 1–26.

34. Johannes Fried, "Recognizing Millennialism in the Middle Ages," Position paper for the Center for Millennial Studies, online at (http://www.mille.org/scholarship/papers/fried.middleages.html).

35. Landes, "Lest the Millennium Be Fulfilled," 137–211. For a critical perspective on the work of Landes, Fried, et al., see Sylvain Gouguenheim, *Les fausses terreurs de l'an mil: Attente de la fin des temps ou approfondissement de la foi?* (Paris: Picard, 1999).

36. On this see Paul J. Alexander, "The Diffusion of Byzantine Apocalypses in

sense of doctrinal coherence in the midst of conflicting authorities (e.g., Is the "Man of Sin" human? Is he responsible for his actions if he is "possessed by the devil"?); factors in the social and historical context of exegete, be they pedagogical, methodological, theological, or ideological, are brought to bear upon these orienting questions. In other words, the medieval exegete of 2 Thessalonians seeks to clarify rather than apply apocalyptic doctrines, although such clarification is shaped necessarily by both the tradition of interpretation and the exegete's material and ideological conditions. The 2 Thessalonians commentary tradition is not an arena of apocalyptic or prophetic discourse about the current political or social state of affairs. Instead, we see something more complex, a dialectical engagement of innovation and continuity, or what Fraade has called "the stance of sociohistorically grounded traditionality . . . the multivocality of a received yet restless tradition."[37] In other words, early medieval commentaries on 2 Thessalonians constitute a tradition of scriptural inquiry through which the doctrines of Antichrist and the

the Medieval West and the Beginnings of Joachimism," in *Prophecy and Millenarianism: Essays in Honor of Marjorie Reeves,* ed. Ann Miller (Essex: Longmans, 1980), 53–106; and Adso Dervensis, *De ortu et tempore Antichristi, necnon et tractatus qui ab eo dependant,* CCCM 45, ed. Daniel Verhelst (Turnhout: Brepols, 1976), which I treat in Chapter 4. The one possible exception in the commentary tradition is the tenth-century commentary of Thietland of Einsiedeln, which I will also treat in Chapter 4.

37. Fraade's observations on medieval Jewish commentary parallel my own on the Latin West: "This collective nature of the *Sifre's* commentary gives the impression not of a single commentator standing face to face with the text of scripture in the unmediated work of interpretation (as if such were ever fully possible), but of a collector and subtle shaper of received *traditions* who creates a commentary out of such traditions by configuring them not only in relation to the atomized texts of Deuteronomy but also in relation to one another. . . . To what extent did such a redactor, or series of redactors, feel constrained by the authority of the traditions he inherited . . . and sought to transmit, and to what extent did he feel free to pick and choose among them, to rearrange them, and to transform them, even if subtly, in his work of commentary? This is the dialectic of continuity and innovation that characterizes the stance of sociohistorically grounded traditionality . . . the multivocality of a received yet restless tradition" (17).

end of the world are constructed, deconstructed, and reconstructed over the first Christian millennium.

The proper frame for this study is Pauline commentary as a whole, because commentaries on 2 Thessalonians generally appear only as part of a commentary upon the entire Pauline corpus. Medieval biblical hermeneutics, even when it scrutinizes the particulars of grammar and syntax of a single word, always conceives of such work in the context of a whole.[38] In this case, the "whole" is the Pauline corpus, which medieval exegetes read primarily as an authoritative source for and model of theology.[39] This context has significant consequences for the kinds of interpretation found therein. The fact that 2 Thessalonians is seldom if ever taken up independently as an object of commentary means that the interpretations of the particulars of the text always refer in principle to the whole of the Pauline corpus. For exegetes, Paul was more theologian than prophet, and thus the question implicit in their inquiry is about how 2 Thessalonians fits into the corpus of Pauline theology. They seek the Apostle's *doctrine* of Antichist, his "Antichristology," more than his prophecy about what historical person that might be.

These concerns for the *doctrinal* sense of 2 Thessalonians need not suggest either an ivory-tower retreat from history or a sustained conspiracy of "antimillennialist" silence. The near silence of the tradition on prophetic predictions shows the "restless traditionality" of commentary at work—predictions that may come and go are not handed on and preserved, but the text is continuously interpreted and reinterpreted in an attempt to bring some insight and continuity to the reading of potentially incendiary passages. As such, it suggests something about the nature of medieval apocalypticism more generally. The 2 Thessalonians tradition is a sort of "micro-history"

38. Fraade, 13.

39. Karlfried Froehlich, "Which Paul? Observations on the Image of the Apostle in the History of Biblical Exegesis," in *New Perspectives on Historical Theology in Honor of John Meyendorff,* ed. Bradley Nassif (Grand Rapids: Eerdmans, 1996), 279–99, esp. 293–95.

of the pervasive presence of apocalypticism in the medieval imagination, a presence made pervasive by its refusal to bind the text's
meaning and use to particular concrete predictions that fail, while
retaining the power of the eschatological structure of time and history in a sense of psychological imminence.[40]

The context of the Pauline corpus also has significant impact on
questions of method. Pauline commentary developed its own exegetical technique, not entirely literal, but neither an example of
"spiritual exegesis" in full flower.[41] In Pauline exegesis, the practical
rules that can be discerned from the commentaries tend toward a
certain restraint in the discussion of a spiritual sense in the texts.

40. McGinn, " End of the World," 63: "I would suggest that early-medieval
rejection of predictiveness may paradoxically have allowed end-time anxiety a
more pervasive, if necessarily somewhat diffuse, power."

41. Spiritual exegesis rests on the conviction that scriptural writings, as the
word of God, have a surplus of meaning not exhausted by the literal or historical
sense of the text. Indeed, each and every word of Scripture was believed to have
relevance to the life of the soul and the life of the church. In the Latin West, this
surplus eventually was reserved into four pools of meaning, the fourfold sense of
Scripture: Littera gesta docet, Quid credas allegoria // Moralis quid agas, Quo tendas
anagogia. (The letter teaches events, allegory, what you believe, // Moral, what
you do, and anagogy, where you are headed.) These theoretical reserves, however, seldom are found in the practice of biblical exegesis: rarely does one find all of
these senses rendered for a particular text or word. Rather, the fourfold sense of
Scripture preserves the breadth of interpretive possibility. The four senses are
hermeneutical "principles" for interpretation rather than practical "rules" for
reading particular texts; the "fourfold sense" is theoretical, not practical. (On this
see Karlfried Froehlich, ed., Biblical Interpretation in the Early Church (Philadelphia:
Fortress Press, 1985). In practice, one might discuss only the literal sense of a passage, or might add a moral sense, etc., without any necessary allegiance to finding
four senses for each text. I have chosen to use the term "spiritual exegesis" as a
comprehensive category that includes the particular forms of typology, allegory,
moral interpretation, Antiochene theoria, etc. I acknowledge that such a comprehensive term is not without its ambiguities, but I am persuaded by Henri de
Lubac's argument in Histoire et Esprit (Paris: Aubier, 1950) that "spiritual exegesis"
or "spiritual understanding" best embraces the fundamental conviction shared by
all of these particular modes of reading that Scripture possesses a surplus of
meaning that is of spiritual benefit to the believing reader. I have benefited from

Pauline interpretation does not lack spiritual exegesis; in fact, I devote a chapter in this study to one such interpretation of 2 Thessalonians. But these spiritual readings of Paul are moderated by the ancient and medieval sense that Paul's letters are, in a way, "literally" spiritual. Paul openly testifies to and explains what is hidden in other biblical texts: faith in Christ and the Church.[42] Paul himself interprets Scripture spiritually and even invokes the term "allegory" in the discussion of Abraham in his Letter to the Galatians (4:24). He marshals numerous texts from the Hebrew Scriptures to illuminate the mystery of Christ. He is, in the eyes of these exegetes, the model spiritual interpreter of Scripture, and his writing is to be clarified more than expanded or unveiled. The exegete usually tries to "think with" Paul as a theologian, paraphrasing his language and clarifying his meaning, sometimes speaking in the first person as if he were Paul.[43] The goal of Pauline commentary was to uncover a sort of "Pauline dogmatics," for lack of a better term. The commentaries

---

Bradley Nassif's thorough survey of the use of this term in relation to the Antiochene style. (Bradley Nassif, "'Spiritual Exegesis' in the School of Antioch," in *New Perspectives on Historical Theology*, 343–77.) As an aside, it is interesting to note that de Lubac's extensive study of medieval exegesis does not address in any way the role of the Antiochene style in that history.

42. Frank Kermode suggests that the "spiritual sense" is properly a characteristic of narratives (*The Genesis of Secrecy: On the Interpretation of Narrative* [Cambridge, Mass.: Harvard University Press, 1979]), passim. This distinction could explain why Pauline letters are not allegorized: they lack a narrative plot from which to suspend an allegorical or spiritual meaning. However, ancient and medieval Christian writers had little problem allegorizing the most apodictic passages of the Pentateuch (e.g., Irenaeus, *Adversus haereses* 5.8.3, where he interprets Lv 11:2ff.'s dietary prescriptions as a reference to Jews, pagans, and Christians). Thus, spiritual interpretation is tied not to narrative structures, but rather to the perceived content of the a particular scripture. So, too, George Lindbeck's discussion of early Christian exegesis as "premodern narrative interpretation" is inaccurate ("The Story-Shaped Church: Critical Exegesis and Theological Interpretation," in *The Theological Interpretation of Scripture: Classic and Contemporary Readings*, ed. Stephen E. Fowl [London: Blackwell, 1997], 39–52).

43. See, for example, Haimo of Auxerre (PL 117.777–84, and my discussion in Chapter 4, pp. 144–69) and Bruno the Carthusian (PL 153.413–24, and my discus-

on 2 Thessalonians must be understood in light of this particular approach to Pauline texts, in that the context shapes the kinds of issues that exegetes will approach and discuss within them, and in that it may just as easily eliminate other such issues that may in another place hold great import, as in Froehlich's reading of Matthew commentaries.

Despite the substantive similarities that endure in Pauline exegesis throughout the early medieval period, the interpretive history of 2 Thessalonians bears witness to developments or shifts in exegetical strategy. Patristic authors address Paul's text in the intertextual context of the rest of the "canon" of biblical texts and within a general hermeneutical frame of Christian doctrine. With no authoritative interpretations to guide them, they differ quite a bit in their conclusions. But once this initial layer of interpretation encircled the scriptural text, the layer itself became a significant (perhaps *the* significant) factor in early medieval exegesis.[44] Early medieval readers treat the interpretive conclusions of the Fathers as authoritative and thus are confronted with a second, patristic canon upon the scriptural canon. Different exegetes in the first millennium manage this twofold canon with distinct methods, as we shall see. Later, in the eleventh and early twelfth centuries, scholars exploit the careful work of their predecessors but reconstruct their commentaries around a new optically organized pattern, the glossed text. These biblical glosses, in turn, prepare the way for the developed distinctions and arguments of scholastic theology. Such stylistic and technical innovations in the tradition of Pauline exegesis develop as the consequence of granting authority to particular interpretations that

---

sion in Chapter 5, pp. 192–206). Also see Beryl Smalley, *The Study of the Bible in the Middle Ages* (Notre Dame: University of Notre Dame Press, 1964), for her reasons for excluding Pauline exegesis from her study.

44. See Kevin Madigan, "Ancient and High Medieval Interpretations of Jesus in Gethsemane: Some Reflections on Tradition and Continuity in Christian Thought," *Harvard Theological Review* 88:1 (1995): 157–73, for a discussion of scholastic theology's creative use of patristic authorities.

do not necessarily agree. Consequently, the 2 Thessalonians tradition, and thus the doctrine of Antichrist, is shaped in part by developing technologies of reading, technologies that culminate in scholasticism.[45]

The 2 Thessalonians Tradition in Brief

The patristic foundations of the 2 Thessalonians tradition are sunk in the soil of the late fourth century. Peter Brown has described the latter half of the century as the "generation of St. Paul,"[46] since many thinkers turned to the Pauline letters as a primary theological source. The major resources for 2 Thessalonians from this period are the Pauline commentaries of Ambrosiaster, Pelagius, and Theodore of Mopsuestia, Jerome's Epistle 121, and Augustine's *City of God* 20.19. Together, these commentaries and exegetical fragments form the bedrock of the tradition of interpretation of 2 Thessalonians upon which all other commentators will draw.

Patristic opinions on the text generally fall within two fields of Christian apocalyptic thought. Of all the possible "graphs" of Antichrist that could be sketched in the three dimensions discussed above, the large majority of opinions fall within these two fields. In one field, what I will call *apocalyptic realism*, Antichrist is primarily understood to be *imminent* and *external*, with broad variance on the "dread-deception" axis. Apocalyptic realists understand apocalyptic language in general and Paul's brief letter in particular primarily as predictions of the historical events that will precede and/or accompany the Second Coming of Christ. They generally agree (1) that the "desertion" (*discessio*, v. 3) is a departure from Roman authority, either as an imperial political power or as an ecclesial spiritual au-

---

45. Ivan Illich, *In the Vineyard of the Text: A Commentary to Hugh's* Didascalion (Chicago: University of Chicago Press, 1993).

46. Peter Brown, *Augustine of Hippo* (Berkeley and Los Angeles: University of California Press, 1969), 151. See also Martha Ellen Stortz, "Exegesis, Orthodoxy, and Ethics: Interpretations of Romans in the Pelagian Controversy" (Ph.D. dissertation, University of Chicago, 1984), 18ff.

thority, (2) that the "Son of Perdition, Man of Sin" presents an Antichrist who will be a single human being come either to persecute the faithful (dread) or to lead them astray (deception) or both, and (3) that his work is foreshadowed in persecutions by Nero and his successors to the throne. The apocalyptic realist position thus emphasizes the historical, the political, and the future. It asserts that the mystery of evil now at work in the world will culminate within the realm of world events at some point in the future. While this future time may not be chronologically imminent, the apocalyptic realist emphasis on the historical continuity between present evil and future judgment carries the weight of psychological imminence. Chapter 2 will be devoted to the elements of this field of opinion as they emerge from the works of Ambrosiaster, Theodore of Mopsuestia, Jerome, and Pelagius.

The other major field of apocalyptic thought is wary of any direct continuity between historical events and the apocalyptic end, favoring an Antichrist who is *immanent, internal,* and *deceptive.* This perspective begins in the work of Tyconius, the famous African Donatist, but its first full articulation is found in his fellow African, St. Augustine of Hippo, in his letter to Hesychius (Epistle 199) and in *City of God* 20.19. Later, Gregory the Great expands the symbolic application of this perspective. What I call the "Latin spiritual interpretation" of 2 Thessalonians is characterized by (1) agnosticism toward the historical referents of the Temple, the "restraining force," and the forerunners of Antichrist, (2) preference for a spiritual reading of the apocalyptic figures and events as symbols that refer primarily to the present life of the Church and the soul, and only secondarily to the future judgment, and (3) a subsequent emphasis upon moral authority of the text rather than its prophetic historical truth. For the Augustinian reader, any continuity between the text and actual historical events is shrouded in ambiguity, and thus the true import of the text lies in its spiritual and moral truth. Chapter 3 will focus upon this perspective in the thought of Tyconius, Augustine, and Gregory.

The early medieval exegetical tradition of 2 Thessalonians is characterized by its ability to hold these fields of opinion together in some fashion. Chapter 4 studies this integrative approach as it is expressed in the commentaries of the first millennium. At the heart of late first-millennium culture, the Carolingian revival of the ninth century leads scholars to study Scripture and the fathers with greater historical and philological precision. Rabanus Maurus, Haimo of Auxerre, and other scholars undertake commentary upon the whole bible with careful attention to patristic authority. Confronted with a large body of authoritative (but often contradictory) traditions, scholars in the early Middle Ages study the breadth and depth of the fathers' work. From this abundance, they select and organize patristic sources in such a way that they offer a particular interpretation of a biblical text, though certainly not the only one. This interpretive art, represented best by the exegetes of the ninth century, is literally "constructive" in the way it builds an understanding of 2 Thessalonians from the timber cut and seasoned in the forest of patristic writings. This scholarly quality endures the transition into the eleventh and twelfth centuries, when a new generation of scholars makes use of both the material and the method of Carolingian commentaries to build their own interpretations of Antichrist and the end. The works of Lanfranc of Canterbury and Bruno the Carthusian, and the great summary of the exegetical tradition, the *Glossa Ordinaria,* reveal the continuities between early scholastic exegesis and its past.

These scholars of the late eleventh and early twelfth centuries are in the debt of earlier medieval scholarship. The material that they receive from the Carolingians, however, is thoroughly reorganized and balanced by their own theological opinions. Lanfranc of Canterbury, Bruno the Carthusian, and Anselm and Ralph of Laon all construct their commentaries in a new "glossed-text" format. The most abundant fruit of this new way of formatting exegetical material is the *Glossa Ordinaria,* in which the scriptural text is configured on the page in such a way that comments on it can be included between the lines and around the margins. The particular edition that we receive as the Ordinary Gloss[47] was probably compiled throughout the early twelfth century. The *Glossa Ordinaria* becomes the authoritative textbook for scholastic biblical teaching and is thus one of the most influential pieces of biblical commentary in the Christian tradition.

The commentaries of Gilbert of Poitiers and Peter Lombard draw upon the full breadth of the exegetical tradition preserved in the Gloss in their Pauline commentaries. Their commentaries upon some Pauline letters include such emerging methods as the scholastic *quaestio;* but the commentaries on 2 Thessalonians are remarkably traditional. Peter Lombard's 2 Thessalonians commentary, despite its traditional form, nonetheless represents the beginning of the end of the early medieval apocalyptic synthesis. Chapter 5 will examine the exegesis of 2 Thessalonians from the earliest glosses of Lanfranc and Bruno, through the *Glossa Ordinaria,* to the exegesis of Peter Lombard in an effort to trace the fate of this apocalyptic text at the dawn of the twelfth-century "renaissance" in Christian theology.

The history of the text by no means ends there, although my study does. Indeed, in the twelfth and thirteenth centuries, eschatological speculation and Pauline commentary begin to flourish anew. The former springs from the creative, eclectic thought of Joachim of Fiore; the latter is the fruit of the new universities, where biblical exegesis is a constitutive element in the education of professional theological masters. But this twin harvest is so abundant that it would require another study of equal or greater length, and so I end with Peter Lombard, who gives us both the last evidence of the early medieval commentary on 2 Thessalonians and the first evidence of its demise.

47. The variations found in the manuscript tradition make any discussion of an "authoritative edition" somewhat difficult, at least for the present. I have used the edition that eventually was printed by Rusch as the *editio princeps* in the fifteenth century. See my more complete discussion of this problem in Chapter 5, pp. 208–10.

Tracing the history of this brief letter for roughly eight centuries sheds light upon both early medieval Pauline exegesis and the doctrinal elements of apocalypticism in the Latin West at their point of intersection, where Paul the Apostle, like a "wise master builder," lays the scriptural foundations upon which exegetes will construct the traditional figure of Antichrist.

CHAPTER 2

THE MAN OF SIN

Apocalyptic Realism in the
Early Church, 200–400

The early medieval tradition of commentary upon 2 Thessalonians found its authoritative sources in the late patristic period, when a number of Christian intellectuals took up the method of commentary in their attempts to clarify the doctrinal claims of the Church. The fourth and early fifth centuries saw the fervor for apocalyptic speculation wax and wane with the turn of each generation. Such movement of thought produced diversity of interpretation in commentaries on 2 Thessalonians, which were vehicles for the digesting of opinion and the construction of doctrine. This chapter documents and describes the apocalyptic realism of four patristic authors who were foundational sources of the early medieval tradition: Ambrosiaster, Theodore of Mopsuestia, Pelagius, and Jerome. The chapter that follows will address the alternative exegetical strategy, found above all in Tyconius and Augustine. Apocalyptic realism—which treats Antichrist primarily as a human individual who will challenge Christ and the Church in the Last Days and looks to political and/or historical realities to make sense of that challenge—is the dominant discourse in late patristic comments on 2 Thessalonians, revealing that the appeal of the apocalyptic frame of reference did not die with the conversion of Constantine.

Paul and Antichrist in the Early Fathers:
The Prehistory of Commentary

Prior to the conversion of Constantine, theologians and church leaders bore the apocalyptic sense of imminent judgment that one might expect from an institution subject to persecution. Irenaeus, Hippolytus, Lactantius, Tertullian, indeed nearly all of the early Fathers had a vivid sense of the imminent end, and many subscribed to millenarian versions of Christ's return.[1] These early theologians presumed that the structure of history was apocalyptic—that is, that the world headed toward its end: the culmination of the history of sin and rebellion in the figure of Antichrist, and the final judgment of Christ that would vindicate the saints.[2] Most believed that the end was near. In the course of the second and third centuries, the scattered traditions about Antichrist and the end coalesced into a basic script of the apocalyptic plot shared by most Christian thinkers. This early apocalyptic script is the bedrock upon which the foundational commentaries of later Fathers rest—these early Fathers framed the debate on apocalyptic matters within a basic narrative.

Irenaeus of Lyons' *Against Heresies* is the first systematic account of Christian faith. Written to refute the claims of Gnostics, *Against Heresies* gives a theological account of salvation history that represents the emerging orthodoxy of the "Great Church."[3] In Book 5,

---

1. While the classic assumption was that millennialism, the belief in an earthly intermediate reign of Christ, was shared by all the early Fathers until Origen (see for example Adolf von Harnack, *Lehrbuch der Dogmengeschichte*, 4th ed., vol. 1 [Tübingen, 1909], 619), the recent work of Charles E. Hill, *Regnum Caelorum: Patterns of Future Hope in Early Christianity* (Oxford: Clarendon Press, 1992), rev. ed. *Regnum Caelorum: Patterns of Millennial Thought in Early Christianity* (Grand Rapids: Eerdmans, 2001) has demonstrated that there are numerous non-millennialist eschatologies in the second century.

2. See Hill, *Regnum Caelorum*, chs. 1–2.

3. The term is taken from Rowan Greer's discussion of Irenaeus in James L. Kugel and Rowan A. Greer, *Early Biblical Interpretation* (Philadelphia: Westminster

near the end, Irenaeus addresses the figure of Antichrist. His reading
of the Adversary follows the contours of Pauline antichristology:
Antichrist will be the "recapitulation of apostasy and rebellion."[4]
Just as Christ, the second Adam, is the recapitulation of all creation,
Antichrist will be the recapitulation of Adam's sin and all subsequent sins and heresies, all of which reject God's law and will. While
he does not cite 2 Thessalonians explicitly, Irenaeus gives a theological reading of the rebellion (Gr. *apostasia,* Lat. *discessio*) of 2 Thessalonians 2:3: Antichrist himself *is* the rebellion, the recapitulation of
all previous rebellions. When he speculates about the identity of Antichrist, he uses the number 666 (Rv 13:18) to decode several possible names numerologically. "Evanthos" contains the number of the
Beast, but Irenaeus refuses to speculate what that might mean.
More provocative is the name "Lateinos" ("Latin" or pertaining to
the Roman Empire), of which he says, "it is a very probable [solu-
tion], this being the name of the last kingdom.[5] For the Latins are
those who rule at present."[6] Irenaeus here indicates that Antichrist
will be Roman, but he immediately withdraws the claim: "I will not,
however, make any boast of this [coincidence]."[7] Irenaeus draws up
to the brink of a prophetic indictment of Rome, but then steps back.
In his discussion of the time of Antichrist's arrival, he reads the ten
horns of the beast in Daniel 7:21 as evidence that the Roman Empire will be divided into ten kingdoms before Antichrist comes, and
he argues that this will come at the end of the six-thousandth year,
though he does not say when this will fall. In all, Irenaeus gathers
evidence on Antichrist from a variety of sources, many of which engage in forecasting Antichrist's arrival. But he always folds these

---

Press, 1986), pt. 2, ch. 1. For a discussion of Irenaeus, see Robert M. Grant, *Irenaeus of Lyons* (London: Routledge, 1997).

4. Irenaeus of Lyons, *Adversus haereses (Adv. haer.)* 5.28.2, ed. W. W. Harvey,
ANF, vol. 1 (Cambridge: Cambridge University Press, 1857), 557.

5. In Dn 7, as interpreted by Irenaeus in *Adv. haer.* 5.28.1.

6. Irenaeus, *Adv. haer.* 5.30.3.

7. Ibid.

readings of Antichrist into a broader theological and less specifically historical understanding of recapitulation.

Hippolytus, the disciple of Irenaeus, is the first to devote an entire treatise to the Adversary *(On the Antichrist)* and the first known author of a complete commentary on a book of Scripture, his *Commentary on Daniel*. Both works are significant sources of thought on Antichrist. In many ways, Hippolytus echoes Irenaeus's testimony: Antichrist as recapitulation, the division of the empire prior to Antichrist's advent, and so on. He adds a general biographical sketch culled from earlier sources: Antichrist will be of Jewish origin; he will rebuild the temple in Jerusalem, gather disciples, and send them out to spread his message, restore the Roman Empire, and persecute Christianity. David G. Dunbar's study of Hippolytus's eschatology has shown that most if not all of this information can be found in other earlier sources,[8] and it appears that his interest in apocalyptic matters was motivated not by an expectation of Antichrist's imminent arrival, but rather by a desire to cool such expectations around him.[9] Hippolytus bears witness to what Dunbar calls "a kind of 'mainline' eschatology which may have been quite widespread during the closing decades of the second century."[10]

Tertullian, contemporary with Hippolytus, shares for the most part in this mainline eschatology, but he shows ambivalence about the role of the Roman Empire in salvation history. On the one hand, in his work *De spectaculis,* he critiques Roman spectacles and shows and he contrasts these with the true spectacle that is coming—Christ's return in judgment. He cannot help but delight in the overturning of Roman imperial society, when emperors and "governors

---

8. David G. Dunbar, "The Eschatology of Hippolytus of Rome" (Ph.D. dissertation, Drew University, 1979), and "Hippolytus of Rome and the Eschatological Exegesis of the Early Church," *Westminster Theological Quarterly* 45 (1983): 322–39.

9. Landes, "Lest the Millennium Be Fulfilled," passim.

10. Dunbar, "Hippolytus of Rome and the Eschatological Exegesis of the Early Church," 339.

of provinces, too, who persecuted the Christian name" will be cast "into the lowest darkness."[11] On the other hand, Tertullian is the first author to apply the concept of the "restrainer" from 2 Thessalonians 2:6 to the empire, since he knows that "the great catastrophe threatening the whole world, the very end of the age with its promise of dreadful sufferings, is held back by the continuing existence of the Roman Empire."[12] Not good in itself, the empire is a necessary evil used by God's providential will to forestall the arrival of the Man of Sin himself. This providential role which Tertullian casts for the empire will be one of the central concerns of the 2 Thessalonians tradition.

The "Christianization" of the empire after Constantine's conversion in 312 cools the apocalyptic energies that are still evident in Tertullian and Hippolytus. Eusebius of Caesarea, the leading intellectual of the Constantinian regime, has no regard whatsoever for the apocalyptic dreams of those who went before him and sees the Constantinian peace as the "firstfruits of future rewards."[13] In the age of Christian empire, the apocalyptic frame of crisis and judgment is passé. In fact, apocalyptic anxiety and hope are transmuted into millennial confidence that the Church is thriving in "Christian times," a conviction that even the young Augustine shares.[14]

A few short years later, the tide turns yet again. The last thirty

11. Tertullian, *De spectaculis* 30.

12. Tertullian, *Apologeticum,* 32. Tertullian is also the first author to give sustained exegetical attention to 2 Thessalonians as a whole. In *Against Marcion* 5.27, Tertullian attacks Marcion's editing and interpretation of the letter. Tertullian's intention is to argue that 2 Th refers to Antichrist and not to "the Creator's Christ," as Marcion has asserted. The argument is largely a critique of Marcion and thus offers very few interpretations itself. It does not enter into the commentary tradition at all, and has no identifiable relevance to the development of apocalyptic thought.

13. Eusebius of Caesarea, *Ecclesiasticae historiae* 3.39.13; *Oratio de laudibus Constantini* 3.5.

14. See Robert Markus, *Saeculum: History and Society in the Theology of Saint Augustine,* rev. ed. (Cambridge: Cambridge University Press, 1988), ch. 2.

years of the fourth century see an end to the cheerful confidence of people like Eusebius. Although Christians under the emperor Theodosius are now granted full legal status and recognition, their confidence in the prospects of the faith in history and in the happy relationship between "Christ and culture" falters. The Church is beset by what Brian Daley calls a "new sense of vulnerability and impending doom."[15] Why this occurs is difficult to say. But it is no small coincidence that this return to apocalyptic thinking follows closely upon the heels of the reign of Emperor Julian the Apostate (361–363).

Under Julian's reign, Christian teachers are restricted and public pagan sacrifices abound. Julian, a former Christian, had written a polemical treatise, *Against the Galileans,* in which he picked apart Christian scriptural claims. Perhaps his most alarming anti-Christian tactic was a plan to rebuild the Jewish temple in Jerusalem. He may have intended to disturb Christianity's confidence in its own supercession of the Jewish temple cult, but the plan only demonized Julian all the more. This pagan interlude came to a swift end when Julian died at the hands of the Persians, just after work had begun on Jerusalem's temple mount, but its effects lingered in the Christian consciousness for years to come. Well into the fifth century, Christians were still attempting to refute his claims. The reign of Julian tempered the exuberance of the "Constantinian" Church with a brief but pointed reminder that Christianity's place within the empire was by no means secure.[16] This, plus the ongoing threat of aggressive wandering Germanic tribes in the outer territories of the

15. Brian E. Daley, "Apocalypticism in Early Christian Theology," *Encyclopedia of Apocalypticism,* ed. Bernard McGinn, vol. 2 (New York: Continuum, 1998), 23.

16. Robert L. Wilken, *The Christians as the Romans Saw Them* (New Haven: Yale University Press, 1984), 164–84. For more information on Julian, see Glenn Bowersock, *Julian the Apostate* (Cambridge, Mass.: Harvard University Press, 1978). For the issue of the rebuilding of the temple, see Robert L. Wilken, *John Chrysostom and the Jews: Rhetoric and Reality in the Late Fourth Century* (Berkeley: University of California Press, 1983), ch. 5, and *This Land Called Holy* (New Haven: Yale University Press, 1994).

empire, may have sent a rather alarming signal to Christians in the Latin West.

Perhaps this is why, according to Sulpicius Severus, Bishop Martin of Tours (d. 397) believed that the Antichrist was alive as a young boy and that "he would assume power as soon as he comes of age."[17] Sulpicius Severus himself confesses that "the times of our age are difficult and dangerous, since the churches are polluted by unprecedented evil and all things are in confusion."[18] In a similar vein, Maximus of Turin's sermons reveal his sense that the times are perilous and call for moral renewal and reform as the Last Judgment approaches.[19] Throughout the Western Empire, Christian intellectuals begin to wonder if in fact the center cannot hold.

Such anxiety may be responsible as well for the sudden turn to commentary on the letters of Paul. Prior to 360, while many of the Fathers of the Church clearly drew upon Pauline theology, none that we know of save Origen ever turn to comment upon the Pauline literature in any formal way. Then, in the fifty years between 360 and 410, no less than six Latin commentaries and at least two Greek works on Pauline texts are written. Marius Victorinus, Ambrosiaster, Jerome, Augustine, Pelagius, the so-called Budapest anon-ymous commentator, Theodore of Mopsuestia, and John Chrysostom all devote meticulous attention to Paul in what has been called the "Renaissance of Paul." The name should not deceive: this renaissance was not a "new birth" of optimistic humanism as its later namesake, but rather the reflection of a dark turn in Christian thought. Wilhelm Geerlings has noticed that this period also produced a series of exegetical works in Job, and he suggests that Paul and Job prove to be fruitful sources for a generation of scholars disenchanted with the triumphalism of the Constantinian generation and preoccupied with the darker issues of theodicy and

---

17. Sulpicius Severus, *Dialogues* 1.41, ed. C. Halm, CSEL I, p. 197.
18. Sulpicius Severus, *Chronicle* 2.46.1.
19. Maximus of Turin, *Homily* 85.1–2.

fatalism.[20] Whatever connections there may or may not be between the apocalyptic turn and Pauline commentary, it is at least the case that the Apostle and the Adversary are both present to mind for late fourth-century Christians. The tradition of commentary on 2 Thessalonians is born in an age of anxiety.

Of course, some form of exegesis, or interpretation of the authoritative texts of Scripture, has been a mode of Christian reflection from its earliest years.[21] Paul, the evangelists, and the other New Testament authors all interpret the events of the life, death, and resurrection of Jesus by referring them to the language and events of the Jewish Scriptures.[22] Similarly, Christian theologians of the late second century, such as Tertullian and Irenaeus, construct their arguments against Gnostics and Marcionites through the interpretation of both the Jewish Scriptures and the developing canon of

20. Wilhelm Geerlings, "Hiob und Paulus: Theodizee und Paulinismus in der lateinischen Theologie am Ausgang des vierten Jahrhunderts," *Jahrbuch für Antike und Christentum* 24 (1981): 56–66. One wonders whether this explains the decidedly non-fatalistic exegesis of Paul found in thinkers such as Pelagius and John Chrysostom, however.

21. What Pierre Hadot has called the "exegetical mode of thinking" certainly predates Christian reflection. Indeed, elements of commentary can be found within the Hebrew Scriptures themselves; e.g., Ez 22:1–16 as commentary upon the Holiness Code in Lv 20. See Kugel and Greer, pt. 1. Also James A. Sanders, *Torah and Canon* (Philadelphia: Fortress Press, 1972); idem, *From Sacred Story to Sacred Text* (Philadelphia: Fortress Press, 1987), especially ch. 5, "Canonical Hermeneutics: True and False Prophecy." Hadot himself has traced the ascendance of the "exegetical mode of thinking" in the Hellenistic philosophical schools of Platonism, Aristotelianism, Stoicism, and Epicureanism. Pierre Hadot, *Philosophy as a Way of Life,* ed. Arnold I. Davidson, trans. Michael Chase (Cambridge, Mass.: Blackwell, 1995); *Qu'est-ce que la philosophie antique?* (Paris: Gallimard, 1995); and "Théologie, exégèse, écriture dans la philosophie grec," in *Les regles l'interpretation,* ed. Michel Tardieu (Paris: Cerf, 1987). Early Christian exegetes were a part of both traditions of thought.

22. See Robert M. Grant, with David Tracy, *A Short History of the Interpretation of the Bible,* 2nd ed. (Philadelphia: Fortress Press, 1984), chs. 2, 3, and 4. Also Kugel and Greer, pt. 2, ch. 2, "Christian Transformation of the Hebrew Scriptures."

Christian Scriptures.[23] Disputes over points of doctrine in the early Church are very often disputes over the proper interpretation of these texts.

But formal commentary, or lemma-by-lemma exegesis, comes into Christian use in the early third century.[24] As I have said, the first commentary upon a complete book of the Bible we know of is Hippolytus of Rome's work on Daniel (ca. 201–204), but the first Christian to offer running commentaries on much of the Old and New Testaments (including the Pauline epistles) was Origen of Alexandria. As a philosopher trained in the Platonic tradition, Origen is quite familiar with this sort of formal commentary upon the works of an authoritative thinker. In the Platonic, Aristotelian, and Stoic schools,

discussing a thesis consists in discussing not the problem in itself but the meaning that one should give to Plato's or Aristotle's statements concerning this problem. Once this convention is taken into account, one does in fact discuss the question is some depth, but this is done by skillfully giving Platonic or Aristotelian statements the meanings that support the very solution one wishes to give to the problem under consideration.[25]

23. The pivotal role of Irenaeus in the development of the Christian bible is discussed in far greater detail than this study can afford, and with great clarity, by Greer in Kugel and Greer, pt. 2. For what we might call the agonistic history of the reception of Paul in earliest Christianity, see Dennis Ronald McDonald, *The Legend and the Apostle: The Battle for Paul in Story and Canon* (Philadelphia: Westminster Press, 1983); Elaine Pagels, *The Gnostic Paul* (Philadelphia: Trinity Press International, 1975); Andreas Lindemann, "Paul in the Writings of the Apostolic Fathers," in *Paul and the Legacies of Paul*, ed. William S. Babcock (Dallas: Southern Methodist University Press, 1990); Froehlich, "Which Paul?" 279–99.

24. One might consider 1 John an early exception, as itself a lemma-by-lemma commentary on the prologue of the Gospel of John. See Raymond E. Brown, *1, 2, 3 John.* Anchor Bible Commentary (New York: Doubleday, 1982), 65ff.

25. Hadot, *Philosophy as a Way of Life,* 76. Hadot's "exegetical mode of thinking" could be supplemented (at least in the case of Christian exegesis) by Peter Gorday's description of the "economic" interpretation found in Origen and other patristic thinkers: The Fathers always read a particular part of Scripture in light of the entire economy of God's revelation as found in Scripture. Gorday's theory is

This sort of synthetic philosophical exegesis was part of Origen's education; as a Christian theologian, he exploits it to interpret much of Christian Scripture. Origen may have been the first Christian thinker to study the Pauline letters in formal commentaries; unfortunately, only his Romans commentary survives.[26] Curiously, after Origen, evidence of formal commentary upon Paul disappears for about a century and a half. While many of the theological luminaries of the late third and early fourth centuries show the enduring influence of Pauline themes,[27] none of them produce formal Pauline commentaries that survive. Until, that is, the prolific half-century from 360 to 410. Of the eight commentators on Paul I mentioned, only five come to bear upon the early medieval tradition. Four of these are "apocalyptic realist" readings of the text and will be treated in this chapter. The other, Augustine of Hippo, represents the alternative exegetical strategy that I will treat in the next chapter.

The Ambrose Tradition (1): Ambrosiaster

One of the earliest Latin commentaries on Paul is an anonymous work by the figure whom Erasmus of Rotterdam dubbed "Ambrosiaster." This appellation is appropriate, not because the work is indebted to Ambrose or bears any real similarities to his

---

developed fully in his published dissertation, *The Principles of Patristic Exegesis: Romans 9–11 in Origen, John Chrysostom, and Augustine* (New York: Edwin Mellen Press, 1983). A briefer summary, focusing upon Origen alone, can be found in "Paulus Origenianus: The Economic Interpretation of Paul," in *Paul and the Legacies of Paul,* ed. William S. Babcock (Dallas: Southern Methodist University Press, 1990), 141–63.

26. The scholarship on Origen as biblical exegete is far too expansive to list here. Some classic works are Henri de Lubac, *Histoire et Esprit, l'intelligence de l'Écriture d'apres Origène* (Paris: Aubier, 1950); Jean Daniélou, *Origen,* trans. Walter Mitchell (New York: Sheed and Ward, 1955); Joseph Wilson Trigg, *Origen: The Bible and Philosophy in the Third-Century Church* (Atlanta: John Knox Press, 1983).

27. Gorday, 303 n. 2; Maurice Wiles, *The Divine Apostle* (New York: Cambridge University Press, 1967), 7.

work, but because it comes to us through the tradition as an authoritative work of Ambrose.[28] Numerous attempts to discover the identity of the real author have yielded only guesses at names. But whether our author was Isaac, a converted Jew, or Decimus Hilarianus Hilarius, proconsul of Africa, or Maximus of Turin,[29] or some other figure we will never discover, Latinists have ascertained from internal evidence that his commentary was written some time in the pontificate of Damasus between 366 and 384. Alexander Souter hazards an educated guess that the author is a well-educated layman of high birth, possibly the holder of high administrative posts in the Roman bureaucracy.

His only extant works are the Pauline commentary and the *Questions on the Old and New Testaments,* previously attributed to Augustine. In these we can detect the signs of a theological mind well-read in the Western theological tradition. Ambrosiaster is influenced most significantly by Irenaeus, Tertullian, Pseudo-Clement, Victorinus of Pettau, and Hilary of Poitiers.[30] His influence, in turn, is substantial for the Latin West. Augustine is indebted to him at least for the terminology of his doctrine of original sin,[31] and Pelagius borrows generously from his work. Jerome seems to use his work, but he nowhere admits his debt. Jerome and Ambrosiaster may have disagreed bitterly over Jerome's translation of the Gospels, and Jerome was certainly not above holding a grudge.[32]

28. The text is printed in *PL* 17, in the "Appendix to the Works of St. Ambrose." The best textual edition is found in *CSEL* 81 (ed. Henry Joseph Vogels [Vienna: Hoelder-Pichler-Tempsky, 1969]), and all references will be to this edition.

29. This latest possibility was pondered by Othmar Higgelbacher, "Beziehung zwischen Ambrosiaster und Maximus von Turin? Ein Gegenüberstellung," *Freiburger Zeitschrift für Philosophie und Theologie* 41 (1994): 5–44. Higgelbacher's argument is evaluated by Andreas Merkt, "Wer war der Ambrosiaster? Zum Autor einer Quelle des Augustinus-Fragen auf eine neue Antwort," *Wissenschaft und Weisheit* 59 (1996): 19–33.

30. Alexander Souter, *A Study of Ambrosiaster,* Texts and Studies (Cambridge: Cambridge University Press, 1905), 31.

31. See Stortz for a thorough discussion of this relationship.

32. Alberto Pincherle, *La formazione teologica di sant' Agostino* (Rome: Edizion

Ambrosiaster is a typical exemplar of what Joseph W. Trigg has called the "Latin tradition" of commentary.[33] Each letter's commentary is prefaced by a brief statement setting the letter in its historical context (in relation to Paul's mission) and its literary context (its relation, if any, to other letters). He follows the text carefully, seldom digressing from his explanation of the sense of each lemma. His comments are generally short and to the point, with some attention to grammar and a good bit more to theology interspersed throughout. He offers an understanding of the literal sense and does not often offer more than one interpretive option. Although he questions the Pauline authenticity of Hebrews, he is rarely controversial or heterodox. His interests are ecclesiological, legal, and eschatological.[34] His most distinctive trait is perhaps his close identification of "sin" and "the devil." Sin itself achieves the status of a personal supernatural power; Ambrosiaster's world is the theater of conflict between the soul and the devil.[35] His agonisitic account of reality and his eschatological passions are played out in his interpretation of 2 Thessalonians. In fact, one can find in this very brief commentary hints of all the theological issues that preoccupy this "great unknown" of the fourth century. Ambrosiaster's exegesis of 2 Thessalonians is both a synoptic glimpse at his own theology and the first "block" of the exegetical Antichrist tradition.

The Letter as a Whole: The Argumentum

Ambrosiaster's commentary begins with a prologue to introduce the issues the letter raises. The original authorship of the prologue is not clear, but it is at least theologically and logically con-

Italiane, 1947); Theodore DeBruyn, *Pelagius's Commentary on St. Paul's Epistle to the Romans* (Oxford: Clarendon Press, 1993), ch. 1; J. N. D. Kelly, *Jerome: His Life, Writings, and Controversies* (New York: Harper and Row, 1975), 90, 149.

33. Joseph W. Trigg, *Biblical Interpretation* (Wilmington, Del.: Michael Glazier, 1988).

34. Souter, *Study*, 155.

35. Comm in Roman., ch. 7.

sistent with Ambrosiaster's commentary. The author of this *argumentum* reads this letter as a sequel to 1 Thessalonians. He sees no conflict or disagreement between the two; rather, each letter addresses particular topics, most of them eschatological. The first letter treats, "among other things, the coming of the Lord and the resurrection of the saints."[36] In this second letter, Paul speaks of "the destruction of the Roman Empire, the appearance and damnation of Antichrist, and of the dissatisfaction of some of the brothers."[37] With—or as—the prologue's author, Ambrosiaster understands 2 Thessalonians as a second chapter in Paul's eschatological instruction to the Thessalonian community. The first treats the positive elements of the end, the "reward"; the second presents the negative elements, the "crisis" and the "judgment." But while the positive elements can be presented in a straightforward fashion, the more "critical" moments are discussed in vague, guarded language.

The prologue also notes that the Apostle's words on the destruction of Rome are given "obscurely, for he was unable to write openly."[38] The author gives no further explanation, and thus the question of *why* Paul was unable to write openly is left for the reader to conclude. But it seems that the author intends to imply that the threat of imperial persecution leads Paul to speak in vague, general terms. He situates Paul's letter in the context of persecution, and he attributes the obscurities to the dissimulation necessary in a hostile environment. It is unlikely that this detail is original to Ambrosiaster, since it appears later in authors who have no apparent knowledge of his work.

Ambrosiaster's understanding of the end shares the basic con-

---

36. *"inter caetera etiam de adventu domini quaedam scripsit, et de resurrectione sanctorum."* Ambrosiaster, *In epistolam 2 ad Thess.* (CSEL 81, 235–44), *Argumentum* ll. 3–5.

37. *"de abolitione regni Romani, et de antichristi apparentia et damnatione, et de quorundam fratrum inquietudine."* Ambrosiaster, *Arg.* ll. 6–7.

38. *"in qua significat, licet obscure (neque enim aperte potuit scribere)."* Ambrosiaster, *Arg.* ll. 5–6.

tours of the "mainline" eschatology we saw in Irenaeus and Hippolytus. All agree that Antichrist will come in the future as a false messiah of Jewish origin. He will appear in the wake of the breakdown of the empire, persecute the Church, and rebuild the temple in Jerusalem. The downfall of Rome and the revival of the Jewish temple cult are thus intimately associated with the coming of Antichrist and the return of Christ. Whether Ambrosiaster uses Hippolytus or some other specific source directly or draws upon the "common knowledge" of this "mainline eschatology" enduring into the mid fourth century is difficult to say. At the very least, Ambrosiaster is consistent with this tradition of association, and he therefore testifies to the endurance of "eschatological exegesis"[39] in the Latin Church of the late fourth century and to the firm foundation of the *apocalyptic realist* tradition of 2 Thessalonians exegesis.

2 Thessalonians 1: "In the Image of the Just Judgment of God"

The letter begins with Paul's praise for the Thessalonian community for their growth in faith, charity, and endurance in a time of persecution. For Ambrosiaster, it is proof that the community received Paul's first letter and benefited from it. The church's situation provides an inspirational model for the other churches and comes as an "image *(exemplum)* of the just judgment of God."[40] Paul promises reward "in the kingdom of God for which you suffer." Ambrosiaster emphasizes the sense of justice and retribution in the passage. The Thessalonians have merited by their endurance the reward promised to the saints who "do not hesitate to spurn the world" in the love of God.[41] The persecutions themselves are *exempla*, "images,"

39. Dunbar, "Hippolytus of Rome," passim.

40. *"in exemplum justi judicii Dei."* Ambrosiaster 1.4. The passage is usually rendered in English as "example" or "evidence of the just judgement of God" (NRSV), which can present problems to English interpreters. The sense of the Latin "exemplum" as "image" or "likeness" makes Ambrosiaster's reading a bit easier to understand.

41. *"et mereantur consequi quae promissa sunt sanctis in die justi iudicii dei, cuius amore mundum spernere non dubitarunt."* Ambrosiaster 1.4.

of what awaits both the persecutor and the persecuted in judgment: "glory for these who suffer, damnation for those who persecute."[42]

Paul claims that this judgment will come "when the Lord Jesus comes from heaven with the angels of his power" (2 Th 1:7). Then Jesus will judge "those who do not know God and those who do not obey the gospel of our Lord Jesus Christ" (1:8). Ambrosiaster understands the judgment to be meted out to the pagans, "who do not know that God is the Father of Jesus Christ," and to the Jews, "who say they know God but do not believe in the gospel of Christ."[43] They will all be judged by Christ, who will appear "brilliant and wonderful" to those who believe and "severe" to those who do not believe.

Ambrosiaster understands the first chapter[44] to give an apocalyptic theodicy. In judgment, persecution is reversed; the suffering of innocents is replaced by glory; the triumph of persecutors is conquered by perdition. Indeed, even the survival of the Jews (which is a problem for Ambrosiaster) and the triumph (if ever brief) of the pagans is explained by their destruction at the end. The coming of Christ in judgment finally balances the scales of justice. This first chapter, then, gives Ambrosiaster the "what" of the eschaton—what will happen to the just and the wicked. In chapter two, Paul moves to speak of the "how"—How will the events leading up to judgment unfold?

---

42. *"ipsae enim pressurae exempla sunt futurorum meritorum in his qui patiuntur ad gloriam, in illis autem qui persequuntur ad perditionem."* Ambrosiaster 1.4.

43. *"paganos, qui ignorant deum patrem esse Christi Jesu, et Iudaeos, qui dicentes se scire deum non credunt evangelio Christi."* Ambrosiaster 1.9.1.

44. Of course, it is a bit of an anachronism to speak of any of these patristic thinkers as referring to the "first chapter." However, in the case of 2 Thessalonians, the chapter breakdown does, in fact, seem to come at a moment of transition in the text, and the commentaries seem to treat it as a whole. Thus, what we call chapter 1 does in fact constitute an intelligible section of the text, and I will continue to refer to it in our customary fashion.

2 Thessalonians 2:1–4: "Let no one seduce you in any way."

Having praised the Thessalonians for their perseverance, Paul now turns to warn them about false predictions of the end. For Ambrosiaster, such false predictions are the work of the devil, intended to seduce the faithful into worshipping him. The devil will appear "under the name of the Savior" to "beguile those who believe in Christ."[45] However, the devil's plan is foiled, because Paul "designates the time and the signs of the coming of the Lord."[46] Using a typical apocalyptic *topos*, Paul gives the signs of the end as special knowledge for the elect to prepare for the final tribulation. Paul's predictions are the best defense against the attacks of the devil.

In 2:3, Paul predicts that Christ will not return unless first the failure *(defectio)*[47] of the Roman Empire occurs and Antichrist appears. Ambrosiaster understands these events as sequential rather than simultaneous: First Rome will falter, then Antichrist will come. Ambrosiaster gives an initial survey of these events and a "first impression" of Antichrist. He "will kill the saints after he has restored freedom to the Romans, but in his own name."[48] He will then take the seat of Christ in the "house of the Lord" and claim to be God himself. Ambrosiaster takes this as an indication that he will either come "from the circumcision" or "be circumcised," that is, either be born of the Jews or become a Jew, so that the Jews may believe in him.[49] But Ambrosiaster's discussion of this verse lacks any explicit

45. *"ut sub nomine salvatoris apparens . . . ut decipiat credentes in Christum."* Ambrosiaster 2.2.1.

46. *"tempus et signa adventus domini designavit."* Ambrosiaster 2.3.2.

47. While *defectio* can mean either "failure" or "rebellion," the context seems to draw the meaning toward "failure," although not to the necessary exclusion of the other. Note that Ambrosiaster is using an older Latin text of the letter. His work predates the Vulgate edition of the Pauline epistles, and his commentaries are a reliable source for a version of this earlier Latin text.

48. *"qui interficiet sanctos, reddita Romanis libertate, sub suo tamen nomine."* Ambrosiaster 2.3.2.

49. Ambrosiaster cites Jn 5:43 here, probably drawing on Irenaeus, *Adversus*

reference to the rebuilding of the temple in Jerusalem,[50] and the exact nature of Antichrist's relation to the Jews is left highly ambiguous.

Ambrosiaster's Antichrist is a supernatural figure, for he has some knowledge of the future. His plan unfolds as it does because "he knows that the coming Lord presses upon him."[51] Antichrist is thus aware of his place in salvation history; in a sense, he *knows* that Christ will not come until he has done his work. In this way, his place is distinct from the attempts of the devil to pose as Christ already come, as we noted above. The devil's initial scheme is foiled because it is not part of the providential plan; this latter attack on the faithful is, in its own way, providential. Antichrist appears at this first introduction to be a self-conscious actor in the events of the end, leading astray some of the faithful and all of the Jews.

2 Thessalonians 2:5–7: "For the mystery of iniquity is already at work"

In verses 5 and 6, Paul reminds the Thessalonians of what he had already taught them, so that they now know "what restrains, that he may be revealed in his time." Ambrosiaster understands this to be Paul's simple summary of what he has said above. "What restrains" is the course of events given in verse 3: first the failure of the Roman Empire, then the appearance of Antichrist. The "restraining force" is the power of historical causality and temporal progression. The coming of Antichrist and then that of Christ are restrained by the fact that events that must precede them have not yet occurred. Nev-

---

haereses 5.30.6, as proof that Antichrist will come to the Jews "in his own name" and be accepted by them. Note, however, that this is not a point that Ambrosiaster emphasizes; he is far more interested in Antichrist's parallels in Roman paganism.

50. Although perhaps it could be understood to imply or assume this, since he clearly associates the "session in the temple" with the Jews. Nevertheless, it is an interesting omission in light of Julian's plans to rebuild it in the years just before Ambrosiaster wrote.

51. *"sciens enim venturum dominum ad se comprimendum."* Ambrosiaster 2.4.2.

ertheless, some signs of the end are already present, since the "mystery of iniquity" is already at work.

For Ambrosiaster, the mystery of iniquity is the persecution of the Church by the Roman Empire:

The mystery of iniquity was initiated by Nero, who, in the zeal for idols and with the instigation of his father the devil, killed the apostles. [It continued] up to Diocletian and most recently Julian, who began his persecution with a certain flair and subtlety but was not able to complete it, since it was not permitted him from on high.[52]

The "mystery of iniquity" is present in any imperial opposition to Christianity, represented above all by the revival of pagan cult. For Ambrosiaster, the pagan gods are a sort of mask for Satan; in the guise of the "mob of gods" *(turba deorum),* Satan mocks the "manifestation of the one true God" *(unius veri dei manifestionem inludat:* i.e., the Incarnation). Julian and his predecessors are the "ministers" *(ministris)* of Satan; they will continue in their iniquity "for as long as the kingdom of the Romans will stand,"[53] when it will be "taken from the midst" *(donec de medio fiat,* 2:7).

2 Thessalonians 2:8–10: "And then he will be revealed"

Having alluded to the foreshadowings of the end, Paul again projects forward to the time when Antichrist will be revealed. And again, Ambrosiaster focuses upon the role of Satan and providence. The devil will know that his destruction is imminent, since the Roman Empire will have fallen and "he will have been cast down from the heavens upon the earth." In his desperate effort to lead the faithful astray, the devil will use Antichrist for his work.

He will suborn himself in Antichrist and perform "certain signs of power through him." Antichrist's works are actual and real; they

---

52. *"Mysterium iniquitatis a Nerone coeptum est, qui zelo idolorum et apostolos interfecit instigante patre suo diabolo, usque ad Diocletianum et novissime Iulianum, qui arte quadam et subtilitate coeptam persecutionem implere non potuit, quia desuper concessum non fuerat."* Ambrosiaster 2.7.

53. *"quamdiu steterit regnem Romanorum."* Ambrosiaster 2.7.

are not illusions. Paul calls them "lying signs" because they lead people into false belief. They are performed only "with the just God's permission." Through the "signs of power" worked through Antichrist, Satan will commend himself to be worshiped like a god. Indeed, Satan deliberately imitates God:

Just as the Son of God, *born or made man*, demonstrated his divine nature with signs or works of power, so Satan will *appear* in a human being, so that he may present himself as a god with lying works of power.[54]

Note that Satan can only "appear" in a human being, while the Son was "born or made man." This distinguishes Christ from Antichrist in nature: only in Christ is supernatural power actually incarnate. It is in this cheap imitation that Antichrist's (and thus Satan's) primary work consists.[55] In this, Antichrist is the fulfilled manifestation of the "mystery of iniquity already at work":

For the revelation of the mystery of iniquity is this: when Antichrist will have appeared, he will be thought to be like the god of those whom—earlier, at his command—the masses worshiped as gods, and of whom he himself is the first or highest.[56]

In this passage, Ambrosiaster connects Antichrist's future coming with the Roman pagan pantheon. When he appears, Antichrist will be the head of all these "gods" that Ambrosiaster equates with demonic powers. Here Ambrosiaster echoes the Pauline theme of personal consummation, whereby the mystery now present, but dif-

54. *"ut sicut filius dei divinitatem suam homo natus vel factus signis ac virtutibus demonstravit, ita et satanas in homine apparebit, ut virtutibus mendacii ostendat se deum."* Ambrosiaster 2.8.1.

55. Whether to speak of Antichrist as "the devil incarnate" or to use any such parallel language for him would be a disputed question for much of the ancient and early medieval period. As late as the end of the sixth century, Gregory I and others would still assert that Antichrist was to be the devil incarnate. See McGinn, *Antichrist,* 94–97, and 298 n. 51. McGinn and I interpret the particular passage quoted above from Ambrosiaster differently.

56. *"revelatio vero mysterii iniquitatis haec est; cum apparuerit Antichristus, cognoscetur ipse esse quasi eorum deus, quos prius nutu eius ut deos coluit vulgus, quorum sit ipse primus aut summus."* Ambrosiaster 2.8.2.

fuse, is made manifest fully in one person. This great evil that is gradually unveiled is idolatry: the Roman cult and its power to deceive. The devil, at each appearance in the commentary, desires above all to divert people from worshiping the true God. Paul's prophetic teaching equips the "saints" with the knowledge necessary to pierce through these deceptions so "they may know what they should be wary of."[57]

2 Thessalonians 2:11–16: "And so, brothers, stand and hold fast to our traditions"

Those who are deceived, according to Paul, will perish with Antichrist. They have spurned the love of truth that could have saved them. Ambrosiaster adds that they have been handed over to the devil; God deserts those who do not want to be saved. It is clear that Ambrosiaster allocates responsibility for damnation to the deliberate act of each person's will in the face of truth. Even when Paul speaks of God sending "the operation of error," Ambrosiaster does not waver. The "operation of error" is "to put faith in false things." God sends this hardness of heart upon those who have already rejected the gospel, "that, having been made guilty by a weightier sin, they can be damned without contradiction as enemies of the truth and patrons of iniquity."[58]

But the Thessalonians, says Paul, are among those that God has taken up for salvation from the very beginning in the sanctification of the spirit and true faith (2:13). He thus encourages them to persevere in their faith (2:15). For Ambrosiaster, Paul's words reflect God's foreknowledge of those who will persevere in faith. As Martha Stortz has demonstrated, Ambrosiaster's notion of predestination is limited to divine foreknowledge and contains no sense of divine forejudgment. And even his sense of foreknowledge is less concerned with knowledge of a soul's desire (as in Pelagius) than

57. *"ut sciant quid caveant."* Ambrosiaster 2.8.2.
58. *"ut possint propensiori delicto rei facti sine contradictione damnari veritatis imimici, fautores autem iniquitatis."* Ambrosiaster 2.11.

with knowledge of the soul's perseverance in the faith.[59] Here, too, Ambrosiaster is concerned above all with who will "finish what they have begun."[60] When Paul balances his exhortation to perseverance with the petition that "our Lord Jesus Christ himself and God our Father . . . [may] comfort your hearts and strengthen them in every good word and work" (2:16–17), thereby preserving the ambiguity between human perseverance and God's confirmation, Ambrosiaster instead reads this as a "heartening doxology" of sorts, such that the knowledge of salvation history might inspire perseverance:

[God] so loved us that he gave his own son for us, God for humans, the lord for servants, the true son for adopted children, that his death may be our life and his resurrection may be our justification, and his second coming may be the repose of our life and eternal glory, that such hope may be the consolation of the present struggles.[61]

Ambrosiaster clearly holds human beings accountable for their failures and rejection of the gospel. God has foreknowledge of their decisions, but he does not ordain them. When he sends "the operation of error" upon those who have rejected the gospel, it is only in response to their prior rejection.

2 Thessalonians 3: "Do not be weary in doing what is right"

Paul now turns away from his teaching about the last things and discusses the life of the community. Specifically, he addresses what Ambrosiaster calls the "dissatisfaction of some of the brothers."[62] Paul is concerned to correct those who are "walking immoderately and not according to the tradition they received from us." Ambrosi-

---

59. Stortz, 54–56.

60. "*impleant quod coeperunt.*" Ambrosiaster 2.15.

61. "*qui in tantum dilexit nos, ut filium suum daret pro nobis, deum pro hominibus, pro servis dominum, pro adoptivis filium verum, ut mors eius vita nostra sit et resurrectio eius iustificatio nostra, secundum autem adventus eius requies vitae nostrae et gloria in aeternum, ut ista spes consolatio sit presentium pressurarum, per quam fundati crescerent in bonis operibus et doctrina.*" Ambrosiaster 2.16.

62. "*et de quorundam fratrum inquietudine.*" Ambrosiaster l. 11.

aster takes this opportunity to speak about the health of a community, Paul's method of teaching by action, and the proper discipline to be administered to those in error. It is clear, however, that Ambrosiaster understands this section of the letter to be a distinct "chapter" of Pauline teaching, not at all related to the rest of the letter. It is an exercise, above all, in Paul's moral teaching, and Ambrosiaster makes no explicit effort to connect it to the apocalyptic teaching given in the first part of the letter.

Ambrosiaster's interpretation of 2 Thessalonians sketches a very particular picture of the end, and, consequently, of the present that anticipates it. His exegesis expresses his particular theological concern for providence and the role of Satan. His scenario is entirely historical or what I have called "realist"; his interpretation demonstrates great concern for how "the mystery of iniquity" unfolds in concrete historical realities. This process of unfolding follows God's providential plan, such that the devil cannot act to deceive or persecute the Church unless it is permitted to him by God. His apocalyptic scenario is full of supernatural conflict; Christian life is one of struggle against the assaults of the devil. The devil is above all a deceiver; he tries to lure believers away by posing as God and thus leading them into idolatry. But his deception has its concrete, historical expression in the pagan cult of the Roman Empire.

This imperial "mystery of iniquity" began with Nero—long the arch-persecutor in Christian (and Jewish) thought—and it continues in Diocletian and Julian. Note that the two emperors he lists after Nero are the two most associated not only with persecution, but with an explicit attempt to revive Roman religion. Perhaps, in the shadow of Emperor Julian's pagan revival, Ambrosiaster was all too aware of the seductive appeal of the cults and sacrifices of traditional Roman religion. Perhaps his emphasis on persistence in the faith is related to the apostasy of baptized Christians such as Julian himself. Whatever the reasons, Ambrosiaster clearly associates the threat of iniquity with the "idolatry" embodied in the imperial pantheon and mystery religions.

Thus, when the Roman Empire fails and Antichrist appears he will restore the freedom of the Romans to kill the saints. And he, like the Roman emperors, will lead believers astray by posing as God. Indeed, he will appear to be the god of the gods of Rome. While Ambrosiaster concedes to the tradition that Antichrist will come from the Jewish people, he is far less concerned with his role among the Jews than with the restoration of paganism. Ambrosiaster's Antichrist is, above all, the false idol, the personification of the devil's deceptions, and this personification finds its clearest exemplar in Rome.

The Ambrose Tradition (2): Theodore of Mopsuestia

Some time in the early Middle Ages, a manuscript of Ambrosiaster's commentaries on Romans and 1 and 2 Corinthians was separated from the rest. To complete the set, a scribe joined them to another set of commentaries from Galatians to Philemon. The new whole was ascribed to Ambrose and copied. It survives in several manuscripts, generating yet another "Ambrose" authoritative for the medieval Latin West.[63] Despite the potential for confusion, this editor's error must be counted a *"felix culpa,"* for it is in this way that the latter Pauline commentaries of Theodore of Mopsuestia survive in Latin translation. And in this way, the heritage of the School of Antioch, of which Theodore is a principal representative, was passed on to the Latin West.[64]

The School of Antioch is best known for its famed assault on the

63. See Swete's introduction to his edition of Theodore's letters, H. B. Swete, *Theodori episcopi in epistolas beati Pauli commentarii.* 2 vols. (Cambridge: Cambridge University Press, 1882), i–lxxi.

64. It must be admitted, however, that any such influence was sporadic at best. However, it is worth noting that even this sporadic influence is significant when it appears in the work of exegetes such as Rabanus Maurus and Lanfranc of Canterbury, each renowned among his contemporaries for his work on the Scriptures. (See my discussion of Rabanus and Lanfranc, pp. 124–25, 180).

hermeneutical walls of Alexandrian allegory. Antiochenes preferred a hermeneutical method that approaches interpretive stumbling blocks by paying close attention to the historical situation, literary form, and rhetorical style rather than by using of rules of allegory.[65] The school flowered under the headship of the prolific Diodore of Tarsus (d. 394). Diodore wrote explicitly against the method of allegorical interpretation in a lost treatise entitled *On the Difference between Theoria and Allegoria,* and his polemic was carried on in the exegetical works of his disciples Theodore of Mopsuestia, John Chrysostom, and Theodoret of Cyrrhus.

Theodore of Mopsuestia (ca. 350–428) was raised from an early age in the schools of Antioch. As a youth, he sat with his colleague John Chrysostom at the feet of Libanius the rhetorician. Diodore of Tarsus tutored him in his advanced theological and exegetical study, and it is under him that Theodore probably wrote his first exegetical work on the Psalms. Ordained a priest in 382, Theodore preached and wrote in Antioch until he was elevated ten years later (392) to the episcopal see of Mopsuestia. He composed his commentaries on the Epistles of Paul in ca. 410–415. These commentaries give insight into both Theodore's exegetical power and his mature theology.[66]

His exegetical method is characterized by his painstaking attention to the contextual, grammatical, and theological details of each text he studies. Each letter's commentary is prefaced by a detailed argument in which Theodore identifies the particular purpose and historical situation for which the letter was written and its continued relevance to Theodore's audience.[67] In such a form, the commen-

---

65. John C. Cavadini, "School of Antioch," *Harper Collins Encyclopedia of Catholicism,* ed. Richard McBrien (New York: Harper Collins, 1995), 67–68; Bradley Nassif, "'Spiritual Exegesis' in the School of Antioch"; Trigg, *Biblical Interpretation;* Froehlich, ed., *Biblical Interpretation.*

66. On the relationship between Theodore's exegesis and his theology, see Rowan Greer, *Theodore of Mopsuestia: Exegete and Theologian* (Westminster, Md.: Faith Press, 1961).

67. Philippians is the only exception to this observation in the extant complete commentaries.

tary on each letter can stand alone as a complete whole. Each letter offers a particular situation and a particular set of problems that Paul addresses, and Theodore interprets each letter independent of, though not unrelated to, the rest.

Theodore's concerns in interpretation are primarily theological, and often specifically Christological. His theology is decidedly Trinitarian in Nicene-Constantinopolitan form.[68] In his exegesis, he often analyzes Paul's syntax, punctuation, and vocabulary, but always with the intent of shedding light on his theological meaning. This powerful combination of grammatical and theological analyses suggests that Theodore was well-suited to his posthumous title, *"the* Antiochene Interpreter."

The particularly Antiochene character of his exegesis appears most clearly in his argument against allegory in the Commentary on Galatians. Antiochene thinkers such as Theodore took exception to the disregard with which he believed the Alexandrians held the literal, historical sense of the biblical text. The Antiochene *theoria,* or "contemplation," searches for a deep spiritual meaning that is within or closely related to the literal sense. Theodore thought that the Alexandrians "played tricks with the plain sense of the Bible and want[ed] to rob it of any meaning it contains." He cautions them, "if they play tricks with history, they will have no history at all."[69] Theodore is thus very concerned to protect the historical referent of the scriptural text. Without it, the coherence of the biblical revelation breaks down.

Theodore guards the literal, historical sense of the text for both exegetical and theological reasons. The theological warrant for his concern is the centrality of a realistic understanding of salvation his-

68. See his *Catechetical Commentary on the Nicene Creed,* ed. A. Mingana, Woodbrook Studies 5 (Cambridge: Heffer and Sons, 1933).

69. *"qui studium multum habent intervertere sensus divinarum scripturarum et omnia quae illuc posita sunt intercipere"* and *"ad quos volebam illud dicere, ut historiam intercipientes, ultra non habuerint historiam."* Theodore, *In epistolam ad Galatas* IV.24, Swete, 74–75.

tory in his doctrine of redemption. Theodore understands history to be divided into two ages. In the first, present age, humans are mutable and mortal; in the second age, initiated by Christ's resurrection, they can become immutable and immortal. The Christian life in history is an exercise in divine *paideia,* or education, so that the Christian person may move from mutability to immutability. Those who live in the time between the resurrection of Christ and the general resurrection participate partially in the future reality through membership in the Church and participation in the sacraments.

Alternatively, Theodore speaks of the Christian life as a struggle against the tyrant, Satan. That struggle is made possible, rather than superfluous, by the victory of Christ. Redemption is mediated by God, through Christ, to Christians in their present circumstance through the sacraments, and through these, the Christian is empowered to conquer Satan. But such a conquest, and thus redemption itself, is fulfilled only in the general resurrection. Theodore's theology and exegesis are eschatological.

Theodore's theology also contained elements that led to posthumous condemnation. His Christology spoke of the "man assumed" and the Word who assumed him by grace as two distinct subjects united in one *prosopon.* This "Word-man" Christology was viewed as proto-Nestorian by Cyril of Alexandria, and when in the early sixth century opinion favored Monophysite theology, Theodore was one of the "Three Chapters" condemned by an edict of Justinian in ca. 534–536.[70] It is likely that the Latin translation of his commentary on Paul issued from this controversial condemnation, since Theodore and his Antiochene school enjoyed great support in the Western churches, who clearly held a "two-nature" Christology. Theodore's commentaries were translated perhaps in an effort to give the Western churches stronger support for their defense, or perhaps as a way to give Theodore a more Latin dress. Whatever the

70. On Theodore's Christology, see Richard A. Norris Jr., *Manhood and Christ: A Study of the Christology of Theodore of Mopsuestia* (Oxford: Clarendon Press, 1963).

reason, the Western efforts failed; Theodore was condemned finally at the Second Council of Constantinople in 553, and the western Church was forced to endorse the judgment.[71] Thereafter the commentaries would survive, whether by subterfuge or by accident, only under the noble mantle of the name of Ambrose.

The Latin text bears the scars of translation. The biblical text is sometimes faithful to the Vulgate, but often the editor gives a direct translation of the Greek text used by Theodore.[72] The Latinity of the commentary has been judged "eccentric" and "faulty."[73] Some words have been taken over directly from the Greek, and in some cases the translator has maintained Greek word order. It does not appear, however, that the "suspect" elements in Theodore's theology have been doctored or manipulated; rather the translator has taken great pains trying to capture the precise sense of Theodore's thought in Latin. It is safe to assume, then, that the Latin text is at least an adequate rendering of Theodore's commentary on 2 Thessalonians.

The Letter as a Whole: The Argumentum

Theodore's *argumentum* carefully constructs a hypothetical historical context for the letter. For Theodore, Paul sees three issues in the Thessalonian community. First, they have continued to suffer

71. W. H. C. Frend, *The Rise of Christianity* (Philadelphia: Fortress Press, 1984), 837–53. While Theodore's theology was certainly popular—so popular that his condemnation caused schism in the Latin Church for some forty years—I do not mean to argue that Latin Christologies in subsequent years were derived from Theodore's work. Rather, Theodore found a home in the west because the theological climate was one already receptive to his thought. See John C. Cavadini, *The Last Christology of the West* (Philadelphia: University of Pennsylvania Press, 1993), for a full discussion of Western Latin Christology and its relation (or nonrelation) to Antiochene traditions.

72. Swete, xli–xliv. A comparison of the Vulgate text of 2 Th with that found in this commentary shows that, by and large, it follows the sense of the Vulgate. Perhaps the only significant difference is in 2 Th 2:3, where there is a transliteration of the Greek *apostasia* rather than the Vulgate's *discessio*.

73. Swete, lviii.

the attacks of persecution, but, "by the power of God," they have endured them. Second, they have been told that "the end of the present age was imminent," and this new teaching is proffered as if it had come from Paul himself. Third, some to the Thessalonians had not benefited from his first letter, but instead had persisted in their bad habits. The Apostle writes his second letter with these three issues in mind. First, he praises the community for their endurance and patience, and he encourages them to continue. Then he teaches them that they shouldn't expect the consummation of time to be imminent. "Among other things," he speaks of the manner of the advent of Antichrist. Finally, he excoriates those "undisciplined" members of the community and advises others in the community as to how to handle them. Having developed this historical context, Theodore steps back and affirms the continuing relevance of the letter: "We are taught very carefully about all of this from what follows."[74] Theodore affirms both the letter's particular historical location and the elements that are still important to his contemporaries.

2 Thessalonians 1: If you are content to suffer for him

Theodore's analysis of the letter proceeds by quoting individual lemmata and following them with a twofold move of paraphrase and logical transition to the next verse. He often introduces the paraphrase with a formulaic phrase such as "For he wants to say . . ." (vult enim dicere). The logical transition is just that: a transitional thought that attempts to link each lemma to the next. For example, commenting on 2Thessalonians 1:4, "such that we ourselves boast in the churches of God about your patience and faith in all your persecutions and all the tribulations you have endured," he writes:

"Indeed, boasting about you in every place we go, we report the strength of your faith, giving praise because, afflicted with so many torments, you

---

74. "cautius vero de omnibus instruemur ex illis quae in subsequentibus habentur." Swete, 42.

have endured in that same state of strength." He said "which you have endured" rightly; this was very worthy of admiration, since they endured the torments brought against them with strength of spirit. Then he speaks of the benefit of their sufferings.[75]

He then moves on to the next verse. Through this repeated action, Theodore attempts to stay close to Paul's text, clarifying it verse by verse through paraphrase and following the course of the argument with the logical transition.

In the first chapter of the text, Paul takes up the first task identified in Theodore's argument; namely, to praise the Thessalonians for their endurance in suffering and to exhort them to continue. Paul's praise for the community is accompanied by a reminder of their promised benefit. The benefit of their sufferings, according to Theodore, is that they will enjoy a place in the kingdom of heaven. Insofar as the Thessalonians "are content to suffer joyfully for Christ, he will be seen in them in his glory in the present age."[76] By speaking of the Thessalonians as "content to suffer," Theodore makes them more active agents than Ambrosiaster had. More than passive victims, Theodore's Thessalonians submit to suffering willfully, even "joyfully" (cum alacrite). In so doing, the Thessalonians manifest the glorious presence of Christ in this life, giving a foretaste of the future kingdom. With these words of encouragement, Paul has dispatched his first task in the letter, and so he moves on to the next.[77]

---

75. "'denique et nos omni in loco de vobis gloriantes referimus fidei vestrae firmitatem, laudantes, eo quod et tormentis variis affecti in eodem statu permansistis.' bene autem dixit quas sustinetis, eo quod hoc demiratione dignum erat, quod forti animo sustinerent inlata sibi tormenta. deinde dicit et ipsius passionis utilitatem." Swete, 44.

76. "sic enim et Christus in vobis gloriosus secundum praesens saeculum videbitur, quando cum alacritate adquiescitis pati pro eo." Swete, 48. I have rendered secundum as "in" rather than "after" on the basis of the translator's use of the term in other parts of the letter to clearly indicate a sense of "in this case." See, for example, Swete, 59, commenting on 2.17: "qui gratia (inquit) sua aeternam illam consolationem nobis donavit (id est, futurorum bonorum spem), ipse et secundum praesentem vitam hanc prosperet corda vestra."

77. "quae ergo conveniebant dici ad laudem eorum qui in adversis firmi persisterunt,

2 Thessalonians 2:1–3.5:
"When the Prescription of God Shall Cease"

Theodore has discerned that Paul's second task in this letter is to persuade the Thessalonians that the "day of the Lord" has not yet come. The Thessalonians should be sure to interpret Paul's discussion of the resurrection in his first letter to refer to the future.[78] Neither should they believe any other teaching about the matter. Theodore's Paul believes that the possible sources of error on this account are either false prophecy or forgery, and he "vehemently desires to make them cautious."[79]

He assures them that Christ will not come until Antichrist comes first. The arrival of Antichrist is the first apocalyptic event; the rest follow upon it. The "apostasy"—*apostasia* here, in a transliteration of the Greek—refers not to the Roman Empire, or in fact to any political or imperial reality, but to "the time when all but a few will fall away from piety and run to him,"[80] that is, to Antichrist. The "apostasy" is not chronologically or logically prior to the revelation of Antichrist; instead, it is logically and chronologically consequent, caused by Antichrist himself.

Antichrist himself is properly called *homo,* "man" or "human being," because he will in fact be a human being, just like Jesus, the *homo assumptus* of Theodore's "Word-man" Christology: "He will be a man, with a demon working everything in him, just as God in the Word seems to have accomplished everything in that man who was assumed for our salvation."[81] Antichrist, the antitype to Christ,

---

et ad exhortationem ut in eadem persisterent sententia, in hisce visus est consumasse. hinc vero incipit de consummatione saeculi disputare, docens eos non existimare sibi finem mundanum imminere." Swete, 48.

78. Swete, 48–49.

79. *"et vehementius eos cautos facere volens."* Swete 49.

80. *"'apostasiam' vero vocavit tempus illud, eo quod paulo minus omnes tunc discedent a pietate, et adcurrent ad eum."* Swete 50.

81. *"homo erit, daemone in eo omnia inoperante, sicut et in illum hominem qui pro nostra salute sumptus est, Deus Verbo omnia perfecisse videtur."* Swete, 50–51.

will attempt to imitate him in everything, even calling himself "Christ." He is called the man *of sin* because "he will serve sin and his cause will appear before many people."[82] Theodore draws upon the traditional doctrine of Antichrist's opposition that finds its origins in Irenaeus and Hippolytus, but in his thought this traditional discipline finds its natural complement in an "antichristology" based on the Christological model of assumption. The parallel is not direct, however; Theodore distinguishes between the two theologically. For example, Theodore is careful to distinguish the nature of Antichrist's appearance from the revelation of God in Christ. While Paul speaks of Antichrist as "revealed," Theodore takes pains to make clear that Antichrist is "manifested," not "revealed" in the technical sense.[83] Also, whereas God in the Word indwelt the *homo assumptus* "as in a son" in his Christology,[84] Theodore makes no use of filiation language in relation to Antichrist, even when the text provides an opportunity. Antichrist is called the "son of perdition," not because he is the "son of the devil" (as other authors will conclude), but because he will necessarily be cast into perdition, or hell, when Christ returns. The language of filiation is applied only in a loosely metaphorical sense, suggesting his destiny, rather than his work or origin.

In fact, Theodore offers no account of Antichrist's origin. His relation to the Jews is conspicuous by its absence. Not only does this commentary lack any statement of his emergence "from the tribe of Dan" or any such thing, but also there is no discussion of his preaching to the Jews or rebuilding the temple. Theodore interprets the session "in the temple" instead as a presence "in the temples, that is, in the houses of prayer."[85] Antichrist will take Christ's seat in the

82. *"peccatum ministrabit, et multis hominibus huius causa existet."* Swete 51.
83. Swete, 55.
84. *On the Incarnation, Book VII,* as translated by Richard A. Norris Jr. in *The Christological Controversy* (Philadelphia: Fortress Press, 1980), 117.
85. *"sic enim et 'in Dei templis,' hoc est, et in domibus orationum, ingrediens sedebit, quasi quia ipse sit Christus et propter hoc debeat ab omnibus adorari in ordinem Dei."*

churches, claiming to be Christ himself. This too, I think, is understood symbolically, as a statement of his usurpation of Christ's proper place in Christian worship and prayer. His appearance and work is thus entirely an intra-ecclesial phenomenon. Antichrist will pose as Christ and try to convert the faithful from "their proper doctrine."[86]

But for the present, says Paul, Antichrist is restrained from coming. Theodore acknowledges that Paul's meaning here is unclear, and he addresses two possible answers. First, he says, there are some who say that Paul refers to the Holy Spirit as "what now restrains." In this view, the miraculous works of the Spirit will decline and eventually cease to occur in public.[87] Theodore rejects this option since, in his opinion, the works of the Spirit have all but ceased and Antichrist has not yet come.[88] Of course, the Spirit has not totally failed, because some of the saints will not fall away. "For then there will be some who do not accept his teaching and who will be famed for struggling against him with their piety."[89] Thus, while the "mighty works" of the Spirit have ceased, her confirming power will persist even during the reign of Antichrist. The Spirit's works, then, cannot be the restraining force.

The second and better interpretation of 2 Thessalonians 2:7 is an understanding of providence. According to Theodore, God alone restrains the devil, who "wanted to do this long ago." God "has established the time of the end of this age, and only then will he per-

Swete, 52. Swete suggests that the change in number for "templis" may very well go back to Theodore, since he was not always precise in quoting his sources.

86. "a propria eorum secta discedere suadens." Swete, 51.

87. Swete attributes this view to Severianus, and it appears to have been a significant enough possible answer in Antiochene circles that several of the major Antiochene interpreters—Theodore, Theodoret, and John Chrysostom—saw fit to respond to it. Note that it will reappear in the thought of Gregory the Great.

88. He concedes that the works of the Spirit have not *totally* ceased, "eo quod et ab aliquibus adhuc per orationem fiant aliqua, licet si et rare." Swete, 53.

89. "erunt enim et tunc qui non suscipient eius doctrinam, qui et clari erunt contemplatione pietatis decertantes adversus eum." Swete, 53.

mit Antichrist to be seen."[90] "That which now restrains" is, simply, God's prescription that he be restrained. The devil struggles in vain against the providential decree of God, since Antichrist appears by the permission of God at the time that God has chosen, the "end of this age."

For the present, Satan must be content to work secretly. The "mystery of iniquity" represents this secret work, where the devil uses "his own" in "particular efforts to tear those who are added to the faith away from holiness of life."[91] Theodore indicates here that the work of the devil is found not in persecution, but in the daily temptations faced by those newly converted to the faith. Whom Theodore classifies as "the devil's own" is unclear, but he certainly refrains from any association with Nero and his like. Again, the apolitical, ecclesial nature of Theodore's interpretation stands in strong contrast to what we have seen in Ambrosiaster and what even his Antiochene contemporary, John Chrysostom, taught.[92] Theodore prefers to understand the attacks of the devil in the present in a far more subtle, individual, moral sense; each Christian as he or she enters the Church struggles with the devil.[93]

90. *"eo quod diabolus quidem dudum voluerit hoc idem facere, Deus vero interim retinet eum, eo quod tempus statuit consummationis saeculi istius, secundum quam videri concedit eum."* Swete, 54.

91. *"per singula momenta per suos a pietate temptans divellere eos qui ad fidem accedunt."* Swete, 54.

92. See John Chrysostom, "Homilies on Thessalonians," in *Nicene and Post-Nicene Fathers*, ed. Philip Schaff, Series 1, vol. 13 (Grand Rapids: Eerdmans, 1965).

93. The parallel with portions of his *Catechetical Homilies* is notable: "Now, however, that the great and wonderful grace, which was manifest through Christ, freed us from the yoke of the Tyrant and delivered us from his servitude, and granted us this wonderful participation in benefits, I have recognized my benefactor. . . . I abjure, therefore, Satan, flee from communion with him, and engage myself that henceforth I shall not run towards him not shall I have any intercourse with him, but I shall flee completely from him as from an enemy and an evil doer, who became to us the cause of innumerable calamities, who does not know how to do good, and who strives with all his power to fight us and overcome us." *Catechetical Homilies*, quoted in Greer, *Theodore of Mopsuestia*, 69.

Antichrist will finally come when "the prescription of God shall cease." His career will be funded "by the working of Satan," since he will travel throughout the world persuading everyone to abandon their faith. His means of persuasion will be the many "lying signs and prodigies," which, according to Theodore, means that they will be "more phantasm than actual work."[94] He will continue in his deceit until "suddenly Christ appears from heaven and, with only a cry, makes him cease from his work." The devil will be handed over to eternal punishment, and Antichrist will be destroyed with "those who are perishing."

"Those who are perishing" are for Theodore "those who are deserving of perdition." They did not persist in "the truth of love"[95] when Antichrist appeared. Paul says that God "sent them an operation of error"; Theodore concludes that he *really* means that God allows this operation to come to them. In fact, they are entirely responsible for their own perdition, since they "attend to the seduction and believe in the lie."[96] For Theodore, this passage has nothing to do with God's predestination or foreknowledge; it is descriptive only of the destiny of those who do not persevere in the faith, and thus become "unbelievers" *(increduli).*

Believers, on the other hand, have been chosen to enjoy salvation, and thus receive the "grace of the Spirit," the "faith in the truth." They will receive "eternal consolation" in the future, and now, in this present life, Christ "prospers their hearts." Paul prays for their continued prosperity and exhorts them to stand fast in what he has taught them. Theodore echoes these sentiments with roughly equivalent paraphrases. But it is clear that, for Theodore, both the "chosen" and the "unbelievers" are responsible for their fate: though

94. *"ostendens quoniam in phantasmate magis quam in opere facit ea."* Swete, 57.

95. Note that he inverts the text, which reads "love of truth." Note, too, that Theodore says nothing here about those who rejected the Gospel forthright. He is concerned only with those who do not *persist* in the truth of love.

96. *"non permanentes in veritate intendunt seductione et credunt mendacio."* Swete, 58.

God has permitted the "operation of error" in Antichrist, the "unbelievers" have freely submitted to his persuasion. And though God has "chosen" the Thessalonians "for salvation," they still must cling to the hope promised to them and persist in "patience and love."

2 Thessalonians 3:6–18: "Working with modesty, they may eat their bread."

Theodore has addressed two of Paul's three tasks in the letter; he now turns to the third. The last section of the letter is directed at the "undisciplined," whom Paul "vehemently chastises" *(vehementer corripiat).* Theodore is careful to specify precisely whom the Apostle is addressing, for the text seems to indicate that all should work to earn their own bread. But this command is inconsistent with Paul's instruction to the Corinthians, where he argues that it is necessary "that those who have been left free for teaching receive supply for the body from the disciples."[97] Thus, Paul cannot have meant this command to be quite so absolute; instead, he intends to address only those do not work and are not "anxious for the better things" *(qui neque de melioribus sollicitus est).* There are those, then, for whom physical labor is an unnecessary burden. They are those who teach, and they should be supported by their community. Only those who do not have such a reason to refrain from labor should feel the sting of Paul's rebuke. Only they, says Theodore, are the *"indisciplinati"* of whom Paul writes.

Theodore thus defends the right not to work under certain conditions. He is not explicit, but one can not help but think that he has in mind those of his own vocation, the bishops and priests, who are supported by their community. His distinctions are drawn carefully to separate zeal for "better things" from mere idleness. Paul himself, who worked for his own sustenance, says that he did this not because he had no right to ask for support from the community, but

---

97. *"videtur enim ipse Corinthiis scribens longa prosecutione id explicasse, quoniam illis debetur qui doctrinae vacant, ut a discipulis corporalium percipiant ministerium."* Swete, 62.

because he wished to give them an example. It is worth noting that Theodore understands this passage to have no thematic connection to the previous sections' eschatological concerns. Paul raises it as another separate problem to be addressed in the community. Having issued his judgments, he draws the letter to a close with his own signature, to assure the community of its authenticity. With that, the letter—and the commentary—ends.

Theodore's commentary, not unlike that of Ambrosiaster, is very disciplined in its approach. In his argument, Theodore sets out three problems in the community and three answers of the Apostle. In the commentary itself, Theodore carefully follows each of the three lines of argument and never wavers with an aside. Only rarely does he speak in the first person, and this only to discuss several possible interpretations of difficult passages. He weaves paraphrase, grammatical clarification, and analysis of argument into a tight, cohesive interpretation of Paul's letter.

The interpretation he offers of the eschatological sections represents a distinctive contribution to the apocalyptic realist family of interpretations. He understands Antichrist to be a real historical figure who will come in the future. His appearance is restrained for the moment by the direct decree of God, without any mention of a terrestrial mediator of this decree (e.g., the Roman Empire). He will persuade large numbers of the believers to abandon their holiness of life through deception alone. Antichrist is only the "false Christ"; he will exercise no tyrannical powers to persecute the Church. Instead, he will pose as Christ and lead the churches (note the plural) from true worship of God in Christ. His work will be public and explicit, and in this way it is distinct from the assaults of the devil in the present. For indeed, this present "mystery of iniquity" is encountered now in individual temptations. But neither the devil's present work nor the future coming of Antichrist has any relation to the Roman Empire or the Jews. Theodore refrains from any and all extraecclesial apocalyptic referents.

Thus he departs significantly from the "mainline apocalyptic eschatology" that we have briefly sketched in relation to Ambrosiaster. While there can be no doubt that Theodore's apocalyptic vision is thematic,[98] literal, and historical, it is equally clear that it is a vision of the travails and triumphs of the faithful *within the Church*. Theodore has no world-historical vision in which Christians engage in combat with or fall prey to external political or military forces. If his commentary is representative, it suggests that, at least in the East, the "mainline eschatology" of the early third century may not have survived into the fifth century even among the more historically minded interpreters of Antioch. Nevertheless, such an eschatology endured and thrived in the West, as the commentary of Pelagius, Theodore's contemporary,[99] conveys.

The Jerome Tradition (1): Pelagius

It is more than a little ironic that the "heresiarch" that Jerome slandered with epithets such as "the dolt weighed down with Scots' porridge" and "that big, bloated alpine dog, able to rage more effectively with his heels than with his feet,"[100] should leave an exegetical legacy to the West under Jerome's own name. But such are the ironies of the history of Pauline commentary, a history in which the purported errors of several major contributors have blotted their names from tradition's book—their names, but not their work. Both Theodore of Mopsuestia and Pelagius have reemerged from their

98. By "thematic," I mean to indicate that it is the primary sense in which he understands apocalyptic language. Augustine does not deny that Antichrist will some day come as a real person, but this interpretation is not thematic; i.e., it is not the interpretation he wishes to emphasize.

99. Perhaps his personal acquaintance, as well. Souter clearly thought so (cf. Alexander Souter, ed., *Pelagius's Exposition of the Thirteen Epistles of Saint Paul*, Texts and Studies 9 [Cambridge: Cambridge University Press, 1922], 196) This rumor, however, may have arisen in an effort to associate Theodore's thought with Pelagianism in the "Three Chapters" controversy to strengthen the opposition to Theodore in the Latin West.

100. Kelly, 311.

disguise in recent times, almost demanding an appellate hearing, and often faring rather well.

Numerous books in the later twentieth century have been devoted to the reevaluation of Pelagius's thought,[101] and answers to Gerald Bonner's question "How Pelagian was Pelagius?"[102] have varied from "not very" to "absolutely." But whatever the final verdict on Pelagius's orthodoxy, his exegesis is valuable testimony to the "Renaissance of Paul" in the fourth and fifth centuries and, in its pseudonymous form, a significant contribution to the medieval tradition of Pauline interpretation.

Little is known of the early life of this controversial figure. The current view contends that he was born in western Britain (rather than Ireland or Scotland) some time in the middle of the fourth century, that he was not ordained, and that he observed a moderate ascetic regimen. We do know that he came to Rome and was active there among the aristocracy from about 380 until the imminent arrival of Alaric the Visigoth convinced him to flee the city with many others in 410. It is perhaps unfortunate that Pelagius and his followers fled to North Africa, where his thought was a most unwelcome affront to the theological sensibilities of anti-Donatist Africans such as Augustine. While the assault on his teaching swelled and finally boiled over in Carthage, Pelagius fled east to Palestine and found his ideas warmly received by the Eastern Church. Indeed, he found it difficult to convince his hosts that his thought was deemed heretical.[103] (Although Jerome labored tirelessly to prove it so.) Pelagius

101. See Gerald Bonner, *Augustine and Modern Research on Pelagius* (Villanova: Villanova University Press, 1972), for a survey of work until 1970, and see Stortz, "Exegesis, Orthodoxy, and Ethics," and B. R. Rees, *Pelagius: A Reluctant Heretic* (Suffolk: Boydell Press, 1988), for thoughtful reevaluations. Also, the new edition of Pelagius's commentary on Romans by Theodore DeBruyn, *Pelagius's Commentary on St. Paul's Epistle to the Romans* (Oxford: Clarendon Press, 1993), contains a helpful introduction and a thorough bibliography.

102. Gerald Bonner, "How Pelagian Was Pelagius?" *Texte und Untersuchungen* 94 (1968): 350–58.

103. Augustine, *Epistolae* IV and VI, PL 33.66–68.

was no martyr, and it is likely that he stayed in the relative safety of Eastern Christianity and disappeared. The date and location of his death are unknown.

Although Augustine labeled him as "the enemy of grace," Pelagius in fact had a highly developed theology of grace that lay at the heart of his thought. As Jaroslav Pelikan has succinctly summarized, "Grace had a fourfold content for Pelagius: doctrine and revelation; disclosure of the future, with its rewards and punishments; demonstration of the snares of the devil; and illumination of the manifold and ineffable gift of heavenly grace."[104] Having received this grace in all its facets, the Christian believer is empowered, but not compelled, to observe the moral law in the Christian community. He is encouraged by the example of holy men and women; he is challenged by the sinful habits and customs (consuetudines) of the world around him. But above all, the Christian remains responsible for his conduct and moral progress.

Pelagius develops these principles in his Pauline commentary. He wrote his commentary on Paul in the later years of his time in Rome, ca. 405–410. The commentary stands solidly in the "Roman" tradition of commentary on the entire Pauline corpus, a tradition initiated by Marius Victorinus (who intended to comment upon the entire corpus, but didn't complete his task) and continued in Ambrosiaster. Indeed, Pelagius makes extensive use of Ambrosiaster's commentary in his work. Unlike his Latin predecessors, however, Pelagius is interested in and influenced by the works of Origen. He read Rufinus's abridged translation of Origen's commentary on Romans, and perhaps knew something of Antiochene exegesis indirectly through the anonymous Latin commentary uncovered relatively recently by Hermann Josef Frede.[105] Like the Antiochenes, his ex-

104. Jaroslav Pelikan, *The Christian Tradition*, vol. 1: *The Emergence of the Catholic Tradition* (Chicago: University of Chicago Press, 1972), 315.

105. Hermann Josef Frede, ed., *Ein neuer Paulustext und Kommentar*, i. Untersuchungen; ii. Die Texte, Vetus Latina: Die Reste der altlateinischen Bibel, Aus der Geschichte der lateinischen Bibel 7–8 (Freiburg: Herder, 1973–74), 164–85. Cited in DeBruyn, 4.

egetical style focuses first upon the grammatical logic of the literal-historical sense of the text. His Pauline text corresponds more or less to the new Vulgate translation, with occasional reversions to the more familiar Old Latin. He made use of *Primum quaeritur,* a prologue to the Pauline corpus probably composed by the Vulgate translator, and it appears that he consulted the so-called Marcionite prologues to several epistles. But for most, he composed his own *argumentum* to summarize the matter of each letter. Pelagius blended these elements, new and old, into a compact, synthetic commentary that reflected his theological concerns.

Pelagius is very reserved in his comments, giving at most a short paragraph and often just a phrase of explanation, such that the entire text of his commentary could fit in one or two Late Antique codices. It should come as no surprise that Pelagius was interested above all in the moral meaning of Paul's letters. But he does not abstract a "moral sense" from the text over and above the literal; instead, he finds ample evidence within the literal sense of Paul's "good example" *(exemplum* or *forma)* to his audience or the "progress" others make in the life of faith *(proficio, profectus).*[106] Paul's genius, for Pelagius, was that he taught true doctrine and demonstrated what he taught with his own conduct.

The Letter as a Whole: The Argumentum

Pelagius's *argumentum* to 2 Thessalonians is brief and succinct. He does not bother to re-identify his audience or make an explicit connection to the first letter to the Thessalonians. He rather implies a connection by beginning, "It was fitting that, as their faith and love grew more and more, so too would praise for them increase."[107] The letter is written primarily as a continuation of the laudatory first exchange; Paul congratulates them on the further steps they have made since he last wrote. But at the same time, Paul writes to cau-

---

106. See Souter's discussion of this element: *Pelagius,* 69–70.

107. *"Iustum quippe erat ut superius crescente eorum fide et caritate et illorum quoque laudatio augeretur."* Souter, *Pelagius,* 439.

tion them against false teaching of Christ's return and to speak of the one who will pose as Christ. With these two motives in mind, Pelagius moves on to consider the text.

2 Thessalonians 1: "That you may give an example of awaiting God's just judgment"

Pelagius's concern for the moral life predisposes him well to interpret the letter's first chapter. Paul praises the Thessalonians for the example they give to the other churches. They have "progressed" so much that he himself presents them as an example for all to imitate. Their suffering is not the "example of the just judgment of God," as the text seems to indicate. Rather, they themselves are an example of "*awaiting* the just judgment of God" that they believe is coming.[108] They suffer willingly, since they understand that no suffering can match the glory of God.[109]

When Christ does return, he will come with real fire. Pelagius reads literally the verse about the return "to give judgment in flames of fire" (1:8). He understands the judgment to come as a real corporal event, just like the "trial by fire" of the three boys in Daniel 3. He rejects the allegorical interpretation of "those who imagine this to be the punishment of minds." To whom he refers and why this matter should be so significant remain mysteries. Nonetheless, it is clear that Pelagius believes that the coming of the Lord will be visible, tangible, and real.

2 Thessalonians 2

No less real for Pelagius are the events that will precede Christ's judgment. Throughout his treatment of Chapter 2, he correlates Paul's account of these events with the "little apocalypse" of Matthew's Gospel, showing that Paul and Jesus offered the same

---

108. "*ut exemplum detis iustum dei iudicium expectandi, quem ita creditis esse venturum.*" Souter, *Pelagius*, 440.
109. "*Hii digni sunt regno dei, qui gloriam eius scientes, nullam passionem putant esse condignem.*" Souter, *Pelagius*, 440.

gospel. The present errors that face the Thessalonians are the work of the devil[110] and fulfill the prophecies of Matthew 24:23, where "many will be saying, 'Behold, here is Christ,' or 'Behold, there he is.'"[111] But Paul reminds them of the proper sequence of the events of the end.

"For unless Antichrist will have come, Christ will not." This seems to Pelagius to be the clear thrust of Paul's talk of the *discessio* in 2:3. But, unlike Ambrosiaster, he often gives several possible interpretations of a passage. After giving the rather straightforward interpretation above, he considers several ways in which this may come to pass:

> What he calls here *"discessio,"* elsewhere in Latin copies he calls *"refuga."* But both should be understood in this way: that unless the *refuga* (flight), either a runaway from his empire or the desertion of the nations from the Roman Empire, just as it says in Daniel through the figure of the Beast. [Dn 7:24][112]

While the latter attribution is clear and predictable, the former is not. It is possible that Pelagius refers here to a version of the Nero legend, perhaps from the Sibylline Oracles, where Nero fakes his death and flees to the Medes and the Persians.[113] But the reference is in passing, and he never returns to the image or mentions Nero explicitly.

Instead, he turns immediately to discuss the identity of the

---

110. *"Poterat et hoc diabolica excogitare astutia, sicut in multis apocryfis apparet, quae ad fidem perfidiae faciendam apostolorum nomine titulantur."* Souter, *Pelagius,* 443.

111. *"Dicentes: ecce hic Christus, ecce illic."* Souter, *Pelagius,* 443.

112. *"quod autem 'discessio' hic dicit, alibi eum 'refugam' appellavit in Latinis exemplaribus: utrumque autem ita intellegendum est, quod nisi venerit refuga, sive sui principatus desertor, sive discessio gentium a regno Romano, sicut in Danihelo per bestiae imaginem dicit."* Souter, *Pelagius,* 443.

113. For text and translation, see John J. Collins, "Sibylline Oracles," in *Old Testament Pseudepigrapha,* ed. J. H. Charlesworth, vol. 1 (Garden City: Doubleday, 1983), 317–72. Also see John J. Collins's dissertation, *The Sibylline Oracles of Egyptian Judaism* (Missoula: Scholars Press, 1974).

"Man of Sin, the Son of Perdition." For Pelagius, both of these titles signify Antichrist's relationship to the devil, who is called "sin" and "perdition." Antichrist will be "the devil's man"; he is called the "Son of Perdition" because the devil, "who causes the nations to stir [Is 64:2],[114] will possess him in servitude, as if he were born to him."[115] Note that Pelagius is careful to distinguish that Satan treats Antichrist *as if* he were a son, not as an actual son. This distinction sets him apart from the Incarnation of the Son of God, since only God has the power to bring his Son into the world with a human nature.

Pelagius's distinction is evidence of an emerging theological reaction to the parallelisms between Christ and Antichrist drawn by earlier thinkers. In the wake of the controversies over the Trinity and Christology, the theological terms related to incarnation, filiation, and nature become more and more specific. Christian thinkers are more reluctant to use such terms in any sense but with respect to their proper divine referent. Antichrist thus cannot be "the devil incarnate" or "the son of the devil." Although he was still considered to "double" the work of Christ in a perverse, inverse manner, the inferiority of his place and work comes to be emphasized more in the writings of the fourth and fifth centuries, of which Pelagius's commentary is a prime example.

Antichrist's work has an ecumenical context of sorts for Pelagius. In exalting himself over everything holy, Antichrist will claim to correct or augment the sacraments of divine worship, taking the role of a Christian reformer. But he also will rebuild the temple in Jerusalem and restore all the ceremonies of the Law,[116] thereby convincing the Jews that he is the Christ, come in his own name (Jn 7:6).

---

114. This is a curious allusion to Isaiah, since the context of the passage in Isaiah seems to make "the LORD" the subject, while here it indicates the devil.

115. *"Quia eum, quasi sibi natum, servitio possidebit, qui secundum Isaiam conturbare dicitur gentes."* Souter, *Pelagius*, 443.

116. It is important to note that in his interpretation of Romans 3:20, 28, Pelagius views the law that Christ abolished to be the ceremonial laws of sacrifice, not the moral law.

While Pelagius gives no indication of whether Antichrist will be born of the Jews, it is clear that he will work among them. When his time to appear comes, Antichrist will try to undo the work that Christ has done to abolish the Jewish Law.[117]

But his time has not yet come. For now, the "mystery of iniquity" is at work in those who "cut the path in his false teachings, those whom blessed John has said have gone into the world."[118] They will persist until "the kingdom which now reigns" (presumably Rome, but not explicitly so) is taken away. Then Antichrist will appear. Citing the "little apocalypse" of Matthew again, Pelagius suggests that Antichrist's task will be to lead astray even the elect, if he is able, through illusions and the likeness of miracles, just as Jamnes and Mambres did in the Book of Exodus.[119] But in the end he will be slain by the power of Christ. Like his contemporaries Ambrosiaster and Theodore, Pelagius "corrects" Paul's statement that "God sends [those who are perishing] the work of error, that they may believe the lie." Paul clearly means that God "permits" *(permittet)* Antichrist

117. Although Pelagius does not say it, one wonders if he foresees Antichrist as reuniting Christianity and Judaism under his single headship.

118. *"In his qui falsis doctrinis eius praevium faciunt iter, quos beatus Johannes in mundum dicit exisse."* Souter, *Pelagius,* 444.

119. Cf. Ex 7:11–13. Pharaoh's magicians are not named in the text, but in other Jewish, and later Christian, literature, the names "Jamnes" and "Mambres" (sometimes "Jambres") appear generally accepted. See, e.g., 2 Tm 3:8. The two are usually invoked in the "history of magic," which includes Simon Magus and other practitioners of false signs, as we find it in Tertullian (*de Idololatria* 9.6; *de Anima* 57.7) and Pseudo-Clement (*Recognitions* 3.55, 56, 57). Antichrist will represent the consummation of this history as the chief deceiver. The explicit connection of these figures with Antichrist occurs roughly simultaneously here in Pelagius and in Jerome's Letter 121.11, but each has its own particular context. Here Pelagius is emphasizing the analogy between Antichrist's power to deceive the elect and the magicians' deceptions before Pharaoh (see p. 78 for Jerome). It is unlikely that either had knowledge of the other's work at this stage. It is possible that they both draw on another source, but I have not been able to find any earlier attribution. It is also possible, if unlikely, that, as both considered Antichrist's works false, both made this connection independently.

to come, not "sends" *(mittet)* him, since Antichrist is the instrument of the devil and thus could not be sent by the just God. "Those who are perishing" will display the justice of their condemnation. They will not be able to "excuse themselves by the obscurity of the incarnation of Christ" since they who could not believe in the divine works will all too readily believe in those of the devil. Pelagius is careful to show that God is just and that those who will be condemned have freely chosen their fate.

2 Thessalonians 2:13–3:18

Paul assures his Thessalonian audience that they, on the other hand, have been chosen for salvation. Pelagius believes that this knowledge comes as a special charism to the Apostle, citing the vision of the Macedonian man in Acts 16:9 as another example. With this knowledge, Paul exhorts them to "stand unmovable in the faith of the truth." They must cling to, and never add to, the "apostolic tradition," that which "is celebrated in the whole world, like the sacraments of baptism."[120] Pelagius notes that Paul refers to the disobedient within the community as those who are "walking in restlessness." He contrasts these with those who have received the apostolic tradition and thus "sit at peace"; they have no need to wander or search. If they walk at all, it is as apostles at God's call. Paul urges his audience to correct those at fault, and he ends his letter with his own signature.

Pelagius's commentary on 2 Thessalonians shows little in the way of creative or original exegesis, but it does reveal an interpreter who is intent on clarifying the sense of Paul's letter in its scriptural context. More than either of the other interpreters we have studied thus far, Pelagius draws parallels from the text he studies to other

---

120. Pelagius alludes to baptism here, but he makes no further comment. Baptism was one of the central loci of his debate with Augustine. That he mentions it here most likely is due to the centrality baptism held for his thought on justification as the "pivotal point" in the transition from the "death" of sin to the "life of righteousness." See DeBruyn, 35–36 et passim.

Scripture. In the very short commentary on 2 Thessalonians, Pelagius cites or alludes to at least thirty-three other scriptural texts. He cites Matthew's "little apocalypse" (Mt 24) and passages in Daniel and Isaiah to support Paul's account of the "last things" and the coming of Antichrist. Other citations from Acts or other Pauline epistles are used to show the affinities between Paul's teachings and the rest of the New Testament. While Ambrosiaster and Theodore certainly understand this letter to be inspired Scripture, neither gives quite the explicit attention to its "canonical context."[121] Pelagius's interpretive method clarifies the text specifically in its relation to other Scripture.

The coming of Antichrist for Pelagius is the future historical fulfillment of prophecies and types scattered throughout the books of the Old and New Testaments. The *discessio* or *refuga* is possibly what Daniel represents with the "beast with ten horns," and will have occurred when the Roman Empire falls. Antichrist will come only when the "falling away" has happened. He will be like a son to the devil, and he will convince the Jews that he is the Christ and rebuild the temple in Jerusalem. He will tempt the elect to believe in him through his illusions and false miracles. Finally, he will be slain by Christ's return in glory.

Pelagius's account of Antichrist more or less recapitulates what we have called the "mainline eschatology" of the early Fathers, with one exception. Pelagius gives no sense of Antichrist's tyranny, no "dread" to balance the "deception." Antichrist's tools will be false teaching, false miracles, and lies. His predecessors are those who "cut the path in false teaching," not infamous Roman persecutors. As Pelagius was so familiar with Ambrosiaster's commentary, such an omission must be deliberate. For Pelagius, true evil lies not in persecutions at the hands of political powers, but in deception and error.

121. If an anachronism may be permitted. The phrase, of course, comes from Brevard Childs, and its proper referent is such a matter of modern dispute. In a premodern sense, though, the phrase is a bit less troubled.

The Jerome Tradition (2):
Jerome and the Persistence of Apocalyptic Realism

One might think the last figure we will consider in this chapter to be a "hostile witness" to the apocalyptic realist tradition we have begun to trace. Jerome, the most learned and the most cantankerous of the Fathers, feared the millenarian excesses of a too-apocalyptic exegesis of Scripture. Many of his writings warn of the dangers inherent in such work. John P. O'Connell found more than fifty instances of Jerome attacking the "Jews and Judaizers" who proposed to believe in the terrestrial millennial reign of Christ.[122] Jerome admits that this error is an ancient one, and he usually cites the honorable names of Irenaeus, Tertullian, Victorinus, and Lactantius as examples of those who have fallen under its sway. He even edited Victorinus's *Commentary on the Apocalypse* to strip it of any of its millenarian overtones. But Jerome's antipathy toward millenarianism in no way cast doubt upon his faith in, and even interest in, the reality of a historical, personal Antichrist to come. It is the earthy or terrestrial aspect of millenarian teaching that most offends him; he always casts its errors in terms of an attachment to sensuality and materiality. He does not, however, discourage apocalyptic speculation itself; far from it. Jerome devotes a large section of his Daniel commentary to questions about the arrival of Antichrist, and his correspondence is peppered with questions and speculations about the signs of the times. In the "gathering gloom"[123] of his latter years, faced with barbarian assaults on his culture and society, Jerome wondered if the dawning of the end was indeed imminent. Although he is remembered as a great opponent of the "apocalyptic exegesis" of the early Fathers, Jerome left a lasting legacy for realist apocalyptic speculation on Antichrist and the end.

Jerome's treatment of 2 Thessalonians is unique among the

122. John P. O'Connell, *The Eschatology of Saint Jerome* (Mundelein, Ill.: Saint Mary on the Lake, 1948), 64–66.

123. The phrase comes from a late chapter in Kelly, 296–308.

sources I have studied thus far, in that it does not occur within the formal genre of commentary. Jerome wrote commentaries upon only four of the letters of Paul—Galatians, Ephesians, Titus, and Philemon—and these date from his early years, when he was still persuaded by the thought of Origen. The commentaries are thus largely derivative and dependant upon Origen, as Jerome himself admits. Curiously, they are also dependent upon Ambrosiaster, despite Jerome's claim that his own is the first Latin work on Galatians.[124] In these works, Jerome often offers several interpretations of a passage without expressing any preference; the decision is left to the reader. He rarely resorts to allegory and generally strives to understand the literal sense of the texts in question.

Jerome shows similar characteristics, for better or worse, in his treatment of 2 Thessalonians. He turns to the letter in response to a series of eleven questions from a Latin laywoman named Algasia. Scholarly opinion dates the letter in 406, late in Jerome's life. The questions are all devoted to the meaning of New Testament passages, from either the Gospels or Paul's epistles. Jerome's answers to the questions are prefaced by brief comments on the nature of Algasia's questions. He praises her for her diligence in seeking his assistance, comparing her quest to that of Queen of Sheba for Solomon's wisdom. But, never to dwell too long in flattery, Jerome suggests that Algasia's questions show that she either has not read the Old Testament or has not understood it. The Old Testament, this "gate of the East," is essential to understanding the prophetic passages in the New. With this brief hermeneutical introduction, Jerome proceeds to answer each question one by one. Her eleventh question asks, "What does it mean when the Apostle writes to the Thessalonians, 'Unless the desertion *(discessio)* will have first come, and the

---

124. Kelly argues that this willful omission on Jerome's part may be due to a conflict between Ambrosiaster and Jerome over the latter's revision of the Latin Gospels. Ambrosiaster preferred the Old Latin text, and the petty Jerome thus struck his name from his own personal "book of life." Would that he had swallowed his pride for once to preserve for us the true identity of Ambrosiaster!

man of sin will have been revealed,' and so on?" The general shape of Jerome's response is a compendium of teachings on Antichrist, with little if anything actually original to him. While it is difficult to discern what sources he actually had before his eyes, it is likely that he used Ambrosiaster's commentary and Hippolytus's *Commentary on Daniel*. Jerome begins his response by setting the text in its historical context. Paul had spoken in his first letter to the Thessalonians of the resurrection of the faithful and the coming of the Lord. They misunderstood his teaching and thought that he meant that Christ would return before any of them had died. Paul hears of their mistake and responds with a second letter.[125]

Jerome then explains the doctrinal and canonical context. "All of the prophets' scrolls and the faith of the gospels teach there are two advents of the Lord and Saviour: for first he came in humility, and later he will come in glory."[126] He then marshals a predictable series of quotations from the "little apocalypse" of Matthew's and John's Gospels to what will precede the Second Coming (Mt. 24:15–17, 23–27, 30–37; Jn 5:43). Jerome suspects that the Thessalonians were misled by poor speculation on the prophecies of Isaiah, Daniel, and the Gospels. Paul corrects their error by giving them the signs of Antichrist's arrival.

Jerome gives the signs in rapid succession, generally summarizing the eschatological exegesis of Hippolytus. The first sign is the *discessio*, or the *apostasia* in Greek, when "all the nations that now submit to the Roman empire will draw back from it."[127] For now, the Roman Empire restrains his coming. Like Ambrosiaster, but with greater detail, Jerome explains the obscurity of Paul's reference to the Empire's fall with the fear of persecution:

125. Jerome, Ep. 121.11, ed. I. Hillberg, CSEL 66.2 (Vienna: Hoelder-Pichler-Tempsky, 1961), 53.

126. *"Duos autem esse scriptam, quasi instet dies Domini Salvatoris, et omnia prophetarum docent voluminam et evangeliorum fides: quod primum in humilitate venerit, et postea sit venturus in gloria."* Ep. 121.11, 54.

127. *"ut omnes gentes quae Romano imperio subiacent, recedant ab eis."* Ep. 121.11, 55.

He does not want to say 'the destruction of the Roman Empire,' because those who rule think that it is eternal. Thus, according to the Apocalypse of John, the blasphemous name, "Romae aeternae," is written on the forehead of the scarlet harlot. If he had said boldly and openly, 'Antichrist will not come until the Roman Empire falters,' a just cause of persecution of the eastern church would then seem to arise.[128]

Whether he draws this idea directly from Ambrosiaster or both scholars use an idea that was part of the common discourse about the end, Jerome takes an idea and embellishes it with references to other Scripture. The "mystery of iniquity" was initiated by "Nero, most vile" and threatens the welfare of the Church. But Rome, in its arrogance, will be brought down, and then Antichrist will be revealed.

Antichrist will bring iniquity to birth by his coming. He is the "Man of Sin" because he is the "fountain of all sins." He is the son of the devil and the "perdition of all." He will tread upon true religion. His session in "the temple of God" refers either to a rebuilt temple in Jerusalem or (as Jerome prefers) to the Church, where he will pose as Christ. Christ will slay him "by the brilliance of his coming" (v. 8), meaning that he will need no assistance from the heavenly host.[129] Indeed, following Hippolytus, Jerome suggests that Antichrist will be the inversion of Christ in all his actions. "Just as in Christ the fullness of divinity existed corporally, so all the powers, signs, and prodigies will be in Antichrist, but all of them all will be false."[130] These false works were foreshadowed in the illusions of Pharaoh's magicians, and, "as the staff of Moses devoured their

---

128. *"Nec vult aperte dicere Romanum imperium destruendum, quod ipsi qui imperant, aeternam putant. Unde secundum Apocalypsin Iohannis, in fronte purpuratae meretricis, scriptum est nomen blasphemiae, id est, 'Romae aeternae'. Si enim aperte audacterque dixisset, 'non veniet Antichristus, nisi prius Romanum deleatur imperium,' justa causa persecutionis in orientem tunc ecclesiam consurgere videbatur."* Ep. 121.11, 56.

129. NB, this will put Jerome in conflict with Gregory in the tradition; see Chapter 4.

130. *"Et sicut in Christo plenitudo divinitatis fuit corporaliter, ita et in Antichristo omnes erunt fortitudines et signa et prodigia, sed universa mendacia."* Ep. 121.11, 59.

staves, so will the truth of Christ devour the lie of Antichrist."[131] But, Jerome asks, why is Antichrist permitted to have any power at all, false or real?

According to Jerome, God permits Antichrist the power to tempt even the elect so that the Jews can be confirmed in their error. They have rejected Christ, the Truth, because they have not submitted to him. God therefore sends them not a worker of errors, but the font of errors himself. If they have seen the Truth and rejected him, and then later they accept the Lie, they can be judged and condemned justly. Jerome's line of argument is similar to (and perhaps derived from) Ambrosiaster's, but Jerome refers it specifically to the Jews. While for Ambrosiaster the threat of deception and punishment hangs low over the heads of everyone, such that none are sure that they will persist in faith, Jerome foresees punishment for a people that, in his mind, have already rejected salvation: the Jews. With this dire judgment, Jerome's letter ends.

Jerome recapitulates many of the letter's ideas in his Commentary on Daniel.[132] His comments on Daniel 11:17–12:13 indicate that this section was composed earlier as an independent treatise and included later. Suffice to say that Jerome devoted himself with particular zeal to questions about the end in the first decade of the fifth century. This "treatise" within the Daniel commentary introduces only one aspect of Antichrist's career that will be significant for the tradition. Commenting on Daniel 11:45, "He will fix his tent Apedno between the seas, upon a glorious and holy mountain,"[133] Jerome argues that, as Christ ascended from the Mount of Olives, so Antichrist will die there. While he claims to inherit the teaching, his is the first written account of it.[134] This little biographical note on

131. "Quomodo enim . . . virga Moysi devoravit virgas eorum, ita mendacium Antichristi Christi veritas devorabit." Ep. 121.11, 59. See n. 119 above.

132. The date of completion usually given is 407. If the dates are correct, the commentary was completed just one year after the letter. Kelly, 299.

133. "et figet tabernaculum suum Apedno inter maria, super montem inclitum et sanctum." Vulgate edition.

134. Jerome, Commentarius in Danielem, in Sancti Hieronymi Presbyteri Opera, I: Opera Exegetica 5, ed. F. Glorie, CCSL 75A (Turnhout: Brepols, 1964), 933–34.

Antichrist, together with his summary of the tradition in Letter 121.11, will become authoritative for the apocalyptic realist tradition of 2 Thessalonians interpretation.

Summary: The Building Blocks of Apocalyptic Realist Exegesis

In this chapter, I have introduced and analyzed the patristic figures that formed the "building blocks" of apocalyptic realist exegesis of 2 Thessalonians. The four commentaries we have discussed were honed by later interpreters into distinct lemmata (or "blocks," to preserve the metaphor) of apocalyptic opinion. Of the four "canonical" patristic authorities, the mantles of two, Ambrose and Jerome, spread over these apocalyptic realist readings of the letter. Each commentary, of course, carried a distinctive intellectual signature; all, however, shared an emphasis on the nonallegorical, eschatological meaning of Antichrist and the end of time. None, however, show any hint of the suspicion of imminence.

Ambrosiaster is perhaps the most important single source of this realist tendency. The centrality of the Roman Empire, both as the past "mystery of iniquity" and the future "falling away," is most pronounced in his commentary. For Ambrosiaster, Rome's religious cult, with its worship of idols and emperors, prefigures the consummate idolatry of Antichrist. This Roman paradigm portrays both Antichrist's dread (that is, his persecution of the saints) and his deception (his placing of himself as a false idol). Significant also is Ambrosiaster's reliance upon the providence of God, by which the last events unfold in proper time and order. Ambrosiaster's apocalyptic schema is not predictive—it posits no discernible timetable for the end—but it is nonetheless realist. Although it gives no "when" to the end, it acknowledges a clear and definite "what," and that "what" is inextricably bound up with the religious and political reality of the Roman Empire. On the three-dimensional "map" we have described above, Ambrosiaster's apocalyptic schema is external (i.e., Roman), equally dreadful *and* deceptive, and imminent.[135]

The commentary of Theodore of Mopsuestia, the other "Ambrose," also gives a clear sense of "what" without a "when." But this "what" stands in sharp contrast to Ambrosiaster's pagan empire. For Theodore, the last times will be, above all, an ecclesial phenomenon. Antichrist will come as a false Christ whose only role will be to lead the faithful astray from their holiness of life *(pietas)* and thus from the true worship of God in Christ. In contrast to Ambrosiaster, Theodore's Antichrist is internal, deceptive, and imminent. Theodore's exegesis, as an alternative "Ambrose," survives only in a few manuscripts, and might thus be counted a minor influence on the history of interpretation. However, the few survivals occur in important places, in the work of exegetes such as Rabanus Maurus and Lanfranc of Canterbury, and thus must be considered a significant alternative (and perhaps complementary) tradition to the influential Ambrosiaster.

The "Jerome" tradition, in both Pelagius and the authentic Jerome, summarizes the eschatological exegesis of the early Fathers and emphasizes a distinctive anti-Jewish strain in apocalyptic realism. Pelagius's commentary portrays Antichrist as one who will both augment the sacraments of Christian worship and restore the Jewish ceremonial law. He focuses upon Antichrist's false teachings and lacks any notion of his tyranny or political power. Pelagius's Antichrist is both internal and external, deceptive, and imminent. Later commentators often use Pelagius's image of Antichrist as teacher of error to complement the politically charged work of Ambrosiaster.

Jerome contributes little original to the tradition, but his summaries of eschatological exegesis themselves become authoritative. Most significant in his comments is Jerome's focus upon the errors of the Jews. For Jerome, God permits the errors of Antichrist to confirm the Jews (and, apparently, *only* the Jews) in their sin. Antichrist

135. Note that I refer here to "psychological imminence," rather than predictive imminence.

for Jerome is internal, but his coming is heralded by external events. The Man of Sin is more deceptive than dreadful, and he is clearly imminent (perhaps literally imminent in Jerome's later life). Jerome also contributes to the 2 Thessalonians tradition through some of his other works on apocalyptic subjects. As I previously mentioned, his discussion of Antichrist's death on the Mount of Olives becomes a standard element in medieval interpretation. In addition, his favorite description of the effects of Antichrist's work, echoing Christ's prophecy that "iniquity will abound and charity grow cold,"[136] would find a definitive place in the tradition.

It is important to note that none of these figures offered a predictive exegesis of 2 Thessalonians. In this sense, the mainstream of Christian exegesis has moved beyond the chiliasm of the early fathers. Nevertheless, they interpret the letter literally, as referring to historical events within the Church and without. In their minds, Paul's letter refers to a simple teaching that he had previously given; the obscurity of the passage comes from the reader's distance from that conversation, not some hidden spiritual word within the text.

The distinctive feature of the apocalyptic realist strain is the vision of Antichrist as the "one who is coming," an individual person who will perform a specific sort of actions in the future to the detriment of the Church. While certain historical persons may prefigure Antichrist, they are not part of Antichrist per se. Antichrist in the apocalyptic realist vision is thus "to come" and imminent, even if only "psychologically imminent." As a natural extension of the "eschatological exegesis" of Hippolytus and his contemporaries, realist apocalyptic interpretation found in 2 Thessalonians the elements of the eschatological future.

136. E.g., in Jerome's commentaries on Habbakuk 2:5 (PL 25.1294), Wisdom 2:12 (PL 25.1370), Nahum 1:1 & 3:1 (PL 25.1233, 1254), Micah 7:1 (PL 25.1217), and Matthew 24:20 (PL 26.178). O'Connell calls this the "most common Hieronymian formula for describing the effects of Antichrist's works."

CHAPTER 3

MEMBERS OF THE ENEMY BODY

The Spiritual Exegesis of 2 Thessalonians

In the last chapter, I provided a sketch of the variety of patristic commentary on 2 Thessalonians from the Roman exegesis of Ambrosiaster and Pelagius to Theodore's Antiochene interpretation to the erudite and cosmopolitan exegetical summary of Jerome. All testify to the enduring appeal of "eschatological exegesis," or what I have called apocalyptic realism. The imminence of the event is seldom emphasized; nevertheless, all four commentators remain convinced that the primary (and perhaps, the sole) referent of 2 Thessalonians' "Man of Sin, Son of Perdition" is the Antichrist, the individual opponent to Christ at the end of time. The context of the letter seems to demand this interpretation. As I have said, Pauline texts are seldom interpreted spiritually, and 2 Thessalonians is explicitly concerned to assert that "the day of the Lord is not yet here." Paul gives the signs of the times so that the Thessalonians will know when Antichrist is coming. It is not surprising, then, that most commentators took Paul at his word and simply tried to clarify his meaning in the apocalyptic realist sense, as future, historical, and individual.

Nevertheless, the late fourth century witnessed the birth of an alternative—and, in its own way, distinctively Pauline—interpretation: In the enthusiastic climate of the North African Church, theological controversy raged over the true nature of the Church, over who would be saved and who would be damned, and over the nature of sin, grace, and forgiveness. Such enthusiasm was expressed in what Fredriksen has called "an uncomplicated millenarianism" that figured prominently in the ecclesial cultures of North Africa. North African Christians maintained their faith in an earthly kingdom under the rule of Christ, and the Catholic bishop Hilarianus in 397 reminded his flock that the six-thousandth year of Creation was only a century away. This sense of the end was even more vivid in the Donatist Church, which still suffered under imperial persecution.[1]

Perhaps in response to just this sort of North African tradition, Tyconius, an excommunicated Donatist layman, offered a spiritual interpretation[2] of 2 Thessalonians. Some would question the characterization of Tyconius's interpretation as "spiritual exegesis," since it seems a far cry from the allegorical reading of Origen or Ambrose. Certainly, Tyconius did not offer a speculative, allegorical interpretation of the text; nor does he seem hostile to its literal sense. Nevertheless, his interpretation is properly "spiritual exegesis," insofar as he discerns his seven "mystical rules" *(regulae mysti-*

1. Paula Fredriksen, "Tyconius and Augustine on the Apocalypse," in *The Apocalypse in the Middle Ages,* ed. Richard K. Emmerson and Bernard McGinn (Ithaca: Cornell University Press, 1992), 23ff.

2. Some would question the characterization of Tyconius's interpretation as "spiritual exegesis." Certainly, Tyconius did not offer a speculative, allegorical interpretation of the text; nor does he seem hostile to its literal sense. Nevertheless, his interpretation is properly "spiritual exegesis," insofar as he devises his seven "mystical rules" *(regulae mysticae)* to help the reader, such that "whatever is closed will be open and whatever is dark will be illumined." To speak precisely, Tyconius's interpretation is an example of typological interpretation. See Bradley Nassif, "'Spiritual Exegesis' in the School of Antioch," 343–77, for a helpful survey and discussion of recent scholarship on "spiritual exegesis."

cae) to help the reader so that "whatever is closed will be open and whatever is dark will be illumined." Tyconius's interpretation is an example of typological interpretation that referred 2 Thessalonians to the situation of the Church in his time. More precisely, his spiritual interpretation of the text provided a "key and lamp" for the interpretation of the rest of Scripture. As we find it in Tyconius's *Book of Rules,* 2 Thessalonians is the measure, not the measured, in Tyconius's interpretive schema; it is not the text commented upon, but the text consulted for its hermeneutical insight. Tyconius never gave the text formal exegetical attention; yet, his almost implicit treatment of 2 Thessalonians initiated an alternative spiritual exegetical tradition with tremendous influence, through Augustine and Gregory the Great, on apocalyptic thought in the West.

Tyconius

Little is known about the life and death of Tyconius. Gennadius speaks only briefly about him in his *Lives of Illustrious Men:* "Tyconius, an African by nationality, was, it is said, sufficiently learned in sacred literature, not wholly unacquainted with secular literature and zealous in ecclesiastical affairs."[3] He lists four works under Tyconius's name. Two appear to be typical Donatist polemical works, *De Bello intestino* and the *Expositiones diversarum causarum;* both are entirely lost. The third, his *Commentary on the Apocalypse,* was extremely influential on Augustine, Bede, and Beatus of Liébana, but it too is lost.[4] Only the fourth, the *Liber Regularum,* survives. The *Book of Rules* appears to have been composed in the early 380s and may have been the occasion for his excommunication from the Donatist Church in ca. 385. Augustine tells us that Tyconius was a lay-

3. Gennadius, *De Viris inlustribus,* in *Nicene and Post-Nicene Fathers,* second series, vol. 3 (Grand Rapids: Eerdmans, 1952), 389.

4. Kenneth Steinhauser has reconstructed large portions of the Apocalypse commentary from these later commentators who used it as a source. See the published form of his dissertation, *The Apocalypse Commentary of Tyconius* (Frankfurt am Main: Peter Lang, 1987).

man. A bit bemused, the bishop also claims that Tyconius remained outside the Donatist communion but refused to become Catholic.[5] A man without a Church, Tyconius thus disappears from the scene. His *Book of Rules* survived. The *Book* is a collection of seven short treatises on the interpretation of Scripture. The prologue tells the reader that Tyconius devised his little book "on rules" to provide "keys and lamps" to the "secrets of the law."[6] Contrary to the assumptions of most of his readers (Augustine included!), Tyconius's "rules" were not, he thought, of his own making; instead, his "little book" offered an introduction to the Holy Spirit's "mystical rules," which are discovered in Scripture.[7] The reader will thereby be equipped to walk the "vast forests of prophecy"[8] without slipping into error.[9] The seven rules are:

I.   The Lord and His Body
II. The Lord's Bipartite Body
III. The Promises and the Law
IV. The Particular and the General
V.   Times
VI. Recapitulation
VII. The Devil and His Body

5. Augustine, *De doctrina christiana* 3.30, trans. D. W. Robertson Jr. (New York: Macmillan, 1964).

6. *"Necessarium duxi ante omnia quae mihi videntur libellum regularem scribere, et secretorum legis veluti claves et luminaria fabricare."* Tyconius, *Liber regularum,* ed. and trans. William S. Babcock (Atlanta: Scholars Press, 1989), prologue, p. 2. Translations are from Babcock unless otherwise noted. I will refer hereafter to this text as "LR." Note that by "law," Tyconius seems to refer here to all of Scripture.

7. See Charles Kannengiesser and Pamela Bright, *A Conflict of Christian Hermeneutics in Roman Africa: Tyconius and Augustine,* Protocol of the 58th Colloquy, Center for Hermeneutical Studies in Hellenistic and Modern Culture, 16 October 1988 (Berkeley: Center for Hermeneutical Studies, 1989), for the full presentation and discussion of this argument.

8. In this case, prophecy seems to refer to any Scripture with a typological application to the Head and/or Body of Christ.

9. *"ut quis prophetiae immensam silvam perambulans his regulis quodam modo lucis tramitibus deductus ab errore defendatur."* LR, prologue, 3.

Each essay presents a rule and offers numerous examples of its presentation in passages of Scripture. Tyconius's citations are drawn from both Old and New Testaments. The great majority of Old Testament instances of "prophecy" are drawn from (naturally enough) Isaiah (124 times) and Ezekiel (143 times). In the New Testament, he depends heavily upon Paul, citing Pauline epistles 156 times as compared to 107 citations from the rest. 2 Thessalonians itself is cited 8 times at key places—quite a lot for the short letter. This dependence on the Apostle is indicative of Tyconius's profoundly Pauline theological roots. Paul's doctrine of the Church as the Body of Christ and his discussion of law and grace are the twin *fontes viventes* of Tyconius's hermeneutics. For Tyconius, Scripture is a "forest of prophecy" that testifies to Christ, both Head and Body. Scripture is the realm of the Spirit, whose Trinitarian role is established in testifying to the Son.[10] The goal of proper interpretation is to move beyond the human sense of scriptural language to the "mystical," divine meaning.[11] This divine meaning always refers to Christ, and prophetic passages in the Scriptures that refer to Christ can refer either to Jesus Christ, the Head, or to the Church, his Body. "Reason alone

10. Contrast this with the Origenian image of Scripture as the Incarnate Word, of flesh and spirit, as conveyed to the West by Hilary of Poitiers. Tyconius's exegesis is far more connected with his pneumatology than with his Christology. This is not surprising, since the Arian Christological controversy had little compelling influence on North African theology; matters of ecclesiology and pneumatology (viz. earlier polemics against Montanism) were far more important to the Africans. See Pamela Bright, *The Book of Rules of Tyconius: Its Purpose and Inner Logic* (Notre Dame: University of Notre Dame Press, 1988), 174–75.

11. Again, the contrast with Origen is telling. As Charles Kannengiesser has stated, "in Origen of Alexandria, the mystic sense is equivalent to the spiritual sense as opposed to the literal sense. Whereas in Tyconius, 'mystic' is equal to divine, as opposed to human. It is a divine structure, implied in the divine Scripture, which is mystic." Kannengiesser and Bright, 83. Thus, whatever connections Tyconius may have had to the "spiritual interpretation" of the Eastern Church Fathers through Hilary of Poitiers, his "spiritual interpretation" is distinct from theirs. For Tyconius, Scripture has only one true sense, the "mystic" or Spirit-authored sense.

discerns, persuading or, such is the force of truth, compelling us to recognize what pertains to each."[12]

Tyconius's fundamental theological insight is into the division inherent in Christian ecclesial identity. Like the Pauline man, the Church has within its members an irreconcilable struggle of spirit against flesh. Unlike his fellow Donatists, Tyconius believes that the Church in the world is mixed inseparably, with the saved and the damned, the just and the reprobate within its walls. The Body of Christ also contains within it the Body of Satan. This two-fold, conflictual identity of the *corpus bipertitum* is the condition of the Church in history, from the life of Christ to the Last Judgment.[13]

2 Thessalonians gives Tyconius the hermeneutical center for discussing this divided body. Although the text is explicitly eschatological in its literal sense, Tyconius's sixth rule provides the key for unlocking its meaning for the present-day Church. This sixth rule, "Recapitulations," addresses the interpretation of eschatological passages. Tyconius tells us that recapitulations in Scripture "often take this form: 'then,' 'in that hour,' 'on that day,' 'in that time.'" He argues that this typically apocalyptic language should not be understood only to refer to the time of the end; instead, such events are recapitulated throughout time. For example, he cites Christ's words in the "little apocalypse" of Matthew:

"On the day Lot left Sodom, it rained fire from heaven and destroyed them all. The day of the Son of Man, when he is revealed, will be the

12. "*sola ratio discernit, dum quid cui conveniat persuadet vel quia tanta est vis veritatis extorquet.*" LR I, 3.

13. His stand in relation to the imminence of that final judgment is contested. Traditionally, scholars have contended that Tyconius's typological interpretation was yoked to a belief that the *eschaton's* approach was imminent. However, Paula Fredriksen has argued that Tyconius's typology was thoroughgoing: Tyconius interpreted apocalyptic texts or "prophecies" *only* as realized mystically in the present life of the Church. The end remained distant and unknown as the final resolution of the divisions within the Church. See Paula Fredriksen, "Tyconius and the End of the World," *Revue des études Augustiniennes* 28 (1982): 59–75.

same. At that hour, anyone who is on the housetop, with his possessions in the house, must not come down to collect them, and so too anyone who is in the field must not turn back. He should remember Lot's wife." Is it only at the hour when the Lord is revealed in his coming that a person ought not to turn back for his belongings and ought to have remembered Lot's wife—and not also before he is revealed? But the Lord commanded that these things be observed at the hour of his revelation . . . to show that the whole time is the "day" or the "hour."[14]

The "whole time," from the Incarnation to the Second Coming, is the "day" of the Lord. This does not give the present time a sense of predictive imminence; on the contrary, Tyconius later states explicitly that "now is not the time of the end." The era of the Church is, in one sense, eschatological time; it is in the "hour" of the Church that Christ continually is revealed, and thus it is in the same "hour" that the Man of Sin continually is revealed. In this way, Tyconius can use 2 Thessalonians as a template for the present Church.

As I have noted, Tyconius cites or alludes to the letter eight times throughout the *Book of Rules*. Many of these eight appearances occur at crucial points of transition in the text. The first rule introduces the Church-as-Body theme, giving numerous examples of when "reason" tells the reader when Scripture refers to Christ and when it refers to the Church. He gives the example of when the Church is referred to as "God," and cites 2 Thessalonians 2:4 as his example:

it [the Church] is even called "God," as we find in the apostle: "above everything that is called God or that is worshipped,"—that "which is called God" is the Church, and that "which is worshipped" is the

14. *"Die quo exiit Loth a Sadomis pluit ignem de caelo et perdidit omnes; secundum haec erit dies filii hominis, quo revelabitur. Illa hora qui erit in tecto et vasa eius in domo non descendat tollere illa, et qui in agro similiter non revertatur retrom meminerit uxoris Loth. Numquid ill hora qua Dominus revelatus fuerit adventu suo non debet quis converti ad ea quae sua sunt et uxoris Loth meminisse, et non antequam revelatur? Dominus autem illa hora qua revelatus fuerit iussit ista observari, non solum ut abscondendo quaerentibus gratiorem faceret veritatem, sed etiam ut totum illud tempus diwm vel horam esse monstraret."* LR VI, 108–11.

supreme God—"so that he takes his seat in the temple of God *(in templum Dei)*, claiming that he is himself God," that is, that he is himself the Church.[15]

The text demonstrates Tyconius's point that the Church is some-times called God, but it also tells the reader, almost indirectly, that Antichrist claims to *be* the Church.[16] In the following paragraph, as he gives several more examples of the Church referred to as "bride," "sister," and "Christ," he interjects another clue from 2 Thessaloni-ans about Antichrist: "the apostle . . . speaks of the enemy body *(adversum corpus)* as 'the man of sin.'"[17] Again, almost indirectly, we learn that Antichrist, the "man of sin," has the same socio-corporate nature that Christ has in the Church. Already, in a rule devoted to "the Lord and His Body," Tyconius has "hidden" the Man of Sin and his body. As he brings this first essay to a close, Tyconius summa-rizes what he has said:

And so the Body, in virtue of its head, is the Son of God; and God, in virtue of his body, is the Son of Man who comes daily by birth and "grows into the holy temple of God." [Eph 2:21]

Thus far, it seems a clear summary of the rule. But he continues:

For the temple is bipartite; and its other part, although it is being con-structed with great blocks of stone, will be destroyed and "not one stone will be left upon another." [Mt 24:2] Against the continuous coming of

---

15. *"dicti etiam Deus sicut per apostolum: Super omne qui dicitur Deus aut quod col-itur—qui dicitur Deus Ecclesia est, quod autem colitur Deus summus est—ut in templum Dei sedeat ostendens se quod ipse est Deus, id est quod ipse sit Ecclesia."* LR I, 8–11.

16. Note that Tyconius seems here to use Latin text **J**, which has *in templum*, in the accusative case, connoting motion or change, rather than the static ablative *in templo* of **D**, the other version that appears in his work. I do not suggest that Tyconius deliberately selects this version, only that the accusative case is more congenial to his interpretation than the "ablative of place where." See my com-mentary on the text, pp. xix–xxi, and Hermann Josef Frede, ed., *Epistolae ad Thes-salonicenses, Timotheum, Titum, Philemonem, Hebraeos,* 9 fascicles, *Vetus Latina: die Reste der altlateinishcen Bibel* 25 (Freiburg: Herder, 1975–81).

17. The whole text is as follows: *"Et Dominus totum populum sponsam dicit et sororem; et apostolus virginem sanctam, et adversum corpus hominem peccati."* LR I, 10.

that temple we must remain on guard until the Church shall depart "from the midst" [2 Th 2:7] of it.[18]

The contrast is clear: The "Son of Man" grows daily into the temple of God; the "Man of Sin" grows, too, into another temple. The two are mixed together for now, and the Church must "remain on guard" until it "shall depart from the midst" of the other temple. Tyconius turns the common interpretation of 2 Thessalonians 2:7 on its head. While typically, as we have seen, "what restrains" is understood to be the Roman Empire (which will fall) or the decree of providence (which will remove its protection from the Church), here the Church itself "departs" *(discedat)* "from the midst" *(de medio)*. The presence of the Church is, in fact, the restraining force; when the Church departs, the "mystery of lawlessness" will be fully revealed. The logic of the passage is thus fundamentally different for Tyconius. The Church is not the object of the passage's action, but its subject: the Church departs. The Church is afflicted now with the presence of Antichrist, but its *discessio,* its departure, is an escape from evil. The eschaton does not represent an increase (for a time) of the devil's persecution of the Church. Instead, it promises at last the total deliverance of the Church from its present afflictions.[19]

Already by the end of the first rule, Tyconius has laid out his ecclesiological schema, using elements of 2 Thessalonians to develop his themes. The "enemy body," which Paul calls the "man of sin," is

18. *"Corpus itaque in capite suo filius est Dei, et Deus in corpore suo filius est hominis, qui cotidie nascendo venit et crescit in templum sanctum Dei. Templum enim bepertitum est, cuius pars altera quamvis lapidibus magnis extruatur destruitur, neque in eo lapis super lapidem relinquitur. Istius nobis iugis adventus cavendus est, donec de medio eius discedat Ecclesia."* LR I, 12–14.

19. LR III, 55. cf. Gn 19:29 and Lk 17:29. Note that the citation of Luke shows that this notion of the departure is not a theme original to Tyconius. Tyconius seems to be the first to apply it in this way to 2 Thessalonians. In addition, Kenneth Steinhauser argues that the same theme in Tyconius's Apocalypse commentary lies behind Jerome's revision of Victorinus of Pettau's exegesis of Revelation 15:1: The seven plagues of Revelation 15ff. are said to occur "when the church goes out from the midst," *cum ecclesia de medio exierit.* Steinhauser, 42.

in the temple *(in templum)*, claiming to be the Church. The Church, the Body of Christ, goes out "from the midst." Pamela Bright calls this "in the midst/from the midst" dichotomy the "linchpin for Tyconius's ecclesiology."[20] With this lens she finds a cumulative linear argument introduced in the first rule and pursued throughout the *Liber Regularum.*[21] While Tyconius's collection of essays retains its initial purpose of "opening" the various mysterious "prophecies" of Scripture, it also develops a sustained inquiry into the "mystery of iniquity," the enigmatic presence of evil within the Church.[22]

The sustained inquiry is developed as Tyconius returns to the theme at the end of each rule, often invoking or alluding to 2 Thessalonians. As we have seen, Rule I ends with an introduction of the "bipartite" theme and takes 2 Thessalonians to exhort the Church to vigilance. Rule II concludes with the statement "the Lord gives testimony that the one body of Abraham's line, in every case, both grows and flourishes and goes to ruin."[23] Rule III ends with an allusion to 2 Thessalonians 2:3 and Luke 17:29–30: "For it is the time when these things may be said openly and not in riddles, as the 'rebellion' approaches *(imminente discessione)* which is the revelation of the 'man of sin,' when Lot departs *(discedente)* from Sodom."[24] Tyco-

20. Bright, 49.

21. "The selective movement from general christological and ecclesiological concerns to the particular emphasis on an eschatology, and then on to a series of texts referring to the revelation of the man of sin (2 Th 2:3) who is 'coming' 'in the midst' of the church establishes a pattern that may be observed throughout the *Book of Rules.*" Bright, 44.

22. I am indebted to Pamela Bright's analysis of the Tyconian text, the depths of which I cannot summarize in this brief treatment. Particularly noteworthy is her close textual analysis of a "concentric" argument about scriptural hermeneutics and a "linear" argument about Antichrist within the Church.

23. *"Ita Dominus in omnibus Scripturis unum corpus seminis Abrahae in omnibus crescere et florere atque perire testatur."* LR II, 20.

24. *"Tempus est enim quo haec non in mysteriis sed aperte dicantur, imminente discessione quod est revelatio hominis peccati, discedente Loth a Sodomis."* LR III, 54, translation mine. I have translated this with a sense of the present ("For it is the time") rather than Babcock's less determinate "For there is a time," based on the

nius plays on the double meaning of *discessio* here, such that it is both the "rebellion" of the body of Antichrist and the "departure" of the Body of Christ. Rule IV reminds the reader that the saints are engaged in a battle "not against human powers but against the spiritual hosts of wickedness in heaven."[25] Rule V discusses the history of the Church:

For, too, the 100 years during which the ark was built represent all the time, during which the church is being built; and during this time, while everything is perishing in the flood, its helm is manned.[26]

Note here the sense of simultaneity, during which the Church is both built and manned at the helm. Rule VI again alludes to 2 Thessalonians as it concludes:

Thus Antichrist was proclaiming Christ as Lord not in honesty but in pretense. With something quite different in mind, he enters in Christ's name in order to smooth the way for himself . . . asserting with signs and wonders that the works of the inner room represent Christ.[27]

Finally, Rule VII, "The Devil and his Body," ends abruptly with a quote from Ezekiel 28:19, "You have been made for destruction and you will not exist forever."[28] Thus, as each rule draws to a close, the presence of evil "in the midst" is brought to mind. Tyconius warns his readers to be wary, and he assures them that, in the end, evil will be destroyed.[29]

---

argument of Paula Fredriksen, "Tyconius and the End of the World." Tyconius refers to a present reality, not some hypothetical future one.

25. *"Unde apostolus dicit non esse sanctis pugnam adversum humana, se adversus spiritalia nequitiae in caelestibus."* LR IV, 88.

26. *"Nam et C anni quibus arca fabricata est omne tempus est quo Ecclesia fabricatur, et eo tempore in diluvio pereuntibus universis gubernatur."* LR V, 109.

27. *"Dominum autem Christum antichristus non voto sed occasione praedicabat. Alio tendens per Christi nomen ingreditur, quo sibi viam sternat . . . signis et prodigiis cubiculorum opera Christum esse asseverans."* LR VI, 114. What he alludes to as "the works of the inner room" is a bit ambiguous. Perhaps this is an allusion to Matthew 24:24, 26.

28. *"Perditio facta es, et non eris in aeternum."* LR VII, 144, my translation.

29. Again, I am indebted to Bright, ch. 4, for much of this argument.

It should be clear that Tyconius's *Liber Regularum* is far from a simple catalogue of hermeneutical principles; on the contrary, it is a well-crafted composition that explores in Scripture the ecclesiological problem that confronted the Donatist and Catholic churches—the presence of evil within the Church. Tyconius's primary model for this problem is drawn from the language of 2 Thessalonians. In casting his contemporary ecclesiological problem in the language of "the man of sin in the temple," Tyconius creates an innovative typological interpretation of 2 Thessalonians, the elements of which are scattered throughout the text. To extrapolate a single exegesis from these scattered hints is admittedly an exercise in historical imagination, but it will be helpful for purpose of comparison.

Since, as we have noted, Tyconius reads 2 Thessalonians as a template for the condition of the present-day Church, his interpretation of the text doesn't follow a particular temporal sequence. Instead, all of the major images refer to the same reality. The third verse of the text describes the simultaneous, parallel, and opposed movements of the two bodies within the Church. The *discessio* denotes both the "rebellion" in which the "man of sin, the son of perdition" is revealed and the "departure" of the just from the midst of the wicked "as Lot departed from Sodom." The revelation of the "man of sin" is actually that of "the body of sin" within the Church. Similarly, the session in the temple is the presence of the body of Antichrist in the Church, such that they themselves claim to be the Church.[30]

Tyconius in no way denies that a final end will come; nor does he deny that these prophetic passages in Scripture refer to this final end. But they also apply, by the Rule of Recapitulation, to the present situation of the Church, and it is this meaning that Tyconius chooses to emphasize. The typological reading of the presence of

30. As an aside, one cannot help but wonder whether Tyconius later interpreted his own excommunication as one such "departure" from the "body of sin" claiming to be the Church. Of course, there is no evidence to support any such speculation.

evil "in the midst" of the Church leads to a moral meaning that is given almost an imperative sense, "Depart from the midst of evil!" issued to the Body of Christ.[31] This separation will never be final until the end; the Body of Christ must constantly "be on guard," ready to again recapitulate the "departure" from the body of Antichrist.

Tyconius has thus developed a spiritual interpretation of 2 Thessalonians, with both typological and moral elements. This interpretation is peculiarly "Pauline," not in any explicit debt to the Apostle's biblical hermeneutics. Rather, it can be said that Tyconius writes in the Pauline spirit, constructing biblical hermeneutics from Pauline imagery (especially the "Body of Christ") and Pauline themes (e.g., the Rule of Recapitulation conveys Paul's sense of the "already–not yet" celebrated by Oscar Cullmann and Rudolph Bultmann; "law and promise" also figures prominently.) Tyconius's interpretation of 2 Thessalonians in the *Liber Regularum* develops a new Pauline form of spiritual interpretation that would have great influence in the Latin West.

Augustine of Hippo

Such influence was accorded to Tyconius by the esteem with which Saint Augustine regarded his work. The famous Bishop of Hippo, whose doctrinal authority in the later tradition was unmatched, considered Tyconius a heterodox puzzle, but no mean exegete. Augustine devoted much of the third book of his *De doctrina Christiana*—in a way, Augustine's own "book of rules"—to summarizing and reformulating Tyconius's *Liber regularum*. The significance of this move should not be underestimated: For Augustine, proper Christian education was oriented toward the study of Scripture. Such study, the summit and goal of Christian learning, was to be undertaken using a version of Tyconius's hermeneutical rules. That a

---

31. For example, he cites 1 John 5:21 at the end of Rule VI: "With salutary caution, the apostle warns us to avoid such people [of Antichrist]: 'little children, keep away from mere semblances.'"

schismatic's thought would find so important a place in the education of the Christian establishes the significance of Tyconian hermeneutics for Augustine's understanding of Scripture.

Augustine's own deepening understanding of Scripture, especially of Paul, often led to major shifts in his thought. The significance of Romans in the *Confessions'* account of his final conversion is well known. And it is his reading of Paul, particularly in Romans and Galatians, that led him to his insights on grace and sin. Yet Augustine never undertook a systematic commentary on the Pauline epistles. His efforts to comment on Romans were never completed. While he did comment on 2 Thessalonians 2, his comments occur within a specific formal context quite different from a biblical commentary.

He addresses 2 Thessalonians in Book 20 of *The City of God,* a work devoted to the defense of Christianity in the face of the apparent end of "Roma Aeterna." Augustine began writing this *magnum opus et arduum* after Alaric's sack of Rome in 410. Fleeing Rome, many senatorial aristocrats took refuge in North Africa, bringing their antiquarian paganism with them.[32] They also brought hints and accusations against Constantinian Christianity for the failure of the empire. Augustine wrote the *City of God* to refute these allegations and strengthen the confidence of Catholics confronted with social and political disaster.

He proceeds by rejecting forthright any version of Constantinian or Eusebian Christianity. With the sack of Rome, Augustine is faced in present reality with events that to earlier writers were a distant part of the prophetic future. He is thus most eager to discourage any speculation that Antichrist's arrival would be associated in

32. I say "antiquarian paganism" because, as Peter Brown notes, Augustine does not mention the newer forms of pagan religious life (mystery cults, Mithraism, etc.). These aristocrats were deliberately antiquarian, seeking to revive the *litterata vetustas* of the ancient traditions of Rome. Thus, if Augustine was "demolishing a paganism that existed only in libraries," he did so deliberately. See Peter Brown, 305ff., for this discussion.

any way with the fall of Rome. Christians are not properly identified with the City of Rome or any other earthly city; theirs is the Heavenly City of Jerusalem to come. The organizing principle of the *City of God* is the interaction and eventual separation of these two "cities," the "earthly city" and the "heavenly," captured by the bishop's famous dictum, "Two loves built two cities."[33] The earthly city is constituted by the love of self; the heavenly city is built upon the love of God. Augustine brings this grand symphonic schema of the mixed life of the two cities to a climax in Book 19 of the *City of God*. In history, the city of God is "on pilgrimage" in the earthly city, using the latter's resources, but not claiming them as its own. It is not identical with the visible Church; on the contrary, the Church contains citizens of both cities, and it is well nigh impossible to distinguish the two. The two cities are commingled in history; only on the Last Day will the two cities be fully separated. The earthly will be banished to perdition, and the heavenly will be with God.[34]

Book 20 of the *City of God* is devoted to this eschatological resolution. Augustine produced the book in 427 in the last years of his life; it thus represents the mature end of his evolving thought on eschatology. In the early days after his conversion, Augustine had sub-

---

33. "*Fecerunt itaque civitates duas amores duo.*" Augustine, *De civitate Dei* [CD] 14.28, ed. B. Dombart and A. Kalb, CCSL 47–48 (Turnhout: Brepols, 1955).

34. Tyconius's stamp upon this image is apparent. Although Augustine shifts the metaphor some, preferring to speak of "cities" rather than "bodies," he takes from Tyconius the sense that this twofold, mixed condition persists throughout history until the end of time. Several modern scholars have demonstrated that this theme appears in some of Augustine's early work, before he was acquainted with the writings of Tyconius. The *De vere religione* (ca. 390) contains an extended meditation in the Pauline theme of the contrast between the "new man" and the "old," in which Augustine refers to the assembled masses of the "old man" as constituting a kind of "city." This city of the "old man" is to be contrasted with the "kingdom of Heaven." Thus, even before he had read Tyconius, Augustine had broadened Paul's anthropological metaphors into social images of "city" versus "kingdom." But Augustine's initial perception of the opposed parties of "city" and "kingdom" lacks his later emphasis upon the mixed character of the two parties on earth. This insight he almost certainly gained from his reading of Tyconius.

scribed to the Eusebian interpretation of the positive eschatological significance of the Christian Roman Empire. Indeed, his early work shows signs of a thoroughgoing millenarian optimism: In *De catechizandis rudibus,* Augustine says that the narration of salvation history should begin with the story of Creation and end with "the present times of the Church." By the early 400s, however, he began to question the accomplishments of Theodosius, the emperor who had finally established Christianity as the religion of the empire. By Rome's fall in 410, Augustine's faith in the *tempora christiana,* in the evidence of providence in the workings of politics and history, had all but disappeared.[35]

Augustine's rejection of his earlier optimistic eschatology found its clearest expression in his correspondence in 418 with Hesychius, a Dalmatian bishop eager in his apocalyptic expectation. In his one surviving letter, Hesychius rehearses many of the arguments from Scripture common to the tradition since Eusebius. He agrees that we cannot know the "day or the hour" of the Lord's return, but we may still look for the signs of his coming, and thus desire his coming all the more.[36] Augustine responds that we may desire his coming and not know when it is. He urges rather that the Christian should work with what he can know:

Everyone ought to fear the last day of his own life. For in whatever state his own last day finds him, in such a state will the last day of the world overtake him, since as one is on the day of one's death, so will one be judged on the last day.[37]

35. The movement of Augustine's thought is traced in Markus, ch. 2.

36. "*Quod autem nemo possit mensuras temporum coligere, manifestum est. Evangelium quidem dicit: 'De die illa et hora nemo scit.' Ego autem pro possibilitate intellectus mei dico, neque diem, neque mensem, neque annum adventus ipsius sciri posse, sed signa quae sunt adventus videndo et credendo, et exspectare me convenit, et credentibus escam hanc retribuere, ut expectantes diligant adventum eius.*" Ep. 198, PL 33.903.

37. "*quod unusquisque debet etiam de die huius vitae suae novissimo formidare. In quo enim quemque invenerit suus novissimus dies, in hoc eum comprehendet mundi novissimus dies; quoniam qualis in die isto quisque moritur, talis in die illo iudicabitur.*" Ep. 199, PL 33.905.

The admission of ignorance in the face of the unknowable and the concomitant concern to work with what one can know are the hallmarks of Augustine's eschatological (or, properly, non-eschatological) thought. His final advice to Hesychius (and, according to his later comments in *City of God*,[38] his definitive word on the subject) is humbly to avoid any such speculation. "It seems to me, then, that one does not err when he knows that he does not know something, only when he thinks he knows what he does not."[39] As his confidence in the correlation between the so-called "Christian times" and the rule of Providence declined, Augustine thought it proper to Christian humility to refrain from speculation.

Augustine applies this principle of humility to several scriptural texts cited by Hesychius; among these is 2 Thessalonians 2. When Hesychius cites 2 Thessalonians 2 as proof that the early disciples knew of the signs of the times, Augustine responds at length:

> Would that you had not only quoted but had also deigned to expound these words, for, though they are so obscure and hidden in meaning, it does not appear that he said anything about established times or that he revealed any length or interval of time. He says, "that he may be revealed in his time," but he does not say how long it will be before this happens. Then he adds, "for the mystery of iniquity is already at work." What the "mystery of iniquity" is has been variously understood by one or another, but how long it will work is a secret . . . then what follows: "such that who now holds, let him hold, until he be taken from the midst. Then that iniquitous one will be revealed, whom the Lord will kill with the breath of his mouth," teaches us that Antichrist will appear. Although he seems to have described him in somewhat clearer terms as due to be killed by the breath of the mouth of the Lord Jesus Christ, after what amount of time he will arrive is mentioned only obscurely.[40]

38. CD 20.5.
39. *"sed mihi quisquam non videtur errare, cum aliquid nescire se scit, sed cum se putat scire quod nescit."* Ep. 199, PL 33.924.
40. *"Quae verba apostolica utinam non tantummodo ponere, verum etiam exponere dignareris: ita sane obscura sunt et mystice dicta, ut tamen appareat eum nihil de statutis dixisse temporibus, nullumque eorum intervallum spatiumque aperuisse. Ait enim, ut reveletur in suo tempore, nec dixit post quantum temporis hoc futurum sit. Deinde subjunxit,*

In this initial exegesis, then, 2 Thessalonians appears to Augustine as a cipher, and nothing more. The only "facts" he gleans from the text are that Antichrist will come and that Christ will kill him by the breath of his mouth; he can find no indication of time whatsoever.

Augustine's dismissal of predictive, realist apocalyptic speculation in the letter to Hesychius is carried off without explicit reference to or apparent use of Tyconius's thought. Nevertheless, Augustine had been reading Tyconius's work since the mid 390s, and few scholars doubt that reading Tyconius influenced Augustine deeply.[41] Interestingly, Augustine's most explicit and sustained work on Tyconius, the *De doctrina Christiana,* seems to ignore the eschatological dimensions of the Donatist's *Liber regularum.* Augustine pays little attention to the "linear argument" about the presence of evil within the Church and instead focuses upon the "concentric" argument of Tyconius about the proper interpretation of Scripture. It seems that, for Augustine, eschatology and biblical hermeneutics are distinct and thus best addressed separately. For Augustine does not ignore the eschatological; on the contrary, Tyconius's insights pervade the general thematic structure and eschatological exegetical portions of the *City of God.*

It is in the context of this great work that Augustine again turns

---

iam enim mysterium operatur iniquitatis. Hoc iniquitatis mysterium quomodolibet intelligatur quid sit, ab alio autem sic; quamdiu tamen operetur, occultum est. . . . Item quod sequitur, Tantum qui modo tenet, teneat, donec de medio fiat; et tunc revelabitur ille iniquus, quem Dominus Iesus Interficiet spiritu oris sui, docet nos Antichristum manifestum futurum: siquidem ipsum videtur aliquanto evidentiori significatione tetigisse interficiendum spiritu oris Domini Iesu Christi; sed post quantum temporis istud erit, nec saltem obscure locutus est." Ep. 197, PL 33.908.

41. Since Augustine had been reading Tyconius in the 390s (He refers to Tyconius in Ep. 41, ca. 396, but Paula Fredriksen is inclined to see Tyconius's influence even in Augustine's early Pauline commentaries), it seems apparent that he knew of the Donatist's particular interpretation of the text already. It seems likely that Augustine here offers no counter-interpretation for rhetorical purposes, i.e., to emphasize that any literal or millenarian interpretation was nigh impossible. See Markus, 118; Fredriksen, *Augustine's Early Interpretation of Paul* (Ann Arbor: University of Michigan Press, 1979), 209–15.

to 2 Thessalonians 2. His discussion of the text comes within Book 20, as part of a general survey of what traditionally will be called the "last things." Book 20 is a defense of Christian eschatology,[42] and more particularly of the "Last Judgment," which Augustine says he will "assert . . . in the face of the irreligious and the unbelieving."[43] He begins his "assertion" by presenting the problem to which eschatological judgment is the answer. It is called the "Last Judgment" because it is the last of a series: God is always judging, from the fall of Adam to the end. But this presents a problem. Why, if God is always judging, do the wicked prosper? This is the question Augustine seeks to answer with his presentation of the Last Judgment. "It will then be made clear that true and complete happiness belongs to all the good, and only to them, while all the wicked, and only the wicked, are destined for deserved and supreme unhappiness."[44]

Book 20 of the *City of God*, then, taken as a whole, presents a rather straightforward rendering of the eschatological traditions of the Church, without pause or hesitation. In fact, Augustine does not shy away from affirming that

we have learnt that those events are to come about: Elijah the Tishbite will come; Jews will accept the faith; Antichrist will persecute; Christ will judge; the dead will rise again; the good and the evil will be separated; the earth will be destroyed in the flames and then will be renewed. All those events, we must believe, will come about; but in what way, and in what

42. Note that we are already a bit of a distance from Tyconius. Augustine brings up the texts in a book devoted to "last things," while Tyconius in the LR wishes to remain even more eschatologically agnostic and treat such texts only insofar as they describe the inner dynamics of the present Church. While Augustine is sympathetic to the point, the fact that he takes up the text in a section on eschatology reveals a broader sense of salvation history.

43. *"De die ultimi iudicii Dei quod ipse donaverit locuturi eumque adserturi adversus impios et incredulos tamquam in aedificii fundamento prius ponere testimonia divina debemus."* CD 20.1. Translation: *The City of God*, trans. Henry Bettenson (London: Penguin edition, 1984). All translations unless otherwise noted are from Bettenson.

44. *"Omnium namque tunc nonnisi bonorum vera et plena felicitas et omnium nonnisi malorum digna et summa infelicitas apparebit."* CD 20.1; Bettenson, 896.

order they will come, actual experience will then teach us with a finality surpassing anything our human understanding is now capable of attaining. However, I consider that these events are destined to come about in the order I have given.[45]

Augustine endorses wholeheartedly the realistic and historical nature of the apocalyptic prophecies found in Scripture. And, indeed, the *City of God* becomes a significant source in the Middle Ages for the sequence of eschatological events in literature and iconography.[46] However, his grand presentation of the Last Judgment begins with a subversive eschatological disclaimer. When Scripture speaks of "resurrection," he says, the reader must distinguish carefully whether it refers to the resurrection of the soul in the rite of baptism or to the resurrection of the body at the end of time.

When he turns to interpret John's Apocalypse with this very Tyconian exegetical principle in mind, Augustine discovers that much of the teachings about "the millennium" are in fact testimony to the present life of the Church. Satan is now bound, the saints now reign, and both anticipate the final judgment, when Satan will be loosed and cast out and the heavenly kingdom will finally come. Augustine admits that the Apocalypse is quite difficult to interpret, as it shifts rapidly from one resurrection to the next, or as it repeats the same thing in different language. But, he assures the reader, the central truth of the book is quite clear: "God will wipe away every tear from their eyes, and death will be no more, and there will be no more sorrow or crying, nor will there be any more pain."[47]

Having consulted the Gospels and John's Apocalypse, Augustine then turns to other apostolic witnesses to the Last Judgment. After

45. CD 20.30; Bettenson, 963.

46. I am grateful to Richard K. Emmerson for this insight in his unpublished paper, "Antichrist in Late Medieval Illuminated Books: The Continuity of the Augustinian Tradition," delivered at a symposium on the *City of God* at University of British Columbia, "History, Apocalypse, and the Secular Imagination," September 18–20, 1997, and for a provocative discussion afterward.

47. "'Absterget omnem lacrimam ab oculis eorum; et mors iam non erit neque luctus neque clamor, sed nec dolor ullus.'" [Rv. 20:4] CD 20.17; Bettenson, 929.

addressing the apocalyptic teaching in 2 Peter, Augustine at last comes to Paul, the least of the Apostles.

Augustine prefaces his comments on 2 Thessalonians by acknowledging that he has left out many eschatological passages in the New Testament. "But I must not on any account pass over what the apostle Paul writes to the Thessalonians."[48] He then quotes 2 Thessalonians 2:1–12 and offers his exegesis. As he so often does, Augustine begins his exegesis by stating what we know for sure:

No one can doubt that Paul is here speaking of Antichrist, telling us that the day of judgment (which he calls the Day of the Lord) will not come without the prior coming of a figure whom he calls the Apostate, meaning of course an apostate from the Lord God.[49]

For Augustine, the "rebellion" or desertion is Antichrist himself, the one who flees from God and resists him. He uses a variant Old Latin text that has *"refuga,"* "exile," or "apostate" instead of *discessio* and interprets it as follows: "Unless first the Exile, which no doubt is said of Antichrist, whom he certainly calls an exile from the Lord God. For if this is said of all the unjust, how much more can it be said of him?" Augustine thereby circumvents the traditional discussion of the fate of Rome—a topic he is perhaps eager to avoid in 427. The *refuga* denotes the moral condition of this great sinner of sinners, not the apocalyptic—and perhaps too familiar—collapse of the empire.

Augustine proceeds to discuss the reference to the temple. He considers the text somewhat opaque; its literal referent is unclear. He will not attempt to decide whether Paul refers to the temple in Jerusalem or to the Church; instead, Augustine cites a spiritual interpretation that supplements the literal sense:

48. *"sed nullo modo est praetereundus apostolus Paulus, qui scribens ad Thessalonicenses."* CD 20.19; Bettenson, 931.

49. *"Nulli dubium est eum de Antichristo ista dixisse, diemque iudicii (hunc enim appellabat diem Domini) non esse venturum, nisi ille prior venerit, quem refugam vocat, utique a Domino Deo."* CD 20.19; Bettenson, 932.

some people would have it that Antichrist means here not the leader himself but what we may call his whole body, the multitude, that is, of those who belong to him, together with himself, their leader. And they suppose that then it would be more correct to say, following the original Greek, that he "takes his seat *as* the temple of God" [*in templum*], instead of "*in* the temple of God" [*in templo*], purporting to be himself God's temple, that is, the church.[50]

Augustine clearly reads this text through the eyes of Tyconius. Antichrist for him is present within the Church now, as the body of potential schismatics, as much as he will come in the future as a historical figure seated in the Church or restoring the Jewish Temple cult.

Augustine has not abandoned the uncertainty of his first attempt at the text in the letter to Hesychius. Twenty years later, he still finds most of the passages impenetrable. When he considers the meaning of verses 6–7, the restraining force and the mystery of iniquity, he points out first that Paul did not speak explicitly because his audience already knew his referent. But what they knew is now lost, and Augustine confesses, "the meaning of this completely escapes me." Unable to offer his own exegesis, he reviews several prominent interpretations, what he calls "guesses." First he examines the traditional understanding of Roman imperial power as the "restraining force" in verse 6. Augustine recounts the theory that Paul wrote obscurely because he feared Roman persecution. He suggests that this theory implies that Nero is the "restrainer," of verse 7. This implication he connects to the sibylline tales of Nero's escape or resurrection. Augustine expresses disdain for those who associate this passage with the Roman imperial power (he may have Ambrosiaster specifically in mind here) and with the variety of speculations about the return

50. "*Unde nonnulli non ipsum principem, sed universum quodam modo corpus eius, id est ad eum pertinentem hominum multitudinem, simul cum ipso suo principe hoc loco intellegi Antichristum volunt; rectiusquequeque putant etiam Latine dici, sicut in Graeco est, non in templo Dei, sed in templum Dei sedeat, tamquam ipse sit templum Dei, quod est ecclesia.*" CD 20.19; Bettenson, 932. Note that this really has little to do with the original Greek; instead, it has to do either with Augustine's use of Tyconius or with perhaps his independent use of the *Vetus Latina* J. See n. 16 above.

of Nero. In coupling any speculation about Paul's obscure references to Rome with wild fantasies of Nero's resurrection and return, Augustine places them all in the same category and dismisses
them: "For myself, I am astonished at the great presumption of
those who venture such guesses."[51]

A better guess, in Augustine's eyes, is offered by "others" who
seem to share Tyconius's perspective. These "others" think that the
verse "refers only to the evil people and the pretended Christians
who are in the church, until they reach such a number as to constitute a great people for Antichrist." This body of Antichrist is a "mystery of iniquity" because it grows in secret within the Church. The
second half of verse 7 is understood then as an exhortation to the
faithful, saying, "Only let him who holds [faith] hold on, . . . until
the secret power of wickedness, now concealed, departs from the
church."[52] The "others" then refer to 1 John's declamation of the
"many antichrists" who have appeared, proving that "it is the last
hour" (1 Jn 2:18). For Augustine, this indicates that, just as in this
first resurrection "many heretics are going out from the company of
the church, in the same way, . . . at the actual time of the end there
will go forth from the church all those who do not belong to Christ
but to that last Antichrist."[53] Having given what I think is his "best

<hr />

51. "Sed multum mihi mira est haec opinantium tanta presumptio." CD 20.19; Bettenson, 933. He admits that the verse could refer to the Roman imperial power,
but only if it is understood as a tautology, "saying, in effect, let him who now
reigns, reign until he is removed from the scene, that is, until taken away." But understood in this fashion, the verse says little about anything, and Augustine can
thus concede to such an inconsequential reading.

52. "ut in fide quam tenent tenaciter perseverent, . . . donec exeat de medio ecclesiae
mysterium iniquitatis, quod nunc occultum est." CD 20.19; Bettenson, 934. Note that
this is a departure from Tyconius in a significant way. Tyconius's thought is sectarian or, as J. Z. Smith might say, "utopian," and thus the "removal" is *of* the saints
from the mystery of iniquity. Augustine, on the other hand, requires that the mystery of evil be removed *from* the Church. See J. Z. Smith, *Map Is Not Territory: Studies in the History of Religions* (Chicago: University of Chicago Press, 1993), passim.

53. "Sicut ergo ante finem in hac hora, inquiunt, quam Iohannes novissimam dicit,
exierunt multi haeretici de medio ecclesiae, quos multos dicit Antichristos: ita omnes tunc

guess" of these troublesome verses (although he does not claim it as his own), Augustine restates that there are many different possible interpretations of 2 Thessalonians. He then briefly reviews the debate over the "lying signs and portents," and he seems to prefer to think that they are real works, not illusions. But he does not express a clear preference, and he concludes only that the answer will become clear when the events actually take place. In typical form, Augustine remains agnostic about the time and events of the end and diverts attention toward the spiritual reality of Antichrist within the Church of the present.

The only verses that Augustine expounds in his own voice come at the end of the chapter, when Paul tells of God sending the work of error upon those who rejected the love of truth (vv. 11–12). As we have seen, most exegetes take great pains to excuse God from this seemingly unfair act; to the contrary, Augustine takes Paul's statement as evidence for the conviction that emerged with ever greater clarity in Augustine's later years. He states confidently that God, "by a just decision of his own," will allow the devil to perform wonders, "although the devil performs them with a wicked and malignant design." For Augustine, Paul's words confess the mystery of God's providence, which declines to give the gifts of faith and perseverance to the wicked:

Thus they will be led astray after being judged, and after being led astray they will be judged. But when they have been judged they will be led astray by those judgments of God, secretly just and justly secret, that judgment he has never ceased to exercise since the first sin of rational creatures; and after being led astray they will be judged by that last and open judgment administered by Jesus Christ, who is to judge with perfect justice, though it was with utter injustice that he himself was judged.[54]

inde exibunt, qui non ad Christum, sed ad illum novissimum Antichristum pertinebunt et tunc revelabitur." CD 20.19; Bettenson, 934.

54. "Proinde iudicati seducentur et seducti iudicabuntur. Sed iudicati seducentur illis iudiciis Dei occulte iustis, numquam iudicare cessavit; seducti autem iudicabuntur novissimo manifestoque iudicio per Christum Iesum, iustissime iudicaturum, iniustissime iudicatum." CD 20.19; Bettenson, 935.

What he had first discussed concerning Pharaoh in Paul's letter to the Romans thirty years earlier, Augustine now repeats for all the wicked: God's secret eternal justice has found them wanting, and he has thus predestined them for temporal judgment. This doctrine of double judgment is the dark side of Augustine's double resurrection, his eschatological principle. God gives those who are drawn into new life through baptism in the Church the gift of perseverance, and they will receive eternal happiness. Those who are "dead in soul" (20.19) will fall prey to the seductions of evil permitted by God's just decree. Of the truth and clarity of this teaching, Augustine has no doubt.

Thus, after a prolonged discussion of apocalyptic ambiguities in 2 Thessalonians, Augustine ends his exegesis on firm Pauline ground. The issues that returned to him continually in his study of Paul arose yet again in 2 Thessalonians. While Augustine remains humbly agnostic about the details of the events of the end, he remains convinced of their essential truth. And the truth that they confess is that the graceful God judges with justice, both eternally and finally. He ends this chapter, as he began this book, with the assurance that "complete happiness belongs to all the good, and only to them, while the wicked, and only the wicked, are destined for deserved and supreme unhappiness."[55]

This truth, which lies behind Augustine's entire treatment of the "last things," betrays a distinct difference in emphasis between him and Tyconius. While Augustine marshals Tyconian principles to break down the authority of eschatological exegesis, his motives are his own. It is necessary to point out that Augustine's "others," while they seem to be Tyconian in temperament, do not represent Tyconius's interpretation directly. Whether Augustine here represents some "Tyconian" exegetes in North Africa, or whether (as I am inclined to think) he assembles some interpretations around Tyconian exegesis and puts them in the mouths of these anonymous "others,"

55. CD 20.1; Bettenson, 896.

the bishop does not directly represent the views of the Donatist. He and Tyconius agree on the necessity of immanent interpretation of eschatological Scripture. But Augustine's purpose in Book 20 of the *City of God* is one that Tyconius may not ever have sanctioned. Tyconius's scattered treatment of 2 Thessalonians was focused upon (and only upon) the mystery of evil as present within the Church. Antichrist is in the midst of the Church in his body; this is given in Scripture by the "mystical rules" of the Holy Spirit. For Augustine, the literal sense of the text is eschatological: Christ will not come in judgment before Antichrist comes. Having said this, he rushes to include that Antichrist is also present within the Church in his body. Unlike Tyconius, he sees the immanent, spiritual sense of 2 Thessalonians as a level of interpretation that complements, qualifies, but finally does not contradict the literal sense. In this case, the Tyconian interpretation is "spiritual exegesis" in the "Alexandrian" manner he had learned from Ambrose—a layer of interpretation given in addition to the literal sense, allowing Augustine, as Karla Pollmann says, "to have his apocalyptic cake and eat it too."[56] I have argued that this is a rereading of Tyconius's "mystical rules." Ironically, this traditional "spiritual interpretation" leaves Augustine, so often held responsible for the "silencing" of millenarian fantasies,[57] more eschatologically inclined than his source.

Despite the differences between Augustine and his source, both men generated for the first time in the Latin West a spiritual interpretation of 2 Thessalonians 2. Tyconius is the author of the notion of Antichrist's immanent presence "in the midst" of the Church in his "body." Augustine is the author of the form in which these influ-

56. Karla Pollmann, "Moulding the Present: Apocalyptic as Hermeneutics in *City of God* 21–22," in *History, Apocalypse, and the Secular Imagination: New Essays on Augustine's* City of God, ed. Mark Vessey, Karla Pollmann, and Allan D. Fitzgerald (Bowling Green: Philosophy Documentation Center, 1999), 180.

57. See, e.g., Richard A. Landes, "Fear of an Apocalyptic Year 1000," and Stephen D. O'Leary, *Arguing the Apocalypse: A Theory of Millennial Rhetoric* (New York: Oxford University Press, 1994), 73–76.

ential ideas usually would appear in the tradition. It is a strange hybrid of "Alexandrian" and "Tyconian" hermeneutics, folded within Augustine's pervasive admonitory skepticism toward eschatological speculation. While this Augustinian form bequeaths Tyconius's ideas to the tradition of interpretation most directly, still another authoritative voice would join the chorus on the Tyconian theme. The voice of "Our beloved Gregory," the last of the Latin Fathers, had little direct influence on the tradition, but his haunting tones echo in the dark halls of thought on Antichrist, and his influence, though indirect, should not be ignored.

Excursus: Gregory the Great, the Silent Presence

I consider this section of the chapter an excursus because Gregory the Great does not fit neatly into the textual history I am tracing. He gives no extended exegetical attention to 2 Thessalonians, and the tradition of commentary does not take up *directly* any of his scattered comments on one verse or another or any of his numerous meditations on Antichrist throughout his work.[58] Nevertheless, such meditations represent the mature fruition of the Tyconian tradition of thought about Antichrist. The writings of "our beloved Gregory," so popular in the Middle Ages, gave moral (or perhaps "immoral") substance to the body of Antichrist, and this substance permeated any discussion of Antichrist after Gregory's death.[59]

58. I.e., I can find no direct textual dependence, and *almost* no unique conceptual dependence (except the confusion about the death of Antichrist, see pp. 109–10) in the major sources of the tradition.

59. One might argue that Bede is a "silent presence" in the apocalyptic tradition, as well. Bede's Apocalypse commentary seems to share many of Gregory's convictions—he, too, for example, combines a vivid sense of presence with a realist sense of the Antichrist to come. However, Bede's apocalyptic thought, well-described by Gerald Bonner, seems really to apply Gregory's combination to commentary on the Apocalypse, with its unique periodization, etc. He does not actively develop the apocalyptic themes that come to bear upon the 2 Thessalonians tradition, since periodization is not one of its central concerns. Bede's Apoca-

Gregory lived in an age, he thought, on the verge of judgment. He did not doubt that a real, personal Antichrist would come soon to lead people astray. But his reflections on this future coming add little to the knowledge of Antichrist's life and career. Unlike most of the post-Nicene Fathers, however, Gregory asserted without apology that in Antichrist, the devil would become flesh. His belief in the incarnation of the devil probably stems from his theological penchant for symmetry: Antichrist truly is the *opposite* of Christ, and as Christ is the "man assumed by God," so, too, Antichrist is the "man assumed by the devil."[60] Since the fury of the Christological controversies had cooled, this manner of speaking of Antichrist was perhaps less objectionable, and it expressed for Gregory the true conflict between Good and Evil. The figure of Antichrist is no less real, no more metaphorical, than the figure of Christ. While the final victory of Christ is assured, Antichrist remains an adversary to be reckoned with.

The manner of Christ's victory over Antichrist is perhaps unclear. Gregory seems to be the author of some exegetical confusion concerning the death of Antichrist. While Gregory affirmed 2 Thessalonians' assertion that Christ will slay him "by the breath of his mouth" and by the "glory of his coming," (2 Th 2:8),[61] he asserts elsewhere that Michael the Archangel would kill him.[62] As we shall

<hr/>

lypse commentary is perhaps best understood in relation to this study as a parallel case, a text that develops this early medieval synthetic apocalyptic eschatology in the tradition and terms of the Apocalypse, rather than in 2 Thessalonians. Or, if I may put it another way, Bede's apocalypticism is more Johannine than Pauline. Its sources and influence are described in Gerald Bonner's 1966 Jarrow Lecture, "Saint Bede in the Tradition of Western Apocalyptic Commentary," in *Bede and His World: Jarrow Lectures 1958–1993* (Brookfield, Vt.: Variorum, 1994), 153–83; and in E. Ann Matter, "The Apocalypse in Early Medieval Exegesis," in *The Apocalypse in the Middle Ages,* eds. Richard K. Emmerson and Bernard McGinn (Ithaca: Cornell University Press, 1992), 38–50.

60. See, for example, *Moralia* 13.10.13, CCSL 143–143B (Turnhout: Brepols, 1985).

61. *Mor.* 32.15.27.

62. Gregory, *Homiliae in evangelis* 2.34.9, PL 76.1251B.

see, this confusion was accepted and transmitted within the tradition without any clear resolution.

Gregory's final contribution to thought about Antichrist's literal arrival comes in his suggestion that the coming of Antichrist will be (is already?) heralded by the declining efficacy of the Church's charisms of prophecy and healing.

> For prophesy vanishes, the grace of healing is taken away, the power of prolonged abstinence weakens, the words of teaching fall silent, the portents of miracles are gone. Not that the rich heavenly dispensation is taken away, but rather God does not display these things as openly and abundantly as in earlier times.[63]

This dearth of wonderful works within the Church will make Antichrist's works seem all the more wonderful, and the Church will be more prone to go astray.

But even this last point concerning Antichrist's literal arrival leads Gregory to reflect on the presence of Antichrist within the Church, about which he is far more concerned. For he immediately moves on to discuss the body of Antichrist, Leviathan, whose power waxes just as that of Body of Christ seems to wane. The body of Leviathan is made up of all the reprobate, who "do not rise up through their desire to the understanding of their spiritual home."[64] They join themselves to this body by their immoral actions and thus submit to the authority of their head, Antichrist. The body of Antichrist, then, is of one mind, and lives in the concord of its evil desires. As such, it is the perverse replica of the Body of Christ (1 Cor

---

63. "Nam prophetia absconditur; curationum gratia aufertur; prolixioris abstinentiae virtus imminuitur; doctrinae verba conticescunt; miraculorum prodigia tolluntur. Quae quidem nequaquam superna dispensatio funditus subtrahit, sed non haec sicut prioribus temporibus aperte ac multipliciter ostendit." Mor. 34.3.7. The use of the present indicative suggests that Gregory sees these things happening in his time. However, the plethora of miraculous events recounted in the Dialogues may qualify this conclusion. But systematic consistency is not Gregory's strength, and there is no reason to deny that he might have believed both.

64. "qui ad intellectum spiritalis patriae per desiderium non assurgunt." Mor. 34.4.8.

12).[65] While Gregory draws the inspiration for these parallels from Tyconius,[66] he spells them out in greater detail and gives them an explicitly moral meaning, which Tyconius did not.

Like Tyconius, Gregory believes that the body of Antichrist extends through salvation history. He laments,

O how many have not seen the times of that [last] temptation and yet are turned around in the tumult of his temptation! Cain did not see the time of Antichrist, but through his deed he was a member of Antichrist. Judas did not know the suffering of that persecution, but, persuaded by avarice, he succumbed to the law of Antichrist's barbarity. Simon lived far from the time of Antichrist, and yet he joined himself to Antichrist's pride in his perverse desire for the power of miracles. So the sinful body is joined to its head, and the parts are joined to the limb. Even if they do not know that they are, they are joined to him by their vile work.[67]

Antichrist was present from the time of Cain to the present. He is not simply a character in the eschatological theater, he is present wherever evil is present, and all such evildoers are bound to him in mind. So intimate are they to him that Gregory calls them his "testicles" (*testes Behemoth*, cf. Jb 40:12).[68] And so subtle are the lures he uses to draw his members in that "it is necessary that each of us return to the mystery of his own heart and fear the penalty for his action, lest, when merits are demanded, he falls among the number of such people by the strict justice of God's judgments."[69] By our actions we ally ourselves with one body or the other.

<hr/>

65. *Mor.* 33.27.48.

66. Whether direct or indirect, the inspiration is clear.

67. "*O quanti illius temptationes tempora non viderunt, et tamen in eius temptationis procella versantur. Cain tempus antichristi non vidit, et tamen membrum antichristi per meritum fuit. Iudas saevitiam persecutionis illius ignoravit, et tamen iuri crudelitatis eius, avaritia suadente, succubuit. Simon divisus longe ab antichristi temporibus exstitit, et tamen eius se superbiae, miraculorum potentiam perverse appetendo, coniunxit. Sic iniquum corpus suo capiti, sic membris membra iunguntur, cum et cognitione se nesciunt et tamen prava sibi actione copulantur.*" *Mor.* 29.7.15.

68. *Mor.* 32.16.28.

69. "*Sed inter haec necesse est ut unusquisque nostrum ad cordis sui secretum redeat,*

Gregory's meditations on the body of Antichrist recapitulate and emphasize the moral dimensions of Antichrist found in Augustine and Jerome. In addition, he animates the Augustinian and Tyconian tradition with the vivid imagery that so fills his work. Indeed, Gregory's solemn warning for each to examine his own heart is taken almost directly from Augustine's admonition in a homily on 1 John: "everyone must question his own conscience whether he be such."[70] But Gregory links this observation to a discussion of the "testicles of Behemoth." His vision of Antichrist is both conceptual and symbolic.[71]

Gregory's vision emphasizes the historic opposition between these two bodies, each bound by the taut sinews of harmony, one for sin, and one for glory. Salvation history is opposed by a parallel "perdition history" of those united in the harmony of mind to Antichrist. This is an observation that draws upon Augustine's grand historical vision of the "two cities," but there is an important difference. For Augustine, the city of God is on pilgrimage in the earthly city, making use of its politics and life, but not claiming them as its own. At least for the present, the city of God is within the earthly city. Antichrist, on the other hand, is within the Church, as Augustine's *Homilies on First John* amply demonstrate. Gregory combines Augustine's meditations on the "Antichrist within" and breadth of his vision of the "two cities." For Gregory, the historic body of Antichrist is within the Body of Christ. "Perdition history" is played out *within* salvation history, within the Body of Christ. This "playing out

---

et actionis suae damna pertimescat; ne exigentibus meritis, per districtam iustitiam iudiciorum Dei in talium hominum numerum currat." Mor. 29.7.14.

70. Augustine, "Homiliae in epistola 1 Johannis" 3.4 (PL 34.1999). The translation is from John Burnaby, *Augustine: Later Works* (Philadelphia: Westminster Press, 1955), 280.

71. For discussion of Gregory's symbolic thought, see Sandra Zimdars-Swartz, "A Confluence of Imagery: Exegesis and Christology according to Gregory the Great," in *Grégoire le Grand*, ed. Jacques Fontaine, Robert Gillet, and Stan Pellistrandi (Paris: Éditions du Centre National de la Recherche Scientifique, 1986), 327–36.

continues to occur, such that "Antichrist's work is done daily among the wicked."[72] While Gregory's themes each can be traced back to Augustine and/or Tyconius, his combination of these ideas make his vision of the immanent presence of the body of Antichrist, united in sin throughout the history of creation, distinctive and influential in the medieval tradition of thought on Antichrist. Thus, while the exegetical tradition around 2 Thessalonians appears to omit Gregory, his silent presence can be discerned in the work of later medieval exegetes who, like Gregory, would compose variations on the Fathers by synthesizing and harmonizing their thought.

In the capable hands of these three mighty thinkers, a distinctively Latin spiritual interpretation of 2 Thessalonians took root and flourished in the early medieval West. Perhaps one could say that seldom has such influence been exerted by so few words. None of the three composed a commentary on 2 Thessalonians, and only Augustine devoted explicit, thematic attention to the letter in any form that survives to us today. Yet this interpretation became the great counterpoint to the apocalyptic realism that survived under the mantels of Jerome and Ambrose.

I have argued that this spiritual interpretation is both particularly "Pauline" and uniquely Latin in its emphasis on the Church-as-Body, and thus by deduction, the antichurch-as-body. Born in the sectarian thought of Tyconius, it is progressively "catholicized" in the meditations of Augustine and Gregory on the nature of the Church in the world. For Tyconius, Antichrist's body will pose as the Church until the time when the elect "depart" from them as Lot left Sodom. Augustine asserts that the wicked pose as a church and thus will depart from the Church in an act of apostasy under the chief apostate, Antichrist. Gregory extends this presence of Antichrist's body into the distant past, fusing Augustine's thoughts on Antichrist with his salvation-historical vision. For Gregory, the Church is within the world, or, perhaps, the world is within the Church. Antichrist works within her daily to oppose her work of salvation.

72. "Apud iniquos namque quotidie res Antichristi agitur." Mor. 29.7.17.

In each stage of thought, the relationship between the Church and the world becomes more blurred, and thus the presence of Antichrist becomes even more immanent, internal to the life of the Church. It is in this sense that Hervé Savon is right to say that, in Gregory's thought, Antichrist

. . . begins a new career in an age where the Roman church is powerful in spite of the evil of the times, of the Lombard threat and of the conflict with Byzantium. In these times, the personage of Antichrist serves less to render intelligible the conflict of civil society and the church than to dramatize the tensions which the latter experiences.[73]

Thus, the last of the Fathers in the Latin West becomes the first medieval thinker about Antichrist and the first medieval exegete. For within Gregory's life, the Church has gained hegemony over public life and discourse. Within Gregory's exegesis, we can find both the broad expository style of the Fathers and the medieval synthetic approach to patristic thought. It is Gregory, then, who provides the moment of transition for this study. His *Moralia* develop Tyconian and Augustinian concepts in a distinctive way, and thus place him among the Fathers. Yet, his reflections on Antichrist contain elements both of apocalyptic realism and of the Latin spiritual interpretation. Early medieval exegetes echoed and adapted his penchant for including seemingly opposed interpretations. Like Gregory, the Carolingian commentators marshaled their tremendous command of patristic thought around the biblical texts in such a way that their commentaries were as much upon the Fathers as upon the biblical texts. It is to this early medieval exegesis that we now turn.

73. Hervé Savon, "Le Antéchrist chez les oeuvres de Grégoire le Grand," in *Grégoire le Grand,* ed. Jacques Fontaine, Robert Gillet, and Stan Pellistrandi (Paris: Éditions du Centre National de la Recherche Scientifique, 1986), 400.

CHAPTER 4

ANTICHRIST AND HIS
BODY, 500–1000

A late-seventh-century crypt in Poitiers bears a dire inscription that portends the End: "Alpha and Omega. The Beginning and the End. Every day, everything becomes worse and worse, for the end is drawing near."[1] The motif is not new or even uniquely Christian—the notion that the world's decline is a portent of a calamitous collapse is found at least as early as Sallust. But in the centuries after the death of Gregory the Great, as Germanic and later Viking invasions terrorize the Continent and the British Isles, as the Muslim conquest of Spain threatens to overflow into Europe, signs of disaster abound for apocalyptically minded Christians. One might expect to find early medieval scholars reading the "signs of the times," awaiting an imminent day of the Lord, echoing the dire sense of an ending preserved in the tomb inscription at Poitiers.

And yet the truth is more complex. If the early medieval Christian had a dire sense of history, he also revered tradition and its authority. Early medieval exegetes revered the authority of Augustine, and few if any dared to challenge him directly. So great was Augustine's authority that the great doctrinal debates of the early Middle

1. From the Crypt of Abbot Mellebaudis, in *Nouveau Recueil des inscriptions chrétiennes de la Gaule,* ed. E. LeBlant, Collections de documents inédits sur l'histoire de France, no. 248 (Paris, 1892), 260. The translation is mine.

Ages—for example, the debate over predestination—were never un-derstood to be for or against Augustine, but rather over whose inter-pretation of Augustine was correct.[2] Augustine's critique of immi-nent apocalypticism and his immanent ecclesial interpretation of apocalyptic Scripture were taken to heart in the Middle Ages; no scholarly discussion of biblical apocalyptic in the years before 1000 ever proceeded without at least some Augustinian proviso.

One might suspect that this paradoxical juxtaposition of apoca-lyptic anxiety and authoritative Augustinianism could leave me-dieval Christianity in a state of cognitive dissonance.[3] Or one could construe the juxtaposition of the two points of view as a social bi-furcation of lay versus clerical, oral versus literary, or popular versus elite.[4] Indeed, such divisions may be discernible; at first glance it seems plausible that Augustinianism was the preserve of a literate high culture, while a desire to discover the "signs of the times" was a much deeper and more widespread social phenomenon. But a closer view yields more detail. Even within the high-cultural activity of biblical commentary, one finds evidence that the Augustinian cri-tique did not eliminate apocalyptic realism. In fact, what we see in early medieval commentaries on 2 Thessalonians is a synthesis of apocalyptic realism and its Augustinian alternative. Perhaps because Augustine had left the door open in allowing the basic frame of the apocalyptic scenario as the literal, historical sense of 2 Thessaloni-ans, early medieval scholars could assert and develop both positions, and even harmonize them.

2. See, e.g., the predestination debate between Gottschalk of Orbais, Hinc-mar of Rheims, Florus of Lyons, Rabanus Maurus, et al., as discussed in Jaroslav Pelikan, *The Christian Tradition,* vol. 3: *The Growth of Medieval Theology* (Chicago: University of Chicago Press, 1978), 80–95.

3. Festinger's theory of cognitive dissonance postulates that individuals, when presented with evidence contrary to their worldview or situations in which they must behave contrary to their worldview, experience "cognitive dissonance." Dissonance is defined here as an "unpleasant state of tension." L. Festinger, *A The-ory of Cognitive Dissonance* (Stanford: Stanford University Press, 1957).

4. The classic case is Norman Cohn, *Pursuit of the Millennium,* rev. and exp. ed.

Pseudo-Primasius: Pelagius Corrected

From 500 to 750, the Latin West produced only thirty-five known biblical commentaries. Of these, fourteen came from the desk of one man, the Venerable Bede.[5] The other commentaries are by no means insignificant—among them are the works of Primasius, Isidore, Beatus of Liébana, and Ambrose Autpertus. But none of these are significant works on the Pauline corpus. Commentaries on Paul disappear from the continent until the Carolingian revival of the ninth century.

The apparent exception is a Pauline commentary that has been associated with Primasius of Hadramentum (d. 565).[6] The text is mostly that of Pelagius, with additions representing the Latin spiritual tradition of Augustine and Tyconius. In fact, it bears the only known explicit reference to Tyconius's *Rules* in the 2 Thessalonians tradition. Alexander Souter, in his quest to unearth Pelagius's original text, identified the Pseudo-Primasius commentary as a work of Cassiodorus and his school. Cassiodorus himself wrote a brief *complexio*, or summary, of the Pauline epistles that affirmed in a brief

---

(New York: Oxford University Press, 1980), the first edition of which posited that medieval apocalypticism as such was the language of "revolutionary millenarians and mystical anarchists." The Augustinian response is therefore, as such, the discourse of the status quo. More recent, and more thoroughly and subtly argued, is Richard Landes's apocalyptic hermeneutic of "roosters and owls," i.e. apocalyptic enthusiasts and cautious Augustinians. Landes argues for a "conspiracy of silence" on the part of Augustinian owls to erase popular waves of imminent apocalyptic speculation. See Landes, "Lest the Millennium Be Fulfilled," 203; "*Millenarismus Absconditus*"; "On Owls, Roosters, and Apocalyptic Time: A Historical Method for Reading a Refractory Documentation," *Union Seminary Quarterly Review* 49 (1996): 165–85; "Fear of an Apocalyptic Year 1000"; *Relics, Apocalypse, and the Deceits of History: Ademar of Chabannes, 989–1034* (Cambridge, Mass.: Harvard University Press, 1995), 91–101, 289–93.

5. John J. Contreni, "Carolingian Biblical Culture," in *Iohannes Scottus Eriugena: The Bible and Hermeneutics,* eds. Gerd Van Riel, Carlos Steel, James McEvoy (Leuven: Leuven University Press, 1996), 3.

6. It is published in *PL* 67.645D–650D, as a work of Primasius.

paragraph that Antichrist was the "Man of Sin" (2:4) and the Roman Empire was "that which restrains." So apparently he was untroubled by the apocalyptic realist reading. But he had also recommended the reading of Tyconius's *Rules* for the interpretation of the Bible. Already one sees evidence of a twofold interpretation.

Cassiodorus revised the Pelagian commentary on Paul because, although he knew the author as "Gelasius," he detected in it the "poison" of Pelagianism and undertook to root it out.[7] This suggests that the central issues he wished to address would concern grace and free will, and thus would be most prominent in Romans and Galatians and bear little consequence for 2 Thessalonians. Perhaps this is why his personal revisions proceeded only partially though Romans and the corrections to the rest of the Pauline commentary were completed by his students at the Vivarium. However, the revisions to the 2 Thessalonians commentary still bear some elements worth noting.

The Vivarium revisions to 2 Thessalonians yield a text that, taken as a whole, makes it the first commentary to contain apocalyptic realist and Tyconian ecclesial readings without dialectical distinctions. The corrections to 2 Thessalonians show a concern to qualify, but not to overturn, Pelagius's unalloyed apocalyptic realism. Indeed, if Cassiodorus himself had a realist perspective on the end, as his *complexio* suggests, then it is fitting that his students would follow him in this while including the Tyconian reading as well. The Vivarium Pseudo-Primasius text does not develop either tradition of interpretation in any significant way, and it does not appear to have much influence on the subsequent tradition. Neither does it synthesize or harmonize its Tyconian additions with Pelagius's realism. Nevertheless, it bears witness at least to the possibility of the coexistence, albeit a bit muddled, of apocalyptic realism and Tyconian ecclesial exegesis in the earliest Middle Ages.

---

7. Cassiodorus, *De institutione* 1.8.1.

2 Thessalonians 1

The first chapter of the Pseudo-Primasius commentary keeps most of Pelagius's central points, but removes the more polemical comments. For example, the text keeps Pelagius's clarification of 2 Thessalonians 1.5—that the Thessalonians' "example of the just judgment" is best understood as their exemplary *waiting for* the just judgment of God. But it removes Pelagius's explanation that those who suffer willingly are "worthy of the kingdom of God," excising the discussion of will or merit. Likewise, the text maintains Pelagius's affirmation of the real flames of punishment (1.8), but omits his critique of an allegorical or mental understanding of punishment (see Chapter 2 in this volume). The commentary on chapter 1 is thus leaner and less argumentative than the Pelagian original.

2 Thessalonians 2: "What is called God" is the Church

The revised commentary to chapter 2 follows Pelagius in cross-referencing the synoptic "little apocalypses" and speaking of the "work of the devil" in those who falsely profess the faith. When it comes to discuss the *discessio* of 2:3, however, the Vivarium text inserts first a moral possibility: the "falling away" might refer to a desertion of the truth, as well as Pelagius's possibilities (desertion of a ruler or the political dissolution of the empire). Then the Vivarium editor inserts another possibility—the *discessio* might refer to the devil himself, the archetypal figure of "falling away from God." This conclusion seems to draw upon the Augustinian/Tyconian reading of the text, derived, as we have seen, from the translation of *apostasia* as "*refuga*" in the Vetus Latina **D** text. However, the Vivarium insertion is silent about textual variants and seems to include this reading based only upon the authority of Tyconius and Augustine.

The Vivarium text leaves untouched Pelagius's speculation about Antichrist's rebuilding of the temple and reinstitution of the temple cult in reference to 2:4, but it follows this with what seems to be series of Tyconian or pseudo-Tyconian readings of the same verse:

What is called "God" is the church; *what is worshipped* is the most high God. *That he may sit in the temple of God, displaying himself as if he were God,* that is, as if he himself were the church, just as if he were to say "seating himself as the temple of God, displaying himself as if he were the temple of God," or "seating himself as God, displaying himself as if he were God." This according to the *Rules* of Tyconius.[8]

Taking the *Rules* of Tyconius as translations to be read right from the page, the Vivarium editor applies the first and second rules of Tyconius to the text. The first rule explains how Antichrist might exalt himself above "God"; the second allows for a social or corporate Antichrist as an "anti-church." But no more information is given as to why this social reading of Antichrist might be preferable; it is included only as a supplement to Pelagius's realism.

This Tyconian insertion is the only substantive addition to the commentary on the apocalyptic matters in 2 Thessalonians 2, and 2 Thessalonians 3 remains relatively untouched. Pelagius's commentary on 2 Thessalonians seems to lack the controversial claims about grace and free will that led Cassiodorus to take up the task of correction. And yet, given that the commentary remains rather untouched, it is curious that the only substantive addition is one that serves to relativize the apocalyptic realism of the original. While not removing Pelagius's speculations about the career of Antichrist, the Vivarium editor(s?) complements these with a rather hastily spun Tyconian reading. This may be evidence of a certain reticence on behalf of the editors, but one cannot read this too strongly into the text. Cassiodorus himself has already suggested that the *"restrainer"* of 2 Thessalonians 2:7 referred to the Roman Empire. At the very least, the presence of Tyconius in the Pseudo-Primasius text from the Vivarium shows that the two readings, the realist and the Augus-

---

8. *"Quod dicitur Deus, Ecclesia est: quod autem colitur, Deus summus est. Ut in templo sedeat, ostendens se quod ipse sit Deus, id est quod ipse sit Ecclesia: quale est, si diceret, in templum Dei sedeat, ostendens se quod ipse sit Dei templum; aut in Deum sedeat, ostendens quod ipse sit Deus. Istud de Ticonii Regulis."* Ps.-Primasius, *Ad thessalonicenses epistola secunda,* PL 30.648CD.

tinian, might coexist within the same commentary. An attempt to reconcile or synthesize these two commentary traditions would come only in ninth century.

Antichrist and His Body: The New Synthesis in Carolingian Biblical Scholarship

With the revival of learning under Charlemagne and his erudite advisor Alcuin, continental scholars took an active interest in Pauline commentary. But the works the Carolingians would produce were more than patristic revivals; they were commentaries in a different key. Carolingian commentaries on Paul form almost a distinct genre from that of their fabled Fathers. Like patristic Pauline exegesis, the Carolingian exegetical form developed from the grammatical scriptural glosses that preceded it. But the grammatical texts inherited by the Carolingians were no longer the classical exemplars used by the Fathers; rather, they bore a distinctively Irish signature.

Perhaps due to its geographical isolation, perhaps due to its somewhat unique intellectual and spiritual heritage, early medieval Irish Christianity possessed a wealth of knowledge from Christian antiquity undisturbed by accusations of heresy or error. Irish Christian scholars freely and openly quoted from the Pauline commentaries of Pelagius and Theodore of Mopsuestia without disclaimer or apology, and their works were filled with allusions to the sometimes suspect biblical apocrypha. When Irish Christians followed Columbanus to the continent in the sixth, seventh, eighth and ninth centuries, they brought with them a variety of sources that seem to have disappeared from the libraries of the orthodox "continentals."

The legacy of these Irish imports in the history of Latin biblical scholarship has just begun to be uncovered in the recent work of Michael Gorman, Carol Ann Scheppard, Jean-Michel Picard, and others.[9] Irish scholars were unique not only in the breadth of

9. The crucial (and controversial) article from which all such work departs is Bischoff's "Wendepunkte in der Geschichte der lateinischen Exegese im

sources upon which they drew but also in their penchant for detail. Their scholarship, says John Contreni, is "suffused with a concern for detail: number, places, persons, events, customs, lists, languages, and first times someone or something is mentioned."[10] Their familiarity with the biblical apocrypha enabled them to fill their commentaries with interesting "new" facts and details. This abundance of information was organized around a "schematic, almost scholastic, question-and-answer format."[11] As John Contreni has shown, this Hiberno-Latin tradition of scholarship was eagerly taken up by the "founders" of the Carolingian Renaissance, contributing an important ingredient to their exegesis.

But there is a more significant divide between patristic and Carolingian exegesis. A new sense of history and tradition possessed by Alcuin and his heirs lies beneath the surface of their commentaries. More than any other generation before them, Carolingian theologians confessed self-consciously their distance from the ages of the apostles and the Fathers and took it as their intellectual charge to preserve the ancient tradition of faith. As John Cavadini has argued,

---

Frühmittelalter," *Sacris Erudiri* 6 (1954): 119–89. For recent scholarship on the subject, see Michael Gorman, "A Critique of Bischoff's Theory of Irish Exegesis: The Commentary on Genesis in München Clm 6302 (Wendespunkte 2)," *Jounal of Medieval Latin* 7 (1997): 178–233; Carol Ann Scheppard, *Eclogae Tractatorum in Psalterium (Wendepunkte 6B) Corpus Christianorum Scriptores Celtigenae* (Turnhout: Brepols, forthcoming); Jean-Michel Picard, "L'exegese irlandaise de Epitres de saint Paul: Les gloses latines et gaeliques de Wurzburg," paper delivered at the conference *L'étude de la Bible d'Isidore à Rémi d'Auxerre (600–900)*, Paris, 5–6 June 1998. For an overview of the issue of Irish exegesis, see also Franz Brunhölzl, *Geschichte der lateinischen Literatur des Mittelalters*, vol. 1 (München: Wilhelm Fink Verlag, 1975), 193–97; Clare Stancliffe, "Early 'Irish' Biblical Exegesis," *Studia Patristica* 12 (1975): 361–70; Martin McNamara, ed., *Biblical Studies: The Medieval Irish Contribution*, Proceedings of the Irish Biblical Association 1 (Dublin: Dominican Publications, 1976).

10. John J. Contreni, "Carolingian Biblical Studies," in *Carolingian Essays*, ed. Ute-Renate Blumenthal (Washington, D.C.: Catholic University Press, 1983), 95.

11. Contreni, "Carolingian Biblical Studies," 95.

For Alcuin, tradition was important because it guaranteed that contemporaries would have the same access to Jesus as did those who actually lived in Jesus' time. Alcuin remarks that it is only by walking through the estates of the fathers that we will now arrive at the banks of the River Jordan.[12]

For Alcuin, the works of the Fathers had become *the* authoritative interpretation of the Scriptures. In essence, the Fathers' works took shape in the early Middle Ages as a new canon, an interpretation of the inspired books that was itself canonical.

In the steady stream of councils and conflicts over doctrine since the close of the apostolic age, the canon of patristic thought had slowly constellated around the four great Fathers, Augustine, Jerome, Gregory, and Ambrose, the four "evangelists" of this subcanon. As the New Testament's four evangelists were considered the reliable access to Jesus, so too were the four Fathers deemed to reliable interpreters of the New Testament. Other great thinkers were whittled away from the core of orthodox faith: Origen's thought, although still influential, had only indirect influence and was significantly qualified. Theodore of Mopsuestia and Pelagius survived on the continent only in anonymity. In a sense, these works became the "apocrypha" to the new canon of the Fathers. Other thinkers such as Bede and Isidore were respected precisely because they were faithful to the four. The Fathers provided a safe and reliable path to the truths of Scripture; other, more innovative paths were fraught with risk of error and missteps.

The Carolingian task,[13] then, was to open the gate to the Fa-

12. Cavadini, *Last Christology of the West*, 103. See also Willemien Otten, "The Texture of Tradition: The Role of the Church Fathers in Carolingian Theology," in *The Church Fathers in the Latin West*, 2 vols., ed. Irena Backus (Leiden: Brill, 1997), 3–50.

13. I concede that, for the sake of argument, I have made a generalization about "Carolingian scholarship." Certainly, some Carolingian scholars fit this description far better than others. In his recent essay on Carolingian biblical culture, John J. Contreni has pointed to the generational divisions between early Carolingians such as Alcuin, middle Carolingians such as Rabanus, and later Carolingians

thers' path. Their expressed desire was only to present the Fathers' work. One might wonder, then, why the Carolingian scholars did not simply preserve these works as individual wholes, say, in "critical" editions. But, as Jonathan Z. Smith has argued, one of the basic characteristics of canons is their application to other aspects of life that they might not address directly.[14] This was the Carolingian scholar's work: to arrange the thought of the Fathers systematically, in such a way that their teachings on a particular text of Scripture or a particular point of doctrine were easily accessible. In Silvia Cantelli's felicitous turn of phrase, the Carolingians engaged in the "exegesis of exegesis."[15]

Thus Rabanus Maurus, one of Alcuin's great students, speaks in the preface to his *Ennarrationum in Epistolas Beati Pauli* of "extracting what is necessary" from the works of the Fathers, whose own works "are as rich in eloquence as they are broad in exposition." He annotates his excerpts with "one two or three letters on the page" so that, should the reader desire, he may search out the texts of the Fathers himself.[16] Rabanus tries to make his use of patristic sources as trans-

---

such as Haimo. While I concede the need for further distinction, I would argue that even the more innovative of Carolingian exegetes, such as Haimo of Auxerre, still consider their task to consist of organizing the thought of patristic authorities around the biblical text systematically, although their methods may differ considerably from their earlier peers. See Contreni, "Carolingian Biblical Culture," 7–10.

14. Jonathan Z. Smith, "Sacred Persistence," in *Imagining Religion: From Babylon to Jonestown* (Chicago: University of Chicago Press, 1982), 49–52.

15. Silvia Cantelli, *Angelomo e la scuola esegetica di Luxeuil*, 2 vols. (Spoleto: Centro italiano di studi sull'alto Medioevo, 1990), 61. Cited in Contreni, "Carolingian Biblical Culture," 9.

16. "*collectarium in Epistolas Pauli apostoli, prout potui, confeci. In quo quantum mihi licuit, et possibilitas sivit, adjuvantibus etiam consortibus lectionis nostrae, ex sanctorum Patrum dictis in unum collegi quod illi in diversis opusculis suis, prout opportunitas tractatus postulabat, posuere. Quorum scripta, quia iuxta copiosam facundiam eorum latam expositionem habuerunt, brevitati studens, excerpsi inde quae necessaria putavi: ut si cui hoc opus nostrum legere voluntas esset, diversorum doctorum sensus continuatim positos inveniret; cui autem displicuisset, ipse de purissimis fontibus catholicorum expositorum in suis locis, quaeque vellet, hauriret. . . . Illum autem qui lectione nostra uti elegit,*

parent as possible. He, for one, would probably endorse wholeheartedly the notion that he was more compiler than interpreter, more text-critic than theologian.

However, with due respect to the stated intentions of Rabanus and his contemporaries, it remains the case—indeed, it could not be otherwise—that their exegetical work reveals their thought as much as the Fathers'. Rabanus was not disingenuous in expressing his desire to pass on the Fathers without interference, but such hermeneutical transparency is impossible for a scholar to achieve. In the process of excerpting the sayings of the Fathers, the Carolingian scholar included some things and left others out. Like Rabanus, he used what he thought was "necessary" and left the rest. He used some sources for a particular passage and different sources for another. In short, he interpreted the Fathers through his editorial choices, and his particular interpretation reveals a definite theological inclination toward a text or a doctrine. The early Middle Ages, represented most systematically by the Carolingians, thus initiate a hermeneutical revolution in the history of biblical exegesis, since these exegetes construct their own interpretations out of the "building blocks" of previous authoritative interpretations. Their exegesis is an interpretation of interpretations of the text, forming a new and original stage in the history of Christian exegesis.

In the interpretation of 2 Thessalonians, of which four Carolingian works survive, we have four quite distinct readings of the text. Rabanus Maurus opts almost exclusively for the interpretations of his "Ambrose," whom we now recognize as Theodore of Mopsuestia, with a few tips of the hat to the other Fathers. Florus of Lyons and Sedulius Scotus recapitulate the thought of Augustine and "Jerome" (Pelagius), respectively, and thereby exclude other interpretive options. Finally, Haimo of Auxerre constructs perhaps the most creative synthesis of his age, using Ambrosiaster, Pelagius,

---

admoneo ut ubique conspexerit, auctorum nomina, quorum dicta ex libris excerpsi, forinsecus in pagina singulis litteris, aut binis, seu etiam ternis praenota." Rabanus Maurus, *Ennarrationum in Epistolas Beati Pauli, Praefatio,* PL 111.1275A–1276A.

Jerome, Gregory, and Augustine in a commentary that would set the standard of interpretation for generations to come. Each thinker used sources that he considered authoritative and had ready to hand; each gave an interpretation of these sources in their application to the text of 2 Thessalonians.

Rabanus Maurus: Antichrist as the Twofold Denial of Christ

Rabanus Maurus is one of the most influential Carolingian public figures and perhaps the most prolific Carolingian author. As a youth, he studied under Alcuin. As monk and abbot of the monastery at Fulda and, later, as Archbishop of Mainz, Rabanus somehow found time to produce commentaries on almost every book of the Bible and many other doctrinal and ecclesiastical essays while engaging in Gottschalk's predestination controversy and in the intrigue of shifting dynastic politics. Rabanus was one of the Carolingians' great polymaths.

Born in 780, Rabanus was sent as a boy to Tours to study under Alcuin. After a short stay, he returned home to continue his studies, only to come back to Tours for more advanced work ca. 801. He entered the monastery at Fulda, was ordained in 814, and was appointed master of the abbey school in 819. The 810s and 820s were a challenging time in the monastery, since the reforms of Benedict of Aniane were imposed upon Fulda in 817, and there was quite a great deal of discord among the brothers. In this contested environment, Rabanus was elected abbot in 822. As abbot of Fulda, he was thrust into the midst of the Carolingian dynastic crisis under Louis the Pious. Rabanus supported the elder Louis even when he was deposed in 833. When Louis finally died, Rabanus then threw in his lot with Lothar, the titular emperor. When Lothar's imperial efforts collapsed in the spring of 842, Rabanus retired as abbot and retreated to the nearby Petersberg Abbey, where much of his biblical exegesis, including the Pauline commentary, was completed. In time, he reconciled with Louis the German and was ordained Archbishop of

Mainz in 847. For the last nine years of his life, a great deal of his time was spent attempting to refute the "double predestination" arguments of Gottschalk of Orbais, with whom he had already clashed years before.[17] He died in 856.

It is difficult to determine the "apocalyptic climate" of Rabanus's world. Juan Gil has argued that the crowning of Charlemagne on Christmas Day 800 was fraught with apocalyptic significance.[18] By a version of the Annus Mundi accounting of the calendar, Charlemagne was crowned on the first day of the year 6000, an alignment that Gil finds too striking to be a coincidence. Perhaps implicitly invoking the pseudo-Methodian "last world emperor" myth, Leo III sacralizes the Carolingian empire, symbolically initiating the millennium of peace under this "last emperor's" benevolent rule. The coincidences are striking, and Rabanus was a young man in studies, in all likelihood aware of such significant events. But if these events had any notable effect upon Rabanus, it does not seem to come to bear on his apocalyptic exegesis.

Neither is there any evidence that the appearance of a mysterious prophetess, Thiota, who gathered a sizable following around her preaching of the end in Fulda in 847, provoked any particular response from Rabanus—at least not one that appears in his scholarly

17. In the late 820s, Gottschalk was a young monk at Fulda who had been oblated to the abbey as a child. When he became an adult, he protested that the vows made for him by his elder relatives were not valid. He asked that he be released from the monastery and that the property his family had donated to Fulda at the time of his oblation be returned to him. Rabanus refused to grant this to him, so Gottschalk appealed to the Archbishop of Mainz. The Archbishop released him from his ties to Fulda, but his property was not returned. In an effort to reverse the Archbishop's decision, Rabanus appealed to Louis the Pious and wrote his treatise De oblatione puerorum. Whatever action Louis took, Gottschalk did not return to Fulda. This personal "bad blood" certainly influenced the predestinarian controversy twenty years later. John McCullough, Introduction, in Rabanus Maurus, Martyrologium, Liber de Computo, ed. John McCullough and W. M. Stevens, CCCM 44 (Turnhout: Brepols, 1979), xvii.

18. Juan Gil, "Los terrores del año 800," in Actas del Simposio para el estudio de los codices del "Comentario al Apocalipsis" de Beato de Liebana (Madrid: Joyas Bibliográficas, 1978).

work.[19] Thiota appeared while Rabanus was nearby in Petersberg Abbey, just prior to his ordination as Archbishop of Mainz, so one can assume that he knew of these events. But, again, evidence of imminent apocalyptic concern—or its refutation—is scant in Rabanus's exegesis.[20]

Rabanus's commentary on the epistles of Paul comes from the middle years of his intellectual life. It represents the maturity of his thought, but it is free of the polemical arguments that filled his later years. We are fortunate to be able to gain some insight into Rabanus's hermeneutical principles, since, as we have noted above, Rabanus makes his intent clear in a dedicatory letter to his student Lupus of Ferrieres. He desires to draw what is necessary from the Fathers to understand the words of the Apostle. He acknowledges that the opinions of the Fathers may sometimes differ, but he says that he has made no effort to harmonize them; rather, he has included the names of his sources:

Thus I think it necessary that the waiting audience hear first the names of the individual authors before he hears what they have written, so that he knows what one particular author understood in the apostolic text, and so gathering many of these in his mind, he is able to select what is of use to him.[21]

The Fathers thus give several interpretations, all of which are true and authoritative, since "all of them are Catholic doctors, except Origen," whom Rabanus carefully edits to bring out the "Catholic sense" in his thought.[22]

19. On Thiota, see *Annales Fuldenses, ad an. 848*, MGH SS, 1:365.

20. One might argue that such mention is conspicuous by its absence. I remain unconvinced that this argument *ex silentio* is sufficient to posit significant apocalyptic pressure in the ninth century.

21. "*Unde necessarium reor ut intentus auditor per lectorem primum recitata singulorum auctorum nomina ante scripta sua audiat, quatenus sciat quid in lectione apostolica unusquisque senserit, sicque in mentem suam plurima coacervans, potest de singulis iudicare quid sibi utile sit inde sumere.*" PL 112.1276A.

22. "*doctores enim ipsi omnes catholici fuerunt, excepto Origene, eius tamen sententias tantummodo, quas catholico sensu prolata credidi, sumpsi.*" PL 112.1276B.

For Rabanus, the tensions and contradictions within the thought of the Fathers are no threat; their pluralism testifies to the riches of Scripture. And these riches are for the use of the reader.[23] Rabanus did not seek to further biblical scholarship per se; the focus of attention is upon the formation of the reader, not the strict accuracy of the text. Scripture's riches are not to be hoarded, but used.[24] Rabanus wishes to let this richness speak for itself:

> I have not proffered much of my own thought in this work (as I have done in my other little works) because I believe that it will suffice for one to discover what is disclosed in the thoughts of the Fathers.[25]

Above all, Rabanus seeks to produce a *florilegium* of the Fathers that will illuminate the Pauline epistles.

As I have said, Rabanus's commentary on 2 Thessalonians depends in its structure and much of its content on the Pseudo-Ambrose commentary of Theodore of Mopsuestia. It seems that the manuscript of "Ambrose's" Pauline commentary available to Rabanus at Fulda contained the work of Ambrosiaster up to and including Ephesians and then continued on with Theodore's work on Philippians and the rest.[26] Approximately 75 percent of Rabanus's text is taken verbatim from Theodore. Into this adopted text Rabanus injects passages from Augustine, Jerome, Gregory, and John Cassian.

23. Although Rabanus makes no explicit mention of it here, the similarities to Augustine's approach to Scripture in the *De doctrina christiana* is worth noting. Rabanus's own formula for Christian education, *De institutione clericorum,* composed in 819, relies heavily upon Augustine's work.

24. This is the central point of Contreni's essay, "Carolingian Biblical Studies."

25. *"Nec ex meo sensu in hoc opere plura protuli, sicut in aliis opusculis meis feci, credens sobrio lectori sufficere quod in Patrum sententiis editum repererit."* PL 112.1276B.

26. This manuscript, which has long since disappeared, makes Rabanus's work unique among his peers. Indeed, his commentary was more or less abandoned by the scholars of succeeding generations, probably due to the prevalence of the Ambrosiaster-type "Ambrose" manuscripts across the continent. That the work of so fastidious an exegete as Rabanus would depend so heavily upon such

There is no apparent theological reason for Rabanus's dependence on Theodore; he is quite willing to depart from the text when he sees fit, and, in the end, his commentary has quite a different flavor than Theodore's. Rather, it is likely that the "Ambrose" commentary had the advantage of being relatively thorough and concise in its treatment of the texts, an ideal structural template into which Rabanus can insert relevant comments from the others. Rabanus's editorial hand becomes visible only when he alters or departs from the Theodoran text and supplements it with other authorities, but such interventions are nonetheless significant and sufficient to reveal the scholar's theological tendencies in apocalyptic matters.

Rabanus's text begins with Theodore's *argumentum* and continues to quote him precisely through the commentary on 2 Thessalonians 1. Rabanus endorses Theodore's identification of three issues within the letter, where Paul praises the Thessalonians for their perseverance in persecution, cautions them in their belief in an imminent end, and admonishes certain members for their persistence in bad habits. He also supports Theodore's treatment of 2 Thessalonians 1, where the Thessalonians are "content to suffer" for Christ and will manifest Christ's glory in their suffering. Rabanus uses only Theodore to comment upon chapter 1, and he makes no editorial adjustments of the text.

When he comes to chapter 2, Rabanus clearly has more resources to bring to bear on the text. After quoting 2 Thessalonians 2:1–2, Rabanus cites a passage from Gregory the Great's *Pastoral Rule*. The excerpt praises Paul's manner of pastoral correction, since he admonishes them (in chapter 2: "*Rogamus autem vos*") only after praising them for their endurance.[27] Placed as it is in the commen-

---

an obscure manuscript tradition and so quickly disappear from the scene serves as a necessary reminder to the modern scholar of the scarcity of scholarly resources even in the "Renaissance" of the Carolingian era. Swete's examination of Rabanus's use of the text in the introduction to his critical edition of Theodore's commentary is still the authoritative source, especially pp. xxxiii–xlviii.

27. "*Egit enim verus doctor ut prius audirent laudati quod recognoscerent, et postmodum quod exhortati sequerentur: quatenus eorum mentem ne admonitio subiuncta*

tary, Gregory's excerpt summarizes the previous chapter and focuses the commentary upon the subject of chapter 2, the false doctrine of the imminent "day of the Lord." While in Theodore, each of the letter's three topics receive equal emphasis, Gregory, and perhaps then Rabanus, believes that this apocalyptic topic is Paul's central purpose for writing. Having thus qualified Theodore's approach, Rabanus resumes his direct quotation of the Antiochene's text.

Indeed, Rabanus even quotes the alternative Latin text from Theodore's commentary instead of the Vulgate that he himself helped to standardize[28] when the commentary comes to 2 Thessalonians 2:3: "*Quoniam si venerit apostasia primum.* " As Theodore argues, this "apostasy" names the time of Antichrist, when almost everyone will fall away from holy living. Interestingly, Rabanus continues to quote Theodore even when the latter draws parallels between the demon's work in Antichrist and the Incarnation of Christ.[29] As I have noted in Chapter 2, this comment alludes to Theodore's "homo assumptus" Christology, condemned by Justinian in the 530s. Apparently, this parallel "antichristology," shielded behind the orthodox name of Ambrose, is not direct enough an allusion to stir Rabanus's editorial hand.

Rabanus's hand does stir a few verses later, when he comes to Theodore's interpretation of "what restrains" in verse 6. Theodore gives a paragraph of comment on the possibility that "what re-

---

concuteret, laus praemissa solidaret, et qui commotos eos vicini finis suspicione cognoverat, non jam redargueabat motos, sed quasi transacta nesciens, adhuc commoveri prohibeat." Rabanus, *Expostio in epistolam secundam ad thessalonicenses.* PL 113.569C–D. From Gregory, *Regula pastoralis* 3.8.39, ed. Bruno Junic (Paris: Editions du Cerf, 1992).

28. On Rabanus's contribution to the standardization of the Vulgate, see Margaret T. Gibson, *The Bible in the Latin West* (Notre Dame: University of Notre Dame Press, 1993), 6. Swete notes that Rabanus sometimes cites the biblical text from translation of Theodore and sometimes prefers the Vulgate, with no apparent rule for distinguishing between them. Swete, xxxiv.

29. "*hominem equidem eum nominavit justa ratione, eo quod homo erit daemone in eo omnia inoperante, sicuti et in illum hominem qui pro nostra salute sumptus est Deus verbo perfecisse videtur.*" Rabanus, PL 113.570C.

strains" is the Holy Spirit, whose miraculous works will decline and almost entirely disappear as the time of Antichrist approaches. Theodore rejects this opinion, since he believes that the miraculous works of the Spirit have long since ceased and Antichrist has not yet appeared. Theodore admits that the Holy Spirit will not totally fail, since a few of the saints will be preserved to resist the enemy. Nevertheless, he believes clearly that, save this preserving power, the works of the Spirit have declined. Rabanus excises this entire discussion.[30]

The reason for Rabanus's excision is unclear; Jacobi and Swete believe that his Germanic Christian culture was still in the thrall of the miraculous, and thus Theodore's argument was distasteful for cultural reasons. This may be true. But a more suggestive possibility (though it can be no more than this) arises if the famous Pentecost hymn, *Veni Creator Spiritus,* can be said to reflect at least the spiritual theology of Rabanus's environment at Fulda, or at most that of the man himself.[31] This hymn demonstrates a well-developed spirituality of the Holy Spirit. The fourth quatrain lauds the Spirit's "perpetual power" by which he "firms up the infirmities of our bodies."[32] If, indeed, the abbey of Fulda possesses such an active notion of the Holy Spirit's continuing work in the Body of Christ, the abbot of

30. While I must concede the *possibility* that Rabanus's source manuscript may lack this portion of the text, which would excuse Rabanus from responsibility for the omission, I find it unlikely, since his text is otherwise more or less reliable. Swete and Jacobi agree; cf. Swete, 53n4.

31. As Brunhölzl notes, the attribution of authorship to texts intended for liturgical use is sticky business. See Brunhölzl, 339–40. But there does seem to be evidence that the *Veni Creator Spiritus* was in use at Fulda in the second half of the ninth century. Even if it did not originate with Rabanus, it is likely that he knew it and that it reflects the spirituality of the Fulda monastery. See also Luke Wenger, "Hrabanus Maurus, Fulda, and Carolingian Spirituality" (Ph.D. dissertation, Harvard University, 1973).

32. *"Accende lumen sensibus / Infunde amorem cordibus / Infirma nostri corporis / Virtute firmans perpeti."* *Hymnus in Pentecosten (Veni Creator Spiritus),* attributed to Rabanus Maurus in Analecta Hymnica Medii Aevi 50, ed. Guido Maria Dreves, S.J. (Leipzig: Reisland, 1905).

Fulda might well resist both the opinion that the work of the Spirit will decline (which Theodore himself rejects) and Theodore's argument for its rejection. Whatever the reason, Rabanus recapitulates only Theodore's preferred exegesis of the passage, that "what restrains" is the decree of God's providence that Antichrist should not be revealed until the end of the age.

Since Theodore's commentary has introduced the theme of the consummation of the age, Rabanus decides to break off from his text to consult Jerome on literal meaning of the course of events of the end. He quotes nearly half of Jerome's treatment of 2 Thessalonians in Epistle 121. (See Chapter 2 in this volume.) He rehearses Jerome's discussion of the *discessio* as the rebellion from Rome and his preference for the allegorical-ecclesial interpretation of Antichrist's session in the temple. Rabanus repeats Jerome's assertion that Paul speaks obscurely for fear of persecution and his comparison of Antichrist's defeat by Christ to the contest between Moses and Pharaoh's magi. And there, Rabanus leaves Jerome's text.

It is worth noting what Rabanus does not include from Jerome's letter. First, Rabanus only includes what Jerome says specifically about 2 Thessalonians, cutting all references to 1 Thessalonians and the synoptic "little apocalypse." This omission makes sense on the basis of Rabanus's pledge to include "only what is necessary" to an understanding of this particular text from the Fathers. Jerome's comments on other Scriptures are better reserved for other commentaries. But second, and more suggestive, Rabanus cuts off his citation just prior to Jerome's notorious diatribe against the Jews. (See Chapter 2 in this volume.) For Jerome, the discussion of Antichrist's "lying works" leads quite naturally into a discussion of the purpose of these deceptions, that is, the just condemnation of the Jews. But Rabanus does not follow Jerome's line of argument this far. It is difficult to draw solid conclusions about this editorial intervention. In his other works, Rabanus shows no reticence in claiming that Antichrist will gather the Jewish people around him, deny the divinity of Christ, and claim to be the Messiah, so it is unlikely that this excision is a concession to Judaism's legacy.[33] Perhaps, rather, it grows out of Rabanus's disinterest in Antichrist's miraculous deceptions. For Rabanus, Antichrist's "lying works" are primarily doctrinal and theological—denying Christ—and he often comments on this verse in the Tyconian or Gregorian sense: "But one who denies that Christ is God is an Antichrist: he is opposed to Christ. All those who depart from the Church and are cut off from the unity of the faith are themselves antichrists."[34] This shift from the realist to the spiritual reading can be seen in what follows in the 2 Thessalonians commentary, where Rabanus abandons Jerome for Augustine.

Omitting Augustine's summary dismissal of the Nero myth, Rabanus quotes the portion of the text where Augustine discusses the connection between "what restrains" (v. 6) and the "mystery of iniquity" (v. 7). The mystery of iniquity is the number of "evil and false people" who are hidden in the Church. They restrain from appearing until they reach a critical number and make a "great people" for Antichrist. All this Rabanus culls right from Augustine's *City of God* 20.19,[35] and it leads him to enrich the spiritual interpretation with an excerpt taken from Gregory's *Moralia*.

The "evil and false people" of whom Augustine speaks are those to whom the apostle John refers when he says that there are "many antichrists now" (1 Jn 2:19). Gregory's excerpt connects these various antichrists to the "body of Antichrist," and gives the text a sharp moral edge:

33. Rabanus Maurus, *De universo* XV.vi: "*Christum enim se mentietur, dum venerit, et contra eum dimicabit, et adversabitur sacramentis Christi et veritati ejus. Nam et templum Jerosolymis reparare, et omnes veteris legis caeremonias restaurare tentabit.*" PL 111.428A. Note that Rabanus here appears to use Pelagius's 2 Thessalonians commentary or a derivative, none of which make an appearance in Rabanus's commentary.

34. "*Sed et ille Antichristus est, qui negat esse Deum Christum: contrarius enim est Christo. Omnes enim, qui exeunt de Ecclesia, et ab unitate fidei praeciduntur, et ipsi Antichristi sunt.*" Rabanus, *II Thess.*, PL 112.572B.

35. Augustine, CD XX.xix, CCSL 47, 32; Rabanus, *II Thess.*, PL 112.572B.

I may remain silent concerning the outwardly criminal people, for behold, someone envies his brother silently in his heart, and, if he had the
occasion, he would try to supplant the brother. Whose member is he, if
not the one of whom it is written "By the envy of the Devil, death entered the world" [Wis 2:24]. Another one thinks himself to be of great
worth, preferring himself, since his whole heart is swollen. He believes
that all are inferior to him. Whose member is he, if not of him of whom
it is written, "He sees every high place and is the king over all the sons of
pride." [Jb 41:25][36]

Rabanus includes this moral, corporal sense from Gregory as the
natural sequel to Augustine's quote. While he could have quoted
more from each of these venerable Fathers—and indeed he does in
several other works[37]—in this context, he seems to include just
enough to represent their spiritual, corporal exegesis.

Having now represented (he thinks) the opinions of each of the
four major Fathers, Rabanus returns to his template, Theodore. He
omits only one more passage from Theodore's commentary. When
addressing 2 Thessalonians 2:10, Antichrist's satanic work ". . . in
every seduction of injustice upon those who are perishing,"
Theodore attempts to clarify with a paraphrase: "that he may work
in everyone who is full of injustice and seduce those who are worthy
of destruction."[38] Rabanus omits this paraphrase. Although this
commentary predates Gottschalk's predestinarian controversy by a
decade, already one may glimpse which position Rabanus will en-

36. *"Ut enim de apertioribus criminibus taceam, ecce alius fratrum in corde suo taci-
tus invidet, et si occasionem reperiat, eum supplantare contendit, cuius alterius membrum
est, nisi de quo scriptum est, 'Invidia diaboli mors intravit in orbem terrarum'? Alius mag-
ni meriti esse se aestimans, per tumorem cordis cunctis se praeferens, omnes semetipso in-
feriores credit, cuius alterius membrum est, nisi eius de quo scriptum est, 'Omne sublime
videt et ipse est rex super universos filios superbiae'?"* Gregory, *Moralia* 29.7.15, CCSL
143B, 1444; Rabanus, PL 112.572C–573A.

37. E.g., Rabanus Maurus, *Allegoriam in universam sacra scripturam*, PL
112.851Cff.; *Expositio super Jeremiam prophetam* XV.xlvii, PL 111.1110D; *Expositio in
Mattheum libri octo* II.vii, CCCM 174.

38. *"ut omne quicquid iniustitia plenum est operetur, et seducat eos qui perditione
digni sunt."* Swete, 57.

dorse. His omission suggests that he resists any hint that one is predestined to destruction. He prefers Theodore's much safer discussion of those who do not remain steadfast in faith meriting their own destruction.

When the letter turns away from apocalyptic subjects and moves to the correction of the brethren, Rabanus introduces yet one more voice into the work. In reference to 2 Thessalonians 2:16–17, where Paul speaks of God's strengthening of the faithful with "eternal consolation and good hope," Rabanus cites John Cassian's *Institutes*. This quote adds little exegetical information, serving only to link the verse to another from Hebrews 13. But Rabanus again turns to Cassian for a very lengthy discussion of chapter 3's admonition to work. Indeed, while Theodore's commentary remains the skeleton of Rabanus's work, the excerpts from Cassian constitute two thirds of the body of his exegesis of chapter 3.[39] They speak very little of theological matters and not at all of apocalyptic themes. Instead, they refer to the very practical matters of obedience and fraternal correction. The change in subject matter and tone is so dramatic that the commentary on chapter 3 is almost a separate text. That Rabanus would include this very long discussion can only reflect his desire to cull whatever wisdom the Fathers offered on all Scripture, whether it departed from the sense of the rest of the letter or not. It also may suggest that Rabanus, guided by the Fathers, conceives of the Pauline epistles as useful for a variety of spiritual aims. In 2 Thessalonians, pedagogical concerns, not strictly doctrinal or exegetical aims, guide Rabanus's exegesis. His exegetical desire is to present the whole biblical text, illuminated by the Fathers' wisdom.

As a whole, then, Rabanus's commentary on 2 Thessalonians appears to be a great amalgam of patristic opinion, all organized around the template of Theodore's exegesis. His use of Theodore and his lengthy citation from Jerome indicates that he had no objections to a literal, apocalyptic-realist interpretation of the text. Yet, his strategic insertion of key summary quotes from Augustine and

39. John Cassian, *De coenobiorum Institutis* X, 8–16, PL 49.375–83.

Gregory suggests that he endorses their spiritual interpretation as well. He does not express a preference for one or the other, nor does he seem to see any need to choose. Antichrist is primarily the future individual embodiment of humanity's rejection of Christ, but he is also present in his members in the sins of the faithful.

What does not really emerge from Rabanus's commentary on 2 Thessalonians is an assessment of Antichrist's character as a historical figure. As we have noted, the tradition casts two primary "types" of Antichrist: the tyrant and the deceiver. Does Rabanus imagine Antichrist as the purveyor of dread or of deception? For this, one must turn to other references to Antichrist in Rabanus's works. In these one finds that the Adversary is above all "he who will persecute the Church."[40] In Rabanus's commentaries on Judges, Maccabbees, and other texts from the Old Testament, he sees precursors to Antichrist in Abimilech, Antiochus Epiphanes, and numerous other persecutors of Israel. "There is no doubt in fact that the things which have happened under Antiochus Epiphanes in image—that a most defiled king would persecute the people of God—prefigures the savagery of Antichrist, who will persecute the Christian people and who will despise the will of God."[41] This profile of Antichrist is certainly not absent from Rabanus's commentary on 2 Thessalonians, since the passages from Jerome seem to cover it rather well. But it is remarkably underdeveloped, given that Rabanus seems to know Pelagius's commentary and uses it elsewhere. It is perhaps due to Rabanus's encyclopedic and literal focus in the Paul commentary— indeed, references to types in the biblical record are scant. His aim, again, is not to show the unity of Scripture's witness to Antichrist, but to interpret this particular passage.

For Rabanus, then, the historical Antichrist—the eschatological

40. E.g., Rabanus Maurus, *Expositio in Mattheum libri octo* 1.2, CCCM 174.

41. *"Nulli dubium est quin haec quae sub Antiocho Epiphane in imagine praecesserunt, hoc est ut rex sceleratissimus persecutus sit populum Dei, saevitiam praefiguret Antichristi, qui Christianum populum persequetur, qui indignabitur contra testamentum Dei . . ."* *Commentaria in libros Machabaeorum* I, PL 109.1135A.

Adversary—is a rival king, a warrior, and a tyrant, while the immanent body of Antichrist is moral and theological—members are
marked by heresy and apostasy. It is as if for Rabanus, the threat of
human evil in the immediate future is not political or military, but
within. He believes that this moral collapse of "holy living" will culminate in the end, and this will signal the imminent arrival of the
Adversarial King. What is worth noting is the apparent discontinuity
between the body and the head, the future Adversary himself. The
"members" of Antichrist do not replicate his specific behavior "in
miniature"; the body of Antichrist does not work through civil discord or violent uprising. Rather, their "apostasy" is of a different
sort. The seeds of discord they sow in the Church are moral and theological. Antichrist himself will be a rival king. What unites the two
is the deep structure beneath the particular moral or tyrannical actions—the denial of Christ, which for Rabanus is the primary sense
of the name "Anti-Christ."[42]

If the apocalyptic phenomena of the ninth century came to bear
at all on his reflection, Rabanus seems to run neither hot with millenarian enthusiasm nor cold with a thoroughgoing spiritual reading. His concern for the moral state of the Church does carry with it
an apocalyptic sense: moral and heretical lapses are the work of the
body of Antichrist in the Church. But nowhere does Rabanus suggest that the end is imminent, that the tyrannical adversary is waiting in the wings. Rabanus's reading of Antichrist in 2 Thessalonians
exemplifies the sense of "psychological imminence" as we have described, where the sheer indeterminacy of the approaching end allows for interpretations that say both the Tyconian "already" and
the realist "not yet."[43]

42. *De universo* XV.vi: *"Christum enim se mentietur, dum venerit, et contra eum dimicabit, et adversabitur sacramentis Christi et veritati ejus. Nam et templum Jerosolymis
reparare, et omnes veteris legis caeremonias restaurare tentabit. Sed et ille Antichristus est,
qui negat esse Deum Christum: contrarius enim est Christo. Omnes enim, qui exeunt de
Ecclesia, et ab unitate fidei praeciduntur, et ipsi Antichristi sunt."* PL 111.428A.

43. An additional note on the commentary: Rabanus's careful excisions from
Theodore, Jerome, and Augustine suggest, perhaps tentatively, a few theological

Florus of Lyons: A "Summa" of Augustinian Antichristology

Florus of Lyons (d. ca. 860) was a deacon of the Lyons church who served under three successive bishops (Agobard, Amalarius, and Remigius). As deacon, Florus presided over the transformation of Lyons into a major center of theological education. With the support of Agobard, Archbishop of Lyons, Florus acquired a large number of texts from the monastic libraries around him, making the Lyons library perhaps the best of his time. Numerous manuscripts bear annotations in his hand delineating passages to be excerpted for use in commentaries.

Presiding over such a theological center, Florus contributed frequently to the doctrinal disputes of his day. His vitriolic attacks against Amalarius, a bishop with a very brief tenure in Lyons who attempted to reform the liturgical practices of the cathedral clergy, are well known. But Florus could also be a scholar with mediating tendencies, as his reserved support for Gottschalk of Orbais demonstrates. Yet, even from his moderate position in the debate, he issued a sharp rebuke of John Scotus Eriugena. By all accounts, Florus was a confident and aggressive theologian.

His exegetical work is the embodiment of the "Lyons school" of scholarship: careful, fastidious research and encyclopedic mastery of patristic sources. While only his *florilegium* of Augustine on the Pauline epistles has been preserved in Migne, research over the last sixty years has demonstrated that his interests were not so narrow. In fact, it seems that he produced or edited similar *florilegia* of Gregory and Jerome on the Pauline epistles.[44]

---

presuppositions and exegetical premises that guide his editorial choices. First, Rabanus believes that the Holy Spirit is "alive and well" in the Church, subject to no decline or cessation. Second, Rabanus seems to resist any suggestion that humans, whether Jews or Christians, are predestined to damnation by some divine mission of error. Finally, he is committed to offering whatever insight the Fathers may offer, whether doctrinal or practical.

44. See C. Charlier, "La compilation augustinienne de Florus sur l'Apôtre:

The commentaries are very brief, clearly intended to be an "index" to the Fathers. As particular verses in Scripture bring up theological topics, Florus cites texts from the Fathers that address this topic. Most of the time he cites patristic sources that address or refer to the text itself. But often he cites other textsthat broach the same topic without any explicit reference to the biblical verse in question. Unlike Rabanus, Florus has a thoroughly theological and topical approach to Scripture: the Bible is primarily the inspired source of theological doctrine.

Florus is selective in his choice of verses upon which to comment; not every verse is quoted; Florus cites only those that appear in the particular Father. For example, the Jerome collection on 2 Thessalonians contains only two citations. The first, concerning 2 Thessalonians 2:3ff., cites the several pages from Jerome's Epistle 121; the second, concerning 2 Thessalonians 3:3, comes from Jerome's *Dialogue against the Pelagians* (PL 23.70.7–20) concerning the power of God's grace to "confirm" the faithful. It is clear that Florus intended no thorough treatment of the linguistic and theological intricacies of the biblical text. This he left to the Fathers themselves.

The Augustine *florilegium* cites from a variety of the famous bishop's works. Florus treats 2 Thessalonians 1 as a series of theological questions about the freedom of the will and the future reward of the blessed. To this end, he cites two passages from Augustine's *De gratia et libero arbitrio,* one from the early *Contra Faustum,* and one from the *Retractationes.*[45] Florus's synopsis of 2 Thessaloni-

---

Source et authenticité," *Revue Bénédictine* 57 (1947): 132–86; A. Wilmart, "Sommaire de l'exposition de Florus su les épîtres," *Revue Bénédictine* 38 (1926): 205–16, and "L'exemplaire Lyonnais de l'exposition de Florus sur les épîtres et ses dernier feuillets," *Revue Bénédictine* 40 (1930): 73–76, for the Augustinian commentary. See Paul-Irénée Fransen, "Description de la Collection Hiéronymienne de Florus de Lyons sur l'Apôtre," *Revue Bénédictine* 94 (1984): 195–228, and "Description de la Collection Grégorienne de Florus de Lyons sur l'Apôtre," *Revue Bénédictine* 98 (1988): 278–317, for the discussion of the other two commentaries.

45. Augustine, *De gratia et libero arbitrio* X.i, PL 44.884ff.; *Retractationum* II.i, CSEL 36; *Contra Faustum* VIII.13, PL 40.446ff.

ans 2 includes both Augustine's dismissive comments about the text's obscurity in the letter to Hesychius and his more generous interpretation in *City of God*. It seems clear that his task is to index all the places in which Augustine refers to 2 Thessalonians or addresses similar topics, without any effort to distinguish between early and late works or any attention to apparent differences between the texts.

With Florus, then, the particular Carolingian desire to be transparent editors of the Fathers most nearly approaches its goal. But I question whether these works are properly called "commentaries." They more resemble outlines or indices, showing no particular regard or reverence for the biblical text itself. These are reference works, and they were valuable as such centuries later to scholars such as Peter Lombard. But this makes them more preludes to commentaries than commentaries themselves.

Sedulius Scotus: "Another Nero, of the Same Title"

We know little about the life and career of Sedulius Scotus. His name indicates his Irish roots. Indeed, some scholars attribute to him membership in an Irish circle of scholars that moved around the Carolingian Empire in the early to mid ninth century.[46] It seems that Sedulius arrived in Gaul ca. 848 and stayed there until 859, when he disappears from the historical record. Franz Brunhölzl has suggested that Sedulius was in Italy for the 860s, basing his guess upon evidence drawn from poems attributed to the Irish bard. But beyond this, his trail totally disappears, and we do not know when or where he died.

The literary prowess of Sedulius Scotus is formidable. In addition to his *Collectanea in Epistolas Pauli,* he is the author of a commentary on Matthew, several grammatical works, a political treatise, at least one play, and numerous poems. He studied and commented

46. Brunhölzl, vol. 1, 450.

upon the grammatical works of Priscian, Donatus, and Eutyches. A Greek psalter with interlinear Latin contains the Greek signature *"Sedulios scottos ego egrapsa,"* suggesting among other clues that Sedulius was at least somewhat literate in Greek. Scholars have long noted Sedulius's combination, perhaps rare in the ninth century, of a developed ecclesiastical piety, as demonstrated by his biblical work, and a humanist sense for wit, humor, and the beauty of the natural world.[47] The wandering Irishman is perhaps one of the most well-rounded individuals of the Carolingian age.

His commentary on the epistles of Paul demonstrates his familiarity with the tradition of Irish exegesis as it took root in and was absorbed by Carolingian scholarship. He begins the work with an original preface that addresses the "seven circumstances" of *persona, res, causa, tempus, locus, modus, materia* in the Irish manner. He follows with what amounts to a short "handbook" to interpret the Pauline corpus, not a great interpretive work. While his use of Pelagius has in the past been taken as a sign of the heretic-exile's rediscovery on the continent, more than likely it testifies to his Irish training, as we have noted above.

Much of the commentary on 2 Thessalonians is a brief synopsis of Pelagius's exegesis upon particular passages. Rather than follow the text verse by verse, Sedulius seems to select only those passages that he feels requires some clarification. He quotes an excerpt from the text and follows it with a brief phrase quoted from Pelagius. Sedulius's interests in the letter's first chapter seem to focus upon questions of judgment and condemnation of the wicked, since he quotes verses 5, 6, 8, and 9, addressing the justice of God's judgment and the manner of punishment. In all, his exegesis of the first chapter fills only twenty-three lines in Migne.

Sedulius devotes more attention to the second chapter. He echoes Pelagius's understanding of Antichrist's work as the restoration of the ceremonial law. However, when he comes to consider

47. Ibid.

the "mystery of iniquity," Sedulius combines Pelagius's comments with an Augustinian turn of phrase:

Iam enim mysterium iniquitatis operatur. Antichrist works through his members, as John says, "There have been many antichrists." In these the mystery of iniquity is at work, these who by false teachings walk on the path of error, who blessed John says have gone out of the world. Just as Christ works through his members, so, too, does Antichrist.[48]

Sedulius incorporates Pelagius's concerns about false teachings and error within a corporate notion of Antichrist. Like Augustine, Tyconius, and Gregory, Sedulius believes that the "mystery of iniquity" is not simply a foreshadowing of Antichrist, but the presence of Antichrist himself. In this way, Sedulius supplements his major source with an Augustinian/Tyconian framework.

Sedulius further supplements Pelagius when he considers the second half of verse 7, "that the one who now holds may hold until he be taken from the midst." Where Pelagius had been vague, Sedulius is explicit in tying this verse to the fate of the "King of the Romans" (Rex Romanorum). He leaves no doubt that the phrase refers to the endurance of Roman rule, and he does not seem to perceive this to be a problem in his own time. But then Sedulius offers another interpretation, making the transition with a simple "Aliter." His second interpretation may be drawn obliquely from Augustine: "As the one who now holds, that is, Nero, he may hold then, another 'Nero,' of the same title."[49] In this reading, Antichrist would be born in the middle of the reign of this second Nero. Drawing on Jerome, Sedulius asserts that Paul was speaking secretly of the Roman Empire because he did not want to incur its wrath. Having taken this

48. "Iam enim mysterium iniquitatis operatur. Antichristus per sua membra agit, ut Joannes dicit: Multi antichristi facti sunt. In his ergo mysterium iniquitatis operatur, qui falsis doctrinis eius praevium faciunt iter, quos beatus joannes in mundum dicit exisse. Sicut enim Christus nunc per membra sua operatur, sic Antichristus." Sedulius Scotus, Collectanea in Epistolam Secundam ad Thessalonicenses, PL 103.223B.

49. "Ut qui nunc tenet, id est, Nero, teneat tunc eiusdem nominis alter Nero." PL 103.223C.

brief excursion, Sedulius then returns to his synopsis of Pelagius, and the rest of the commentary is rather uninteresting.

But this only makes his brief excursion in chapter 2 all the more interesting. Sedulius seems to have found Pelagius's treatment of Antichrist wanting. While he tips his hat to the Latin spiritual interpretation, the Irish bard seems to have preferred an interpretation that was more realist and more political than that of Pelagius. He does not indicate why this might be. It is interesting to note that the collapse of the Roman Empire does not seem to present a problem to him. Indeed, he seems quite comfortable with the conclusion that the "reign of that future Nero" is properly the Roman Empire.[50] Without more decisive evidence, I can only suggest the possibility that Sedulius Scotus accepted the Carolingian *mythos* that the dignity and honor of the Roman Empire had been preserved in the descendants of Charlemagne, the Holy Roman Emperor.[51] In his very brief "handbook" on the Apostle, Sedulius gives an interpretation of 2 Thessalonians that contains elements of both the literal-realist and the spiritual traditions, but as a whole, it falls clearly within the apocalyptic realist field, even supplementing the exegesis of Pelagius to make it more so.

Haimo of Auxerre: The Providential Delay of Antichrist

The gradual recovery of the figure of Haimo of Auxerre has been one of the great contributions to scholarship on the Carolin-

---

50. "Donec de medio, *hoc est, regno mediante illius tunc Neronis, nascatur Antichristus in medio regno alterius tunc Neronis. Hoc de imperio Romano dictum est, et propterea Paulum non id aperte scribere voluisse dicunt, ne calumniam incurreret, quod Romano imperio male optaverit, cum speraretur aeternum.*" PL 103.223C.

51. I.e., the notion of *translatio imperii*, that the Honor of Rome had moved from East to West. A basic survey of this theme is given in Werner Goetz, *Translatio imperii: Ein Beitrag zur Geschichte des Geschichtsdenken und der politischen Theorien im Mittelalter und in der frühen Neuzeit* (Tübingen: J. C. B. Mohr Verlag, 1958).

gian period in the last century. Confused with several other contemporary Haimos and other masters of Auxerre, (Haimo, Bishop of Halberstadt and disciple of Rabanus Maurus; Remigius of Auxerre, who followed Haimo), Haimo the Auxerre master was all but forgotten for nearly a millennium. And yet his commentaries on much of Scripture are among the most innovative and learned in the Carolingian era. His commentary on 2 Thessalonians preserves a great deal of patristic inheritance and is perhaps the most influential upon the later medieval world. In this sense, for my purposes Haimo's commentary on 2 Thessalonians is a hermeneutical center, both of this chapter and of this whole book. It is both an exemplary manifestation of the Carolingian renaissance and the essential link between patristic and high medieval exegesis of Paul and Antichrist.

The monk and master of Auxerre has had something of his own renaissance in twentieth-century scholarship. Since Eduard Riggenbach demonstrated in 1907 that the commentaries attributed in the *Patrologia Latina* to Haimo, the Bishop of Halberstadt, were actually the work of another Haimo at Auxerre,[52] a few scholars relentlessly have pursued a "quest for the historical Haimo." The gains have been real and measurable as these scholars have reclaimed many works for the monk of Auxerre and have found traces and hints of his thought in his Auxerre disciples.[53] John J. Contreni has recovered a sermon on 1 John 5 that suggests that the rumors of our hero's death in 865 may have been greatly exaggerated, that he in fact be-

52. E. Riggenbach, *Die älteste lateinischen Kommentare zum Hebräerbrief* (Leipzig: A. Deichert, 1907).

53. The major works are Riggenbach; Riccardo Quadri, "Aimone di Auxerre alla luce dei 'Collectanea' di Heiric di Auxerre," *Italia Medioevale e Umanistica* 6 (1963): 1–48; H. Barré, "Haimon d'Auxerre," *Dictionnaire de Spiritualité* 7 (Paris, 1969): 91–97; John J. Contreni, "The Biblical Glosses of Haimo of Auxerre and John Scotus Eriugena," *Speculum* 51 (1976): 411–34. Each of these articles contains a more complete bibliography. The most significant recent work is by Burton Van Name Edwards, who has begun to devise a method by which to distinguish Haimo from his successor at the Auxerre school, Remigius. See his introduction to Remigius, *Expositio super Genesim*, CCCM 136 (Turnhout: Brepols, 1999).

came the abbot of Sasceium (Cessy-les-Bois) until his death ca. 875.[54] Through the diligence of four generations of scholars, we may now know more about Haimo than anyone has since his death.

And yet the sum total of biographical details is still small. He was probably born in the early years of the ninth century in Francia. He was a monk of St. Germain at Auxerre. While little is known of his personal life and actions, scattered references in the work of Remigius of Auxerre lead to the conclusion that he was active in the school of Auxerre between 840 and 860. The great majority of his work, including his Pauline commentary, probably dates from this period, but it is difficult to determine which works are authentic or to arrange them in any particular chronological order. As I have noted, it appears that Haimo left the Abbey of St. Germain to become abbot of Sasceium (Cessy-les-Bois) in ca. 865, where he remained until his death ca. 875. But there is no firm evidence of his actions as abbot or any testimony to his role in the doctrinal controversies of his day.

Nevertheless, we do know that Haimo lived and worked in a time and place of shifting political alliances. The Abbey of St. Germain at Auxerre was blessed with imperial favor in 840 when Count Conrad, the brother-in-law of Emperor Louis the Pious, was miraculously cured of an affliction of the eyes at the saint's tomb. The emperor died that same year, and as his sons squabbled over succession, their often violent conflict peppered the countryside around the abbey. On June 25, 841, the joined forces of Charles the Bald and Louis the German defeated the army of their brother Lothar at Fontenoy-en-Puisaye, very near Auxerre.

In the years following, the Abbey of St. Germain enjoyed the patronage (and often the presence) of Charles the Bald. With the partition of the Treaty of Verdun (843), Auxerre landed solidly within the territory of the lockless king, while the title "Emperor" fell to the

---

54. John J. Contreni, "Haimo of Auxerre, Abbot of Sasceium (Cessy-les-Bois), and a New Sermon on I John V, 4–10," *Revue Bénédictine* 85 (1975): 303–20.

much humbled Lothar in his middle kingdom. In fact, the emperor proved that he was no more than a competitor to his rival brothers; even his attempts to use his influence in Rome to secure the support of the Frankish church failed miserably. The Frankish hierarchy, under the formidable influence of Hincmar of Rheims, rejected Lothar's episcopal candidates. When Lothar died in 855, the title of Emperor passed to his son Louis II, who was king of the Lombards, and the Kingdom of Lotharingia eventually was partitioned between the two surviving brothers (Treaty of Meersen, 870). As each of the middle years of the ninth century passed, the influence of the empire receded more and more from Auxerre.[55] This political history of the waning (and, indeed, disappearance) of imperial authority may have had some impact upon Haimo's exegesis of the *discessio* (2 Th 2:3), as we will see below.

In the context of the history of biblical commentary, Haimo stands out among the work of his contemporaries. Beryl Smalley concedes that Haimo "stands on the line that divides the compiler of select extracts from the author of a commentary,"[56] plotting him just short of the breakthrough into original biblical scholarship. But this is more than she is willing to concede to most Carolingians, and thus Haimo gets relatively high marks. Recent scholarship has been more generous. Haimo's scholarship is most distinctively his in its exegetical method. It represents the confluence of theological tradition and methodological innovation, thus, in one scholar's opinion, anticipating scholasticism by nearly three centuries.[57]

55. For more development of the Carolingian political scene, see Rosamond McKitterick, *The Frankish Kingdoms under the Carolingians 751–987* (New York: Longman, 1983), 169–99. For its impact on Auxerre, see Musée d'Art et d'Histoire, *Saint-Germain d'Auxerre: Intellectuels et Artistes dans l'Europe Carolingienne IXe–XIe Siècles* (Auxerre: Musée d'Art et d'Histoire, 1990).

56. Smalley, *Study of the Bible in the Middle Ages,* 40.

57. E. Bertola, "I commentario paolino di Haimo de Halberstadt o di Auxerre e gli inizi del metodo scolastico," *Pier Lombardo* 5 (1961): 29–54, and "I precedenti storici del metodo del Sic et Non di Abelardo," *Rivista di filosofia neoscolastica* 53 (1961): 255–80.

The method of Haimo of Auxerre gives further testimony to the power and influence of Irish scholarship in the Carolingian renaissance. Not, indeed, because Haimo was Irish; he was probably not. But his school of Saint-Germain d'Auxerre was established by—and he himself was taught by—Muretach, an Irish grammarian. Louis Holtz has surveyed Muretach's Irish attention to detail and broad use of scholarly *"quaestiones"* in depth, and he has given a convincing argument for Haimo's scholarly dependence upon this less famous Irishman.[58] It was from Muretach, says Holtz, that Haimo learned the approach to texts that is constitutive of his method and the method of the Auxerrois school.

The first step in Haimo's method consists of proceeding through the text lemma by lemma. He does not quote every word of every verse, but rather he draws out the significant portions in each lemma. True to his Irish master, he gives grammatical and lexical notes to various words in the text, making note of textual variations from the Vulgate or Greek words and their Latin equivalent. To each lemma he gives a clarification, often introduced by his hallmark word, *subaudi, subaudis, subauditur* ("to be understood as"), *ac si diceret* ("as if to say"), or *et est sensus* ("and this is the sense").

Haimo rarely quotes his sources directly, instead giving the "sense" or kernel of their teachings. This summary style permits him to contrast the plurality of interpretations among his authorities,[59] but he rarely makes any attempt to resolve the conflict. Instead, he strings the various interpretations together with a simple

58. Holtz has edited Muretach's commentary *In Donati artem maiorem*, CCCM 40 (Turnhout: Brepols, 1977). His introduction to this edition contains his argument for the relationship between Muretach and Haimo. See also Louis Holtz, "Muretach et l'influence de la culture irlandaise à Auxerre," *L'École carolingienne d'Auxerre: de Muretach à Remi 830–90*, eds. Dominique Iogna-Prat, Colette Jeudy, Guy Lobrichon (Paris: Beauchesne, 1991) 146–56.

59. This sets him apart from Rabanus, who as we have seen quotes his authorities in large chunks of text addressing several lemmata at once. It also sets him even further apart from the Lyons school, where different commentaries were developed for each Father.

transition such as *aliter* ("otherwise"). Indeed, Haimo rarely shows any indication that he finds any logical contradiction between the various opinions; he seems to find it unnecessary to give one proper interpretation. While Haimo often introduces *quaestiones* into his exegetical work, these are seldom used to oppose authorities in the manner of "yes" and "no" answers as Abelard later would; rather, they reflect the curiosity about the details of the text that he inherited from Muretach.[60]

Haimo's debt to Muretach should not be overestimated, however. The sheer breadth of Haimo's knowledge testifies to his immersion in and mastery of the Latin theological tradition. The ease with which Haimo weaves his sources into his commentary and his general reluctance to cite his sources by name can obscure the vast variety of resources he brings to bear upon the interpretation of Scripture. His work of course bears the imprint of the major Fathers, but he also draws upon more contemporary authorities such as Alcuin, Claude of Turin, or Rabanus Maurus. His theology is rigorously orthodox; his exegesis often includes summaries of exegetical errors made by various heretics in the history of the Church, including the recent adoptionist error of Felix of Urgel.[61] He also displays a smat-

60. It is worth noting that he seems to have passed on this method for the most part to his disciple and successor at the School of Auxerre, Remigius. Recently, Burton Van Name Edwards has suggested that differences of method alone cannot be used to distinguish Haimo and Remigius. Instead, careful and disciplined survey of the extant manuscripts is necessary to make such a judgment. See Edwards, ed., *Expositio super Genesim* (Turnhout: Brepols, 1999), XIII–XX. Dominique Iogna-Prat, however, remains convinced that the Paul commentary and the Apocalypse commentary are among Haimo's works. Dominique Iogna-Prat, "L'œrvre d'Haymon d'Auxerre: État de la question," in *L'École carolingienne d'Auxerre*, 157–79.

61. Indeed, Riggenbach considers his overarching concern to defend against heresy as one of the definitive elements in Haimo's thought. Riggenbach and Contreni have accumulated lists of several hundred texts that refer to heretics in general, to Donatists, Novatians, Arians, Sabellians, Photinians, etc. See Riggenbach, 69; and Contreni, "Haimo of Auxerre," 309. It should be noted that while Haimo and his contemporaries had no doubt that Felix's adoptionism was

tering of knowledge of classical Latin texts (he often quotes Vergil) and apocryphal biblical sources. Haimo manipulates a tremendous library of resources in order to interpret the great majority of both Testaments of Scripture, proving himself to be one of the virtuoso exegetes in the Carolingian Renaissance and in the history of Christianity as a whole.

The commentary on the epistles of Paul is a keynote in Haimo's work. Dominique Iogna-Prat has lauded "the originality of its development and its reasoned used of previous commentaries" and called it "a highpoint in the Pauline exegetical tradition."[62] Since Riggenbach demonstrated its proper attribution in 1907, it has been the criterion by which other works are attributed to the elusive Haimo.[63] The work is a comprehensive commentary on the Pauline corpus, including the minor letters to Titus and Philemon. The text as a whole lacks a preface in the surviving manuscripts, but Haimo begins his exegesis of each letter with an extensive *argumentum* setting it in an historical context. The Migne *Patrologia Latina* edition of the text contains some considerable gaps in the commentaries on Galatians, Colossians, and Titus, but preliminary investigations suggest that Migne's version of the 2 Thessalonians commentary is reliable.[64]

---

evidence of the resurgence of heretical Nestorianism, John C. Cavadini's study of so-called "Spanish Adoptionism" has shed serious doubt upon this judgment. See Cavadini, *Last Christology of the West.*

62. Dominique Iogna-Prat, "L'œuvre d'Haimon d'Auxerre," 161.

63. Iogna-Prat, 161.

64. In examination of four independent manuscripts, I found only minor variations in word order and occasional word choice, and none of these affects the sense of the text dramatically. My study of manuscripts was in no way comprehensive. The text survives in some form in 166 MSS, and a thorough critical evaluation of most or even the majority of these MSS was beyond the scope of this project. The MSS I consulted were Admont 160 (A), Bonn (Koblenz, Jesuiten) 288 (B), Bonn (Eberhardsklausen) 289 (C), and Schlägl 194 (D). A and D are twelfth-century Gothic *textualis* on parchment; B and C are fifteenth-century on paper. The variants are few and insignificant. My thanks to the Hill Monastic Manuscript Library and especially Father Gregory Sebastian, O.S.B., for their assistance.

It is fair to say that the commentary on 2 Thessalonians is certainly not the keystone of the Pauline commentary. The full strength of Haimo's great exegetical prowess is better displayed in his commentaries on Romans and Hebrews, where vital and perennial theological issues at the core of the Christian message arise and where the wealth of source material is so much greater. Nevertheless, Haimo's commentary on this less prominent letter is a "high point" in the history of 2 Thessalonians exegesis. The formidable exegetical hands of Haimo forge earlier traditions into a moderate synthesis of perspectives on the crisis and judgment of the end. Curiously, Haimo, whose Apocalypse commentary is *very* Augustinian, excludes the Latin spiritual tradition from his exegesis of 2 Thessalonians. His 2 Thessalonians commentary offers a literal reading of the apocalyptic tradition that he seems to have reserved for Paul alone.[65] While for Tyconius, Paul's letter provides the hermeneutical key his spiritual apocalyptic theology, Haimo's editorial choices suggest that, for him, an apocalyptic realist perspective is the proper preserve of the Apostle: Paul's second letter to the Thessalonians teaches in a literal fashion the events of the end.

The Letter as a Whole: The Argumentum

Haimo begins his commentary on the letter with a lengthy original *argumentum*. He sets the letter in its historical and literary context, connecting it to 1 Thessalonians and its teaching on the resurrection. Haimo deduces that the Thessalonian community was "shaken and terribly frightened"[66] by this teaching. They believed

65. This conclusion is provisional, since it awaits study of the Matthew commentary that may be Haimo's. I have not seen the text, nor have I seen any study of the "little apocalypse" of Matthew 24. If it is authentic, and if the interpretation favors an apocalyptic realist interpretation (as I suspect it would), then apocalyptic realism is not Pauline, and the discrepancy between the Apocalypse commentary and that on 2 Thessalonians tell us more about the former than the latter.

66. "*conturbati sunt, nimiumque perterriti,*" Haimo of Auxerre, *Expositio in epistolam secundam ad Thessalonicenses,* PL 117.777C.

that Paul was telling them that the end was at hand, and they feared that, being young in the faith, they would not achieve the perfection necessary for salvation. Paul writes to them to correct this misunderstanding, telling them that the last day was not, in fact, imminent. Drawing on Ambrosiaster and Jerome, Haimo claims that Paul speaks obscurely of the destruction of the Roman Empire, which must precede the day of the Lord, because he does not wish to incite persecution. In what seems almost an afterthought, Haimo adds, "He [Paul] also speaks of the coming of Antichrist and his slaying."[67] From the very beginning, the reader receives the impression that the letter primarily addresses the issue of the delay of the Parousia and is concerned only secondarily with the figure of Antichrist.

2 Thessalonians 1: The Providence of God

Haimo's treatment of the first chapter of the letter focuses on the doctrine of providence. Quoting 2 Thessalonians 1:4, Haimo cites the traditional teaching: "Just as we have been able to gather from the words of Prosper and other teachers, nothing occurs in this world unless it is done or permitted by God."[68] The "just judgment of God" consists in the fact that the reprobate will suffer in the next life as much as the elect in this life and more. These reprobate, who "do not obey the gospel," (1:8) are "the heretics, the false Chris-

---

67. "*Denuntiat enim adventum Antichristi et interfectionem eius.*" PL 117.777D.

68. "*Sicut ex verbis Prosperi aliorumque doctorum colligere possumus, nihil agitur in hoc mundo, nisi aut faciente aut ipso permittente.*" PL 117.778C. Note that Haimo here cites the authoritative interpreter of Augustine, Prosper of Aquitaine, rather than Augustine himself. For Prosper, and for the Council of Orange (529) that depended upon his writings, the notion that Augustine seemed to permit, that God willed the damnation of the reprobate, was anathema. Thus, providence required that God either do *or permit* all things to happen in the world. Though he had no public role in the predestinarian controversy around Gottschalk of Orbais, it is clear from this text and others that Haimo subscribed to the moderate mainstream position represented by Hincmar of Rheims and his party. See Haimo, *Expositio in epistolam romanos*, PL 117.456C. for a clearer statement of Haimo's doctrine of predestination.

tians, and the Jews."[69] Their judgment will come "in flames of fire" because fire will fill the earth just as the waters of the flood filled it before. This fire will purify the elect and punish the reprobate. Several of Haimo's comments illustrate the grammatical and syntactical concerns he inherited from Muretach. Commenting on 1:6, Haimo clarifies Paul's syntax by stating, "The conjunction *si tamen* is used in this case not for the purpose of doubting, but for affirmation, as if he were saying, 'Since it is just for God to do thus.'"[70] Later, in reference to 1:9, Haimo justifies Paul's reference to the damned "giving punishment" *(dabunt poenas)* by quoting a line of Vergil in which the same idiom is used.[71] The exegesis of chapter 1 offers a prime example of the grace with which Haimo moves from grammar to theology and back again, utilizing both classical and Christian sources.

2 Thessalonians 2: "At the time chosen by God"

Like many of his predecessors, Haimo focuses most of his attention on chapter 2 of the letter; roughly 60 percent of the text is devoted to it. He begins his comments on the chapter by giving what amounts to another *argumentum*, setting chapter 2 in its doctrinal context: "We read of two comings of the Lord—the first in humility, the second in power, when he will come in judgment. This account *(ratio)* is given concerning the latter."[72] For Haimo, the argument of the letter is clear and simple: it teaches about the Last Judgment. Haimo discerns that the letter is not ecclesiological; he does not refer to another "coming of the Lord in his body" in the Tyconian manner. Instead, he judges Paul's intended subject to be literal and historical, and thus he gives it a literal and historical exposition.

69. "*haereticis videlicet, et falsis christianis, atque Judaeis.*" PL 117.778D.

70. "*Si tamen conjunctio causalis in hoc loco non pro dubitatione, sed pro affirmatione, quasi diceret, Quoniam justum est Deo ita agere.*" PL 117.778D.

71. "*Sicut in Virgilio: Et pro purpureo poenas dat Scylla capillo.*" PL 117.779A.

72. "*Duos Domini adventus legimus, primum in humilitate, secundum in potentia, quando veniet ad iudicium, de quo hic ratio agitur.*" PL 117.779B.

For this reason, Haimo depends most heavily upon Jerome's Epistle 121 and Ambrosiaster's commentary in this chapter. With Jerome, Haimo suggests that Paul's admonition against a false "spirit" or "speech" *(per spiritum, per sermonem)* refers to those who claim special inspiration of the Holy Spirit or who interpret Isaiah and Daniel to mean that the Day of Judgment is near. Paul urges them not to fear such dire predictions and gives his teaching about the events of the end to dispel their fears. Like Ambrosiaster and Jerome, Haimo explains that this *discessio* is the time when "all kingdoms will fall away from the kingdom and rule of the Romans."[73] But without further comment, he proceeds to discuss "the Man of Sin," whom he identifies as Antichrist.

Haimo's portrait of Antichrist is an summary of classic Christian apocalyptic. Antichrist is called the "Man of Sin" (2:3) because, "although he may be only a man, he will be the font of all sinners."[74] He is called the "Son of Perdition" because he is the son of the devil by imitation, not by nature, and the devil is the source of humanity's perdition.[75] Haimo nearly quotes Ambrosiaster's discussion of Antichrist's exaltation over the pagan pantheon, "over Hercules, perhaps, and Apollo and Jove, who are falsely called gods." Antichrist will also exalt himself over the elect, "who are called gods without reproach," like Moses (Ex 7) and the clergy (Ex 22). Antichrist will thus lord himself over both pagans and Christians. But, even more, he will exalt himself over "what is worshipped," (2:4) which Haimo takes to mean the Holy Trinity itself, "which alone ought to be worshipped and adored by every creature."

The epitome of his blasphemy will be his session in the temple

---

73. *"Quoniam nisi venerit discessio primum, ut discedant omnia regna a regno et imperio Romanorum."* PL 117.779D.

74. *"Antichristus videlicet, qui licet homo sit, fons tamen erit omnium peccatorum."* PL 117.779D. See Jerome, *Ep. 121,* 58, for the source quote.

75. Such a qualification is culled, but not directly quoted, from the distinctions found in Ambrosiaster and Pelagius between the true sonship of Christ and the lesser power of the devil. See Chapter 2 in this volume.

of God (2:4). Like Jerome, Haimo admits two possible interpretations of this lemma. But he expands Jerome's discussion of the possibilities by including the traditional Hippolytan biography of Antichrist in his exposition of the first possibility. Either Antichrist will be born in Babylon of the tribe of Dan, come to Jerusalem, claim to be the Messiah, gather the Jews around him, and rebuild the city's temple, or he will take a place in the Church, posing as God. Haimo expresses no preference for one interpretation or the other.

Haimo offers the traditional contrast between Antichrist and Christ in several forms. From Jerome and Ambrosiaster he takes the contrast of incarnational characteristics: "For just as the complete fullness of divinity reposed in Christ, so the fullness of evil and every vice will come to dwell in that human called Antichrist because he is opposed to Christ."[76] In a rare allusion to the Tyconian tradition, Haimo states that Antichrist is said to oppose Christ because "he is opposite Christ and all his members," but he says no more along this line. It is clear that Haimo's aim in these passages is to characterize the future historical individual who will follow the *discessio* of the Roman Empire and precede Christ's return.

Having given a summary of the traditional teaching of Antichrist, Haimo returns to discuss the fall of the Roman Empire. Haimo's discussion of the *discessio* or "rebellion" has traditionally been understood to refer to the future fall of the translated Roman Empire in the hands of the Franks. However, this understanding misrepresents the text. For example, in one of the more comprehensive studies of the text thus far, Daniel Verhelst cites Haimo's comment on "what restrains" in 2:6, "since the Kingdom of the Romans has not yet been destroyed, nor have all the nations receded from

---

76. *"Nam sicut in Christo omnis plenitudo divinitatis requievit, ita in illo homine qui Antichristus appellatur, eo quod sit contrarius Christo, plenitudo malitiae et omnis iniquitatis habitabit, quia in ipso erit caput omnium malorum diabolus, qui est rex super omnes filios superbiae."* PL 117.780C. See Jerome, *Ep. 121, 59*, for a close analogue. It is likely that Haimo is also thinking of Isidore's etymological definition of Antichrist in his *Etymologiarum*, PL 82.274.

them,"[77] as evidence that Haimo believes that Rome still endures.[78] However, placing this text in its context, one finds that it is Haimo's paraphrase of the Apostle in the present tense, and thus these words refer to what Haimo believes 2 Thessalonians 2:6 means *to Paul's Thessalonian audience:* "'You know,' he says, 'what restrains' that Antichrist, and what delays him, since the Kingdom of the Romans is not yet destroyed, nor have all the nations drawn away from them."[79] The temporal location of this hypothetical pericope is thus the first century, not Haimo's ninth.

To the contrary, Haimo clearly believes that the rebellion has already occurred. He summarizes his exegesis of 2 Thessalonians 2:4 with the following sentence:

With these words the Apostle demonstrated to the Thessalonians that the Lord will not come for Judgment before the defection of the human kingdoms—*which we already see fulfilled*—and the appearance in the world of Antichrist, who will kill the witnesses of Christ.[80]

---

77. "*quia necdum destructum est regnum Romanorum, nec recesserunt omnes gentes ab illis.*" PL 117.780D.

78. See Verhelst, "La préhistoire des conceptions d'Adson concernant l'Antichrist," *Recherches de théologie ancienne et médiévale* 40 (1973): 80.

79. "*Vos scitis, inquit,* quid detineat *illum Antichristum, et quid moretur illum, quia necdum destructum est regnum Romanorum, nec recesserunt omnes gentes ab illis.*" PL 117.780D.

80. "*His verbis demonstravit Apostolus Thessalonicensibus, non prius venturum Dominum ad judicium, qui regni humani defectio fieret, quod iam nos impletum videmus, et Antichristum apparere in mundo qui interficiet Christi martyres.*" PL 117.780C (emphasis mine). Edmond Ortigues ("Haimon d'Auxerre, théoricien des trois ordres," in *L'Ecole Carolingienne d'Auxerre,* 218) has argued that Haimo here argues that the *discessio* of Rome has a double sense: On the one hand, it has already fallen; on the other, Rome remains with us to the end of time. I don't think that this particular text supports that reading. It is conceivable that Haimo could refer to the *translated* empire, that of Charlemagne and Louis the Pious, as having suffered "the rebellion," that is, the partition of the empire and the clear discord within it. But there is no clear evidence either way. Haimo indicates that Rome has fallen, but we cannot know whether he means in 476 or ca. 841.

Haimo believes that the "rebellion" *(discessio)* or "defection" *(defectio)* of the nations from Rome has already occurred, but that the appearance of Antichrist is still to come. This belief presents him with an exegetical and theological problem: if the Apostle says that the coming of Antichrist will follow the rebellion (2 Th 2:3), and the rebellion has already occurred, then where is Antichrist? What is the cause of his delay? Haimo resolves this conundrum with an argument from providence. Later in the commentary, as he discusses the death of Antichrist on the Mount of Olives, Haimo considers again Antichrist's arrival, as if the solution to the earlier problem just occurred to him:

Indeed, when the Apostle says, "then that perverse one will be revealed after the Roman empire will have been destroyed," he should not be understood to have said that [Antichrist] will come immediately, but rather that first the empire will be destroyed and then Antichrist will come, at a time chosen by God.[81]

He then returns to the death with no further comment. This reconsideration of the "rebellion" resolves Haimo's exegetical problem with an Augustinian theological argument about history. Augustine had discouraged apocalyptic speculation by arguing that all time since Christ is eschatological; Christ initiated the sixth age, and thus no major epochal providential shifts will occur until the end.[82] Similarly, Haimo concludes that his age is eschatological: it lies in the time between the first sign and the last sign of the end.[83] The rebel-

---

81. *"Quod vero dicit Apostolus: Tunc revelabitur ille iniquus postquam fuerit destructum Romanum imperium, non est ita intelligendum, quod statim dixerit illum venturum, sed primum illud destruendum, ac deinde Antichristum venturum, tempore a Deo disposito."* PL 117.781C.

82. Augustine, CD 22.30. As Robert Markus has argued, Augustine insisted "that since the coming of Christ until the end of the world, all history is homogeneous, that it cannot be mapped out in terms of a pattern drawn from sacred history, that it cannot contain decisive turning points endowed with a significance in sacred history." Markus, 20–21.

83. Haimo's argument is less compelling than Augustine's, since his epochmarker is less significant than the very incarnation of Christ. Nevertheless, it

lion has already occurred; Antichrist has not yet come. The coming of Antichrist is unknown and entrusted to the providence of God.

If Haimo believes that the Roman Empire still endures, he would have no reason to introduce this temporal gap in the eschatological drama. But, living as he does at a particular nadir of the Carolingian imperial mythos, Haimo perhaps can state comfortably that the Roman Empire has fallen. While there is always a titular Holy Roman Emperor, Haimo writes in an environment in which the imperial power is held in low esteem (to say the least!), and his kingdom is under the patronage of a rival to the imperial throne. As Charles the Bald, the friend of Auxerre, expands his territory, it is over against his brother the Emperor and the imperial offspring. As it is, Haimo asserts that he dwells in the ambiguous "time in-between." Antichrist could come tomorrow; he could come in a thousand years. The time "chosen by God" is hidden, and thus speculation about the end is futile until Antichrist arrives. Haimo's apocalyptic schema, when Antichrist will arrive and practice his deceptions, is thus vague and deferred into the inscrutable mystery of providence.

However, Haimo still can identify the signs of the "mystery of iniquity" already at work in history. With Ambrosiaster, Haimo concludes that this "mystery of iniquity" refers to the persecution and slaughter of the holy martyrs that Nero began and Diocletian and Julian the Apostate continued. This slaughter prefigures Antichrist's murder of Enoch and Elijah in the last days. Haimo speaks of these Roman evildoers as "members" of Antichrist, alluding to the spiritual interpretation of Antichrist, but he does not exploit the power of the corporal metaphor. Nero and his fellow "kings" are "members" of Antichrist because they "prefigure" him, just as Christ, the "head of the elect" is prefigured in the death of Abel, the sacrifice of Isaac, and David's victory over Goliath. "Members" are types, "shadows"

---

reflects an attempt to come to terms from an Augustinian perspective with a scriptural text that is clearly predictive apocalyptic.

of a future "reality";[84] missing is the vivid sense of corporeality and connection found in Tyconius and Gregory. While Haimo uses corporal language, he does not offer what I have called the Latin spiritual interpretation. Haimo's Antichrist in this commentary does not actually come in his members; they merely point forward in time to him. 2 Thessalonians 2:8 speaks of both Antichrist's arrival and his death. Like others before him, Haimo is careful to point out that the "revelation" of Antichrist is his "manifestation," not to be confused with God's revelation. Antichrist's death is another potential source of confusion. Reading Gregory and Jerome, Haimo concedes that they disagree: Antichrist may be killed by Michael the Archangel, or he may be killed by Christ alone. Paul's declaration that Antichrist will perish "by the breath of his mouth" simply affirms that, whoever the agent of his death may be, he will die by the power of Christ. Haimo includes Jerome's details of that death: He will die "upon his throne on the Mount of Olives in Babylon."[85] Such concrete detail sketches a vivid picture of the real, historical course of events before the Judgment.

But Haimo remains reluctant to affirm that these events assure the imminent arrival of the day of the Lord. He states that there will be a brief respite between Antichrist's death and Christ's Judgment:

It should be noted that the Lord will not come to judge immediately after Antichrist has been killed. Rather, as we know from the Book of Daniel, forty-five days will be given to the elect for penance. In truth, how little the span of time may be until the Lord will come is entirely unknown.[86]

84. I allude to Jean Daniélou's work on typology, *From Shadows to Reality: Studies in the Biblical Typology of the Fathers*, trans. W. Hibbard (Westminster, Md.: Newman Press, 1961).

85. *"Occidetur autem (sicut doctores tradunt) in monte Oliveti in Babylone et solio suo."* PL 117.781C. See Jerome, *Commentarius in Danielem*, Sancti Hieronymi Presbyteri Opera I, CCSL 75A, 933–34.

86. *"Notandum quia non statim veniet Dominus ad iudicium, ubi fuerit Antichristus interfectus, sed (sicut ex libro Danielis intelligimus) post mortem illius concedentur electis*

As Robert Lerner has shown, the seeds of this notion of delay before the Last Judgment are sown in Hippolytus and Jerome.[87] Haimo is the first to introduce the teaching into the tradition of 2 Thessalonians commentary, and he adds his own editorial comment. He seems to suggest that the forty-five days deduced from Daniel may symbolize an undetermined period of time.[88] This bears further witness to Haimo's reluctance to speculate about an apocalyptic timetable of any sort. While he is more than willing to give a "what" of the eschatological end, he refuses to give a "when." The "when" is left to providence, to the "time chosen by God."[89]

Having summarized the doctrines related to Antichrist's death, Haimo returns again to consider his nature and work. 2 Thessalonians 2:9 says that Antichrist's coming will be by the work of Satan. For Haimo this indicates that Antichrist will do whatever he does with the instigation and cooperation of the devil, who will "possess him totally." Nevertheless, Antichrist will remain responsible for his actions.

He will not let go of his senses, so that he might say ignorantly that he did not know God. Nor will he be vexed by the devil like the lunatics. If this were the case, he would have no sin whatever he did. For those who suffer madness have no sin, for they do not know what they are doing.[90]

---

ad poenitentiam dies quadraginta quinque. Quantulumcunque [sic] *vero spatium temporis sit usque quo Dominus veniet, penitus ignoratur."* PL 117.781D.

87. Lerner, 97–144.

88. Lerner interprets Haimo's comment to mean that there will be forty-five days *and then* a "span of time, however small." I disagree with this reading of the text, but the disagreement is insignificant. Either way, Haimo's point is to make the duration of the delay elastic.

89. Again, the similarities to Augustine's tactic in *City of God* 20 are notable. Augustine gives a rich synopsis of the events of the Last Judgment, but he argues that we cannot know when these will occur.

90. *"tamen non amittet sensum, ut ignoranter dicat se nescire Deum, neque vexabitur a diabolo, sicut phrenetici: quia si ita esset, nequaquam peccatum haberet quidquid ageret; sicut illi non habent qui phrenesim patiuntur, qui nesciunt quid agant."* PL 117.781D–782A. Many classical and early Christian medical dictionaries discuss *phrenesis* as demonic possession, but I have been unable to locate a specific reference to the issue of moral culpability.

Haimo has inherited a tradition of commentary in which the devil often is said to "possess" Antichrist (e.g., in Pelagius, Chapter 2 of this volume) or "appear as a man" (Ambrosiaster, ibid.). In spite of this legacy, Haimo carefully protects Antichrist's humanity and culpability. His caution suggests an implicit "antichristology" that for the first time requires positive attributes. While patristic thinkers had denied certain attributes to Antichrist (e.g., he was *not* the devil incarnate, he did *not* work authentic miracles, etc.), Haimo is the first in this exegetical tradition to affirm his humanity clearly and unequivocally. In effect, Haimo's brief comparison asserts that Antichrist is the embodiment of human sin, and thus he must be held responsible for his actions.[91]

2 Thessalonians 2:9 asserts that Antichrist's actions will be "signs and lying prodigies." For Haimo, this refers to the false miracles that Antichrist will accomplish. They are "false" in two senses. First, they will deceive people through magical art and illusion, "just as Simon Magus deceived someone who beheaded a ram, thinking it was [Simon]."[92] Secondly, these wonders that he will seem to work will "lead people into worshipping the Lie." But in either case, Haimo asserts that Antichrist's works are false miracles that he will seem to do. Antichrist is a human being with no true miraculous powers.

91. One might infer from this something like a perverse Athanasian definition, "What the devil has assumed, Christ cannot condemn." Why Haimo would feel so compelled to make this argument is unclear. It is possible that he is responding to Theodore's "antichristology" as preserved by Rabanus Maurus. Or it is possible that he is reacting to Gregory the Great's more or less explicit affirmation that Antichrist is the devil incarnate. (See Chapter 3.) Although Eastern Christian sources had developed this incarnational antichristology in the centuries just prior to Haimo's work (see McGinn, *Antichrist*, 94–97), and although some of these texts (such as Pseudo-Methodius) were translated into Latin in the 700s, it seems unlikely that Haimo is responding to them, since he shows no knowledge of any other aspect of their thought (e.g., the Last Emperor motif).

92. *"sicut et Simon Magus delusit illum qui, putans eum occidere, arietem decollavit pro eo."* PL 117.782A. This vignette can be found in the apocryphal "Acts of the Holy Apostles Peter and Paul," *Ante-Nicene Fathers* 8, ed. C. Richardson (Grand Rapids: Eerdmans, 1981), 482.

Nevertheless, according to 2 Thessalonians 2:10, Antichrist will succeed in his seduction of "those who are perishing," whom Haimo identifies as "Jews and pagans."[93] Jews and pagans will be seduced because they have already refused to accept the truth of Christ and the Spirit. For this reason, Haimo concedes with his predecessors that God permits[94] Antichrist, the "operation of the Lie," to lead them further astray into worship of the Lie. The highest sin for these "Jews and pagans" is idolatry: they turn from God and worship the devil. Paul contrasts these with the "first fruits of salvation," whom Haimo identifies as the apostles, "since they were the first to believe."[95] Those who are converted by the apostles' preaching "add to the body of Christ"[96] and receive "eternal consolation" (2:16) through the promise of the Heavenly Kingdom. Salvation and damnation as Haimo presents them in these passages are rather clear-cut: Those who accept the apostolic tradition will be saved; "Jews and pagans," on the other hand, have already rejected Christ and will worship the devil and be condemned.

His exegesis at the end of chapter 2 through chapter 3 lacks the sharp engagement with the text that he shows earlier. Indeed, his exegesis of chapter 3 occupies only twenty-four lines in Migne and tries to clarify the sense of only a few passages. Haimo's exegetical interest in the letter wanes after 2 Thessalonians 2:10, and his remaining comments seem perfunctory and anticlimactic. Unlike Rabanus Maurus's, Haimo's exegesis is controlled by the thematic content of the letter; once he has handled the delicate issues of the "day of the Lord" and the "Man of Sin," he has accomplished his aim.

Haimo aims to present a thorough summary of the historical

---

93. "id est Judaeis et paganis." PL 117.782B. See Jerome, Ep. 121, 58, for the clearest patristic statement of this position.

94. NB: Like Jerome, Theodore, etc., Haimo insists that God does not send Antichrist directly but permits him to come.

95. "Apostoli primitiae fuerunt, quia primi crediderunt." PL 117.782C.

96. "ut vos acquisisti ad fidem nostra praedicatione, augmentum faciatis corpori Christi." PL 117.782C.

events and characters of the end, complete with an analysis of the theological issues of providence and moral culpability that pertain to them. He leaves no doubt in this commentary that Paul's *discessio* refers to the collapse of the Roman Empire and that this has already occurred. When the Apostle speaks of "the Man of Sin, the Son of Perdition," he refers to a historical individual, fully human, who will come to persecute the elect and lead astray those who have already rejected Christ. That the former has occurred and the latter has not yet come is due to God's providential decree, which obscures the precise time of Antichrist's arrival from human eyes. Christ will slay Antichrist and give a brief respite to the saints before he comes in judgment. But, again, God in his providence alone knows how long this respite will be before Christ comes to reward those who have accepted the Gospel and condemn those who worship the devil.

Given this evidence, it would appear that we could place Haimo firmly within the apocalyptic realist camp. But, as I have suggested in the case of Jerome, such appearances can deceive. Haimo also composed a commentary on the Apocalypse, and this commentary offers a decidedly different perspective. The Apocalypse commentary recapitulates the Tyconian interpretation of the text, carried through Bede and Ambrose Autpertus, casting the Apocalypse as an allegory for the present and future Church. He rarely refers to Antichrist without referring also to "his members," the heretics and sons of pride within the Church.[97] The contrast between the two expositions is so sharp that one might wonder if Haimo has attempted a deception of his own worthy of Antichrist!

But the source of conflict is far less insidious, and it sheds some light upon Haimo's approach to Scripture. His *argumentum* to the 2 Thessalonians commentary gives a clear sense of Paul's purpose for writing: Because the Thessalonians are afraid that the day of the Lord is at hand, Paul writes to them to dispel this fear, "and he

97. Cf. Haimo, *Expositio in Apocalypsim*, PL 117.1092D–1098D, where the first beast of Rv 13 is Antichrist and the second is his body.

shows them that the Roman Empire must be destroyed first." For Haimo, Paul responds to the concrete fear of the Thessalonians with a concrete answer. He gives them what they need: evidence that the end will not yet come. The Apostle's purpose is to give them a literal, historical teaching. Haimo thus interprets this teaching in a literal, historical manner.

The apostle John, on the other hand, receives the Apocalypse as an "intellectual vision" in consolation for his imprisonment on Patmos. John's vision is one in which "such symbols *(sacramenta)* are revealed to him from heaven in his mind."[98] Paul relates events; John receives imagery. Thus in the Apocalypse, "nothing historical should be accepted, because the words themselves, if they are examined carefully, are put forth to teach."[99] The difference between Haimo's expositions of 2 Thessalonians and the Apocalypse is one not of apocalyptic perspective, but of genre. It is the difference between historical and visionary literature.

So, while the Apocalypse commentary contains over 130 mentions of the term "Antichrist," it refers to 2 Thessalonians only three times—a conspicuous absence, to say the least. Even these references are taken in a Tyconian sense: For example, when Christ will "slay [Antichrist] with the breath of his mouth" (2 Th 2:8), this refers either to Antichrist's punishment or to that of his members.[100] Most references to Antichrist recommend just such a corporal Tyconian reading. For Haimo, the "beast rising out of the sea" (Rv 13:1ff.) rep-

---

98. *"divinitus sibi dum in mente tanta ostensa sunt sacramenta."* PL 117.940B.

99. *"In hac autem revelatione nihil historicum est accipiendum, quod ipsa verba, si subtiliter inspiciuntur, docere probantur."* PL 117.938C.

100. *"Et descendit ignis a Deo de coelo, et devoravit illos. Per ignem repentinum interitum Antichristi, vel membrorum illius intelligere debemus. Unde Paulus dicit: Quem Dominus Jesus interficiet spiritu oris sui* [2 Th 2]. *Et in Evangelio ipse Dominus: Cum dixerint pax et securitas, tunc repentinus eis superveniet interitus* [1 Th 5]. *Sicut enim nunc iste mundus plenus est hominibus, sic erit in adventu Filii hominis. Sicque cum repente Dominus venerit ad judicium, quasi ignis, id est sententia damnationis subito descendet de coelo, et devorabit impios, non solum in corpore, sed etiam in anima."* Haimo, *Expositio in Apocalypsim* VII.xx, PL 117.1188BC.

resents Antichrist in his body. His feet are "worldly powers"; the blasphemies he speaks out of his mouth are the words of liars, false apostles, and pseudo-prophets, which continue to plague the Church. Like Rabanus, Haimo sees the body of Antichrist working through deception, separating people from the faith of Christ "in mind," preparing the way for the individual Antichrist's consummate, eternal separation of his body from Christ.[101]

For Haimo, then, both the Latin spiritual interpretation and the literal apocalyptic realism are valid interpretations of the apocalyptic tradition, but they should not be confused. Each is appropriate for its own genre and context. In the last chapter, I argued that this "peaceful coexistence" between the two traditions is demonstrably present in the thought of Gregory the Great, and I suggested that it is characteristic of much early medieval apocalyptic thought. In this chapter, I have shown that such "peaceful coexistence" occurs within each of the Carolingian exegetes of 2 Thessalonians. All agree that realism and the spiritual/ecclesial reading can coexist without contradiction.

In Rabanus Maurus, the historical realism of Theodore and Jerome is tempered and balanced at crucial points by excerpts from Augustine. Similarly, Sedulius Scotus incorporates the spiritual-corporal interpretation into a commentary dominated by Pelagian realism. While the major source for each commentary presents a realist account of the eschatological events, each exegete folds spiritual ingredients into the exposition. In the case of Florus, I can only infer that his devotion to compiling indexes of each Father, without confusion and with separation, is indicative of the value he places

---

101. *"Qui in captivitatem duxerit, in captivitatem vadet. Haec verba sicut pertinent ad omne corpus Antichristi, ita et ad ipsum principem malorum Antichristum, qui duobus modis captivabit homines, primum videlicet a fide Christi eos separans mente, deinde ab aeternorum societate fidelium, quia qui ei obaudierint, perpetuo captivitatis exsilio damnabuntur. Ita et ille prius captivabitur in anima, dum diabolo tradetur ad possidendum. Deinde damnabitur in inferno captivitate perpetua."* Haimo, *Expositio in Apocalypsim* IV.xiii, PL 117.1098A.

on each tradition. He compiles an index for Augustine and for Gregory, but also for Jerome.

With Haimo, this coexistence is organized rationally by the type of scriptural book. Haimo's commentary on 2 Thessalonians gives a thorough summary of the apocalyptic realist tradition because he understands the subject matter to be history and the genre to be catechetical, that is, the teaching of doctrine to the Thessalonian community. In Haimo, as in Jerome before him,[102] 2 Thessalonians becomes the authoritative New Testament resource on Antichrist and the events of the end, and Paul is its apostolic catechist. The Apocalypse, on the other hand, is a spiritual vision, and contains "nothing historical." Its message is not doctrinal but moral and exhortatory, and thus Antichrist is understood in the corporal and spiritual sense.

Such a generic distinction sets Haimo apart from his contemporaries and seems to confirm Bertola's insistence that Haimo anticipates the rigorous distinctions of the scholastic method by several centuries. But if this is so, it is because in Haimo one can see the fruition and maturation of exegetical principles that are thoroughly Carolingian. Each Carolingian exegete I have studied agrees, at least in their practice, that the opinions of the Fathers constitute an authoritative canon of biblical interpretation. Each selects from this canon and manipulates its "bricks and mortar" to construct a synthetic interpretation of the biblical text, and each synthesis bears the signature of its craftsman.

Antichrist emerges from the Carolingian period as both present and foretold. The presence of Antichrist is moral and corporal in the Tyconian sense. The body of Antichrist is at work denying Christ through perverse morality and false belief. The head, the Antichrist foretold in the teaching of Paul the Apostle, will come at the time God chooses and wield the sword against the Church. Sedulius, Ra-

---

102. I have noted already Jerome's willingness to "spiritualize" the Apocalypse exegesis of Victorinus and his concurrent willingness to contribute to apocalyptic realist interpretations in the Commentary on Daniel and in Epistle 121.

banus, and Haimo seem to share the desire to distinguish these two modes of Antichrist, each in their own way. The present threat, they indicate, is within the body of Christ, in false teaching and moral deviance. But the coming threat will be a historical and political power, a tyrant persecuting the Church in some hidden future.

The Ambiguity of the End or the End of Ambiguity?
Antichrist in the Tenth Century

Within a century of Haimo's death, the Carolingian world was crumbling, and perhaps the threat of the tyrant's persecution seemed all the more real. The collapse of Carolingian culture coincided (unhappily, it seems) with the approach of the year 1000. Recently scholars have revisited the issue of the year 1000 and have found it difficult to dismiss the date's apocalyptic significance. While imminent apocalyptic expectation does not loom large throughout the tradition of commentary, as we have already seen, there is at least one, and maybe two, notable exceptions that appear as the end of the millennium approaches. The first is a unique work, an "antihagiography" of Antichrist, composed by Adso, abbot of Montier-en-Der. This work, while it is not a commentary, depends upon the 2 Thessalonian commentary tradition, especially on Haimo. It was immensely popular; Daniel Verhelst has identified some 170 manuscripts of the text in various redactions throughout western Europe. The second text from the tenth century is unique as well, though nowhere near as popular. The commentary of Thietland of Einsiedeln on 2 Thessalonians is an anomalous work that departs significantly from the mainstream of the 2 Thessalonians tradition, and it seems to have no influence upon the later tradition. And yet it may be the only text in the 2 Thessalonians tradition to predict an imminent end. These two works are exceptions to the apparent absence of predictive imminent apocalypticism in the 2 Thessalonians tradition.

Few would dispute that Adso of Montier-en-Der's famous treatise "On the Origin and Time of Antichrist" is a conservative document. "Terror" and "anti-Terror" historians alike concede that Adso's purpose in the document is to show that Antichrist will not come terribly soon, that his advent should not be a cause of concern to the immediate present. The treatise is, in essence, a letter of consolation to the Queen Gerberga, promising that Antichrist's coming is forestalled until the Roman Empire, in a later Frankish incarnation, has finally passed away. But Daniel Verhelst has demonstrated how bold and risky such a claim is in the tenth century, since it ties the eschatological fate of the world to an imperial dynasty limping through intramural conflict and challenges to its authority.[103] Although Adso is largely dependent upon Haimo of Auxerre for the "facts" of Antichrist's biography, this concrete political-historical referent is missing from his source. In his historical claims made on behalf of the "kings of the Franks," the abbot Adso seems to doubt the vague utterances and the ambiguity of Haimo's apocalyptic commentary. If Adso's purpose is conservative, his dismissal of the traditional and authoritative doctrine of moderation may betray a conceptual limit to his conservatism.

The traditional and conservative nature of Adso's treatise in not difficult to divine. Drawing on the insights of patristic exegesis as gathered in the Carolingian commentaries, Adso argues that Antichrist will not come until the Roman Empire has fallen.[104] From another tradition, Adso develops the doctrine of the last world em-

---

103. Daniel Verhelst, "Adso on Montier-en-Der and the Fear of the Year 1000," trans. An van Rompaey and Richard Landes, in *The Apocalyptic Year 1000,* ed. Richard Landes, David Van Meter, and Andrew Gow (New York: Oxford University Press, 2003) I will cite from the prepublication manuscript. This citation from p. [10]. See also Johannes Fried, "L'attesa della fine dei tempi alla svolta del millennio," in *L'attesa della fine dei tempi nel Medioevo,* ed. Ovidio Capitani and Jürgen Miethke (Bologna: Società editrice il Mulino, 1988), 1–16. For background history, see McKitterick.

104. Adso of Montier-en-Der, *De ortu et tempore Antichristi,* ed. Daniel Verhelst, CCCM 45 (Turnhout: Brepols, 1976), 26. I will use the English translation of Bernard McGinn as found in his *Apocalyptic Spirituality,* 89–96.

peror, whose reign will end only when he willingly relinquishes the crown and scepter upon the Mount of Olives in Jerusalem.[105] Adso clearly wants to establish some distance between the present and the eschaton, and he offers the security of political peace and unity under Frankish rule, "possessing Rome anew,"[106] before the end will come. Verhelst has argued that Adso's claims are read most coherently as a conservative reaction to a widespread sense of apocalyptic anxiety.[107] He suggests that we can plunge beneath the moderate and placid surface of the text to find the currents and eddies of a contextual undertow bubbling with anticipation. As the infamous "Year 1000" (variously dated) loomed upon the horizon, its winds stirred the sea.

A brief survey of the apparatus of Verhelst's edition of Adso shows his dependence upon Haimo's 2 Thessalonians commentary. Adso's schema of the last times draws heavily upon Haimo as a source but rejects the ambiguity of Haimo's resolution. He points to the *discessio* and identifies it with the dissolution of the Roman Empire, as Haimo had done. But he ignores Haimo's struggle with the apocalyptic timetable and immediately proceeds to cite "our learned men" in support of his discussion of the Last World Emperor. This apocalyptic monarch will be both Frankish and Roman, since the "dignity" of Rome endures in the Frankish line. He will reign in peace and will then hand over his crown to God upon the Mount of Olives. Only then (but then immediately), Antichrist will appear.[108]

When Adso then turns to discuss the characteristics and career of Antichrist, he again mines Haimo's commentary for information, and he endeavors to harmonize Haimo's interpretations with his own. In the first part of the treatise, Adso asserted that Antichrist

---

105. Pseudo-Methodius, "Revelations," in *Sibyllinische Texte und Forschungen,* ed. Ernst Sackur (Halle: Niemeyer, 1898).

106. *"unus ex regibus Francorum Romanum imperium ex integro tenebit."* Adso, 26. McGinn, *Apocalyptic Spirituality,* 93.

107. Verhelst, "Fear," [9].

108. Adso, 26.

will rebuild the temple in Jerusalem and gather the Jews around him. Haimo's commentary sees this temple restoration as one of two possible understandings of 2 Thessalonians 2:4, "he will be seated in the temple." His second possible understanding proposes that "temple" refers to the church, and that Antichrist will be enthroned in it.[109] Although Adso has already chosen the former understanding, he harmonizes the two possibilities. In Adso's treatise, Antichrist will rebuild the temple in Jerusalem and be enthroned in the church.[110] That he would bother to harmonize Haimo's treatment of the temple issue with his own shows his respect for Haimo's authority. And yet, his earlier disregard for Haimo's understanding of the Roman Empire seems to belie that respect. This apparent discontinuity in Adso's hermeneutical method of appropriating Haimo betrays the conceptual limits of Adso's conservatism.

Adso cannot conceive of the apocalyptic drama in Haimo's mysterious, ambiguous terms. He writes at the request of the queen of the Carolingian court at a time when her husband's power and security upon the throne of the Western Franks is far from assured. In his dedicatory paragraph, Adso seems to allude to Louis IV's tenuous grip upon the throne:

If I were able to gain the whole kingdom for you, I would do it most gladly; but since I cannot do that, I will beseech the Lord for the salvation of you and your sons that his grace may always precede you in your works and his glory may follow you in loving kindness.[111]

In a consolatory letter to his queen, the abbot invests not only his petitions and well-wishes upon her royal line but also his apocalyptic hopes. The epistolary form of Adso's text give him a particular, po-

109. PL 117.780A–B.
110. Adso, 27.
111. *"si potuissem vobis totum regnum adquirere, libentissime fecissem. Sed, quia illud facere non valeo, pro salute vestra filiorumque vestrorum Dominum exorabo, ut gratia Euis in operibus vestris semper vos preveniat et gloria Illius pie et misericorditer subsequatur, ut, divinis intenta mandatis, possitis adimplere bona, que desideratis, unde corona vobis detur regni celestis."* Adso, 20. McGinn, *Apocalyptic Spirituality,* 89.

litically engaged audience and a broader horizon for speculation than the exegetical enterprise of Haimo. But, writing within these broad generic parameters, Adso need not have exploited them with such specific speculations. Whatever his motive may have been, it is beyond the historian's reach. But some elements of the letter's historical context yield several possibilities.

Adso's *De Ortu et Tempore Antichristi* most likely was written around 950. If this date is accurate, it's composition follows a few years after Queen Gerberga negotiated the release of her husband Louis IV from a vassal of Louis's rival, Hugh the Great (in 945–46). Hugh continued to threaten, even attacking their residence at Rheims in 949. Even after peace was arranged between them in 950, Hugh continued to harass the king and queen by erecting forts in Francia to serve as bases for his pillaging relatives and vassals. Louis and Gerberga often called upon the support of her brother Otto the Saxon, King of the Eastern Frankish kingdom to strengthen his position and quiet Hugh. With such a relentless foe, it is even possible that Gerberga may have sought Adso's opinion as to whether Hugh the Great may have been Antichrist. (!)

Whatever the nature of her request, Adso's reply dispels any notion of Antichrist's imminence and of his local origin. Citing the tradition, he is certain that Antichrist will be a Jew of the tribe of Dan and that he will be born in Babylon. As I have noted, Adso's "dangerous" conservatism links the coming of Antichrist with the endurance of the "Kings of the Franks" who possess and perpetuate the "dignity," if not the power, of Rome. It is possible and reasonable to argue that this "dignity" is preserved in any Frankish king, since Adso does not specify and there were precedents for the application of the title to each.[112] This precedent, coupled with the close

112. When Charles the Simple (father of Louis IV) and Henry the Fowler (father of Otto I and Queen Gerberga) met and treated at Bonn in 921, they were addressed as *rex francorum occidentalium* and *rex francorum orientalem,* respectively. M. Bouquet, *Recueil des Historiens des Gaules et de la France,* vol. 9, ed. L. Delisle (Paris, 1869–80), 323.

association of Otto and Louis from 942 to 954, lead to the possibility that Otto's claim to legitimacy as a Frankish king and possessor of Rome "by right" could not easily be denied. Adso may have written with deliberately broad strokes, such that the rightful heirs to either Frankish throne may be included. But even this speculation about the "whom" of Adso's reference begs the more interesting question of "why?"

Why did Adso make any connection at all between the advent of the End and the Frankish royal line? Why did he depart from Haimo, his authoritative source? Again, certainty eludes the historian. But Adso knew from Haimo that Antichrist would come only after the *discessio,* the rebellion from the Roman Empire. He understood that this would culminate in a last world emperor. Charlemagne was certainly the heir to Roman imperial authority, and thus too were his descendants, down to Louis IV. At the same time, Otto the Saxon, from the time of his accession to the Eastern Frankish throne in 936, sought to emulate Charlemagne's career, perhaps in an effort to revive the notion of sacral kingship that the great Carolingian represented. It is at least possible that Adso, in his response to the anxious request of Gerberga, read all of these factors together. It is possible that this combination of factors led him to only one possible conclusion: that the fate of Rome, and thus the fate of the world, rested upon the Kings of the Franks.

Though his purpose is conservative and though he attempts to postpone the imminent arrival of Antichrist, Adso cannot settle for the indeterminate postponement found in Haimo. To leave the hour of Antichrist to the inscrutable hand of providence is impossible. Without this option, Adso's conservative impulse brings him to tie the eschaton to the fate of the Frankish royal house. As Verhelst argues, this connection produces a "dangerous" conservatism, as it places all eschatological hope in a dynasty whose future is by no means secure.[113] But perhaps it is the only plausible conservatism available to the abbot of Montier-en-Der.

113. Verhelst, *Fear,* [10].

And, indeed, perhaps such conservatism is the source of the treatise's success. The abundance of manuscripts of Adso's text (or variants thereof) testifies to its popularity at or around the millennium.[114] For Adso, Antichrist is not only a real historical figure (he is for Haimo, too), but he stands just over the horizon at the end of the reigning dynasty. The threat is not immediate, but it is, to a degree, imminent and real. This combination of conservative forestallment and historical specificity proved fertile for further speculation about the identities of the last world emperor and Antichrist. And such speculation was abundant as the Christian world hovered on the brink of the year 1000.

We see in the relationship between Haimo and Adso the ways in which the 2 Thessalonians tradition was exploited and applied to fit a particular occasion of crisis or anxiety. The function of the commentary tradition is to preserve and synthesize the Fathers; Adso takes this wisdom and applies it to his concrete situation. The commentary tradition stands as a sort of reservoir of orthodox apocalypticism awaiting pastoral or political use or abuse. Commentaries are intimately related to the phenomena of medieval apocalypticism, but rarely are they implicated in concrete prediction of the coming end. Their scholastic and pedagogical aims trump political exigencies.

The apparent exception to this rule is found in a 2 Thessalonians commentary contemporary with Adso, the work of Thietland of Einsiedeln. Only two manuscripts of this text survive, testimony to its relative obscurity in the medieval tradition of commentary. But its curious use and rejection of the commentary tradition that precedes it, all in the interest of addressing current concerns, make it worth examining, evidence at least of the path not taken in the majority of commentaries.

Thietland was abbot of the monastery of Einsiedeln in Swabia

114. Verhelst refers to 171 manuscripts that he has examined. This includes the variants attributed to Alcuin, Albuinus, Anselm, et al.

from ca. 958 to ca. 964. He is known to have written commentaries
on several works of Paul: Romans, 1 Corinthians, Ephesians, Philippians, and 1 and 2 Thessalonians. Of these, the first four are largely
derivative of the commentaries of Atto of Vercelli (d. 960). The
Thessalonian commentaries draw heavily upon Haimo and Augustine, for the most part excerpting chunks of text from each to address particular verses. Insofar as Thietland comments strictly upon
the letter of 2 Thessalonians, his work is unremarkable. He identifies the "rebellion" in 2:3 with "a departure of the nations from the
Roman Empire." Antichrist, the "Man of Sin," is fully a man, opposed to Christ in all things. Thietland quotes Augustine when he
addresses Antichrist and the temple in 2:4, suggesting that this verse
might be understood to mean Antichrist will pose "as the temple"
(in templum). With Augustine, too, he confesses ignorance about the
"mystery of iniquity now at work" (2:7). Thus far, Thietland follows
a rather traditional path of spiritual and realist readings introduced
in counterpoint.

However, when he comes to 2:8, he departs from the path:
"There follows, '. . . and then that wicked one will be revealed.' In
certain copies, 'shall be loosed' is found. Therefore, we must see
whether he is to be revealed or loosed."[115] What follows is a careful
exploration of the "binding and loosing of the serpent" in Revelation 20, a crossing of Revelation and 2 Thessalonians unprecedented
in the tradition of 2 Thessalonians commentaries. His sources are
again both Augustine and Haimo, but now from the Apocalypse
comments of each, and he also departs from their spirit as he does
so. Whereas Augustine and Haimo had treated this section in a de-

---

115. "Sequitur: Et tunc revelabitur ille iniquus: In quibusdam exemplaribus inven-
itur 'solvetur' Unde ergo revelandus aut solvendus sit videndum est." Thietland of Einsiedeln, In Epistolam II ad Thessalonicenses, MS Einsiedeln 38:184ᵛ. Translated by
Steven R. Cartwright, in Second Thessalonians: Two Early Medieval Apocalyptic Commentaries, ed. Steven R. Cartwright and Kevin L. Hughes (Kalamazoo: Medieval
Institute Publications, 2001), 54. My thanks to Steven Cartwright for his transcrip-
tion of the Thietland MS.

terminedly anti-millenarian fashion, Thietland offers the following comment: *"Mille annos ultimam hanc saeculi partem vocat quaerit a Domini nostri passione et nostra redemptione usque ad antichristi adventum. Millenarium ergo numerum pro totius huius temporis posuit perfectione."* I have quoted the Latin here because Thietland's Latin is rough and ambiguous, and the translation matters most here. The first part is relatively straightforward: "He calls this last part of the age, which will have run from the passion of our Lord and our redemption to the coming of Antichrist, 'a thousand years.'" But what follows is more ambiguous. Thietland may be rendering the millennium as a *symbolic* number for the consummation: "He *posits* the 'millennium' as the number for the completion of all this time." Alternatively, he may be predicting the time of the end: "He *fixes* the millennium as the number for the completion of all this time."[116] If this latter is the case, as Cartwright has taken it, Thietland foresees a time in the not-too-distant future—less than a century!—in which the devil will be loosed upon the world: one thousand years from the Passion of the Lord, or ca. 1033.

If the former is true, then Thietland is consistent with Augustine throughout. So, with Augustine, Thietland sees the "binding" of the devil as the limitation of his power to the wicked, who are "the abyss" (Rv 20:3) into which he is cast. Unfortunately, this is the only textual reference that begins to indicate predictive imminence, so it is not clear that Thietland can be invoked as a prophet of the apocalyptic year 1000.[117] Before returning to the text of 2 Thessalonians, Thietland offers an interpretation of Gog and Magog from Revelation 20 that, like Augustine, but with his own philological invention, he claims refers not to some alien tribes or nations, but to the

116. *"Mille annos ultimam hanc saeculi partem vocat quaerit a Domini nostri passione et nostra redemptione usque ad antichristi adventum. Millenarium ergo numerum pro totius huius temporis posuit perfectione."* Einsiedeln 38:185r. Cartwright, 56.

117. Given the paucity of other evidence in the text, I am inclined to think, *pace* my colleague and collaborator Steven Cartwright, that Thietland is, in fact, Augustinian in his symbolic interpretation of the millennium.

wicked among the Church. Gog, he says, means "covered," and Magog is "uncovered." The former refers to the wicked who are hidden
among the ranks of the faithful; the latter refers to the devil himself,
who will be revealed within the wicked before the Second Coming.
After this, Thietland returns to the text of 2 Thessalonians, and the
rest of the commentary is unremarkable.

The evidence from these two texts may suggest an intensifica-
tion of apocalyptic enthusiasm as the years 1000 and 1033 approached. If *psychological* imminence was a persistent presence
throughout the early and high Middle Ages, Adso and perhaps Thietland show that the tradition of *predictive* imminence either survives until the approach of the first millennium or revives in light of
the date. Certainly, the popularity of Adso's text suggests that this
predictive tradition appealed to readers around the millennium and
thereafter (a great number of the Adso manuscripts date from the
twelfth and thirteenth centuries).

However, to suggest that predictive apocalypticism may have ex-
perienced a revival in the tenth century is not to disprove or discred-
it the argument we have pursued throughout. Rather, the two are
largely compatible. The non-predictive apocalyptic tradition that we
see synthesized and passed on in Haimo and Rabanus Maurus is the
condition for the possibility of the existence of texts such as those of
Adso and Thietland. The tradition of commentary preserves the
apocalyptic structure of time and history, preserves both the "already" and the "not yet" of Christian eschatology, without pinning
that tradition on one particular figure or sequence of events. When
events or the calendar provokes anxiety about and/or enthusiasm
for the coming end, scholars such as Adso turn to the commentary
tradition for guidance. More generally, then, psychological imminence is not opposed to predictive imminence; rather, it may be the
condition for the possibility of the latter in the early Middle Ages.
Psychological imminence perpetuates and keeps fresh the energy of
eschatological conviction, saturating the medieval imagination with
symbols of the end. The imagination thus constituted can shape the

perception of a particular turn of events in politics or history or the approach of a significant date on the calendar. The ambiguity of the end can yield for a time to the end of ambiguity; the end is coming at a certain discernible time. When these particular stimuli pass, ambiguity returns, and the eschatological imagination reverts to the posture of constant watchfulness, which, as McGinn suggests, is "a more pervasive, if necessarily somewhat diffuse, power"[118] in the Middle Ages.

Conclusion

The early Middle Ages saw the integration of apocalyptic traditions into a synthetic eschatological vision, ambiguous about the end, but powerful and pervasive in its ambiguity. The 2 Thessalonians tradition bears witness to the dynamic exchange between the realist and spiritual accounts of apocalyptic thinking to preserve an eschatology that is neither wholly de-historicized nor dangerously precise. Such a synthesis preserved the moral power of the apocalyptic tradition in the vision of the "body of Antichrist," those wicked present in the midst of the Church who are, as Rabanus says, "opposed to Christ" in their failure to observe a "holy life." But the persistence of this moral power relies upon its connection to the culmination and embodiment of human evil, the historical figure of Antichrist. So the synthesis is not simply a formal function of the harmonizing tendencies of early medieval theologians, but instead is necessary to the substantive generation of a vital theological eschatology, a productive tension between the "already" and the "not yet." Such a productive tension is carried on and enhanced through the more sophisticated tools of the theological science in the eleventh and twelfth centuries, and it is to these we now turn.

118. McGinn, "End of the World," 63.

CHAPTER 5

SEEING THE
ADVERSARY AFRESH

Paul and Antichrist in Early Scholastic Exegesis,

1000–1160

The year 1000 came and went without the apocalyptic denoue-
ment. And yet the years after 1000 saw the release of tremendous
energy expressed in various social movements such as the Peace of
God, the Truce of God, and the "Gregorian Reform." Seeking a
cause for such broad-based social momentum is perhaps unwise,
and many have demonstrated that there are social, environmental,
and economic factors that contribute to this fundamental but complex change in medieval social and intellectual life.[1] But one cannot
dismiss apocalypticism's role among these other factors in fueling
reformist enthusiasm across the spectrum of religious opinion.[2] If
the shadow of the Second Coming seemed to grow all the more

1. For a survey of the variety of such developments as they relate to the Peace
of God, see Thomas Head and Richard A. Landes, eds., *The Peace of God: Social Violence and Religious Response in France around the Year 1000* (Ithaca: Cornell University Press, 1992), esp. 1–40.

2. See Richard A. Landes, *Relics, Apocalypse, and the Deceits of History* for a detailed discussion of the pivotal years around 1000. An alternative explanation of
events around the year 1000, in response to Landes, is found in Sylvain Gouguenheim, *Les fausses terreurs de l'an mil.*

dark as the millennium approached, one might imagine that apocalyptic hope and anxiety, never absent from the medieval imagination, intensified. Such intensity may have built into a sort of psychic
pressure that, when the end did not come, was released into the passion for *reformatio* that in essence creates the "High" Middle Ages.[3]
This would suggest that one could count the birth of scholastic theology among the fruits of medieval apocalypticism, which makes
the exploration of their intersection in 2 Thessalonians commentaries all the more intriguing.

For it is in the latter half of the eleventh century, after what
seems to be a hiatus in scholarly attention to the Bible, that students
in Rheims, Bec, and Laon, trained in the liberal arts, turn with a
fresh critical eye to examine the biblical text. At Bec, Lanfranc's
work represents a new moment in the organization of knowledge
on the page with the glossed-text format. In Rheims, the scriptural
commentaries attributed to Bruno integrate careful rhetorical study
and the glossed-text format with the judicious use of the *quaestio*
method of theological analysis. Finally, at Laon, the work of
Anselm, his brother Ralph, and their students succeeded in gathering an unprecedented amount of information into a single glossed
bible that would become the authoritative presentation of the exegetical tradition, the *Glossa Ordinaria*. This generation of scholars,
Artur Michael Landgraf's "early scholastics," found in biblical commentary, and in Pauline exegesis in particular, the fertile ground
from which to produce a new approach to intellectual inquiry itself,
the scholastic method.

Lanfranc of Bec: The Early Glossed Text

Lanfranc of Bec, later of Canterbury, is perhaps most famous for
his celebrated student and successor, Anselm of Bec/Canterbury.[4]

3. For an alternative account of the cycle of apocalyptic thinking, see Richard
A. Landes, "On Owls, Roosters, and Apocalyptic Time."

4. The best resource for Lanfranc's life and work is Margaret Gibson, *Lanfranc*

As Anselm is considered the "first scholastic theologian,"[5] one might consider Lanfranc to be the "father" of scholastic theology. But Lanfranc was not a theologian by training. Born to a rich family in Pavia ca. 1010, Lanfranc was educated in the finest school traditions of the tenth century. He was an accomplished teacher of the *trivium*, perhaps at Avranches, before he was converted to the religious life and entered the monastery of Bec in 1042. Lanfranc's teaching of the liberal arts attracted students to the monastery school at Bec throughout the 1040s. But in the 1050s he made a decided turn toward Scripture, applying the skills of the *trivium* (grammar, dialectic, rhetoric) to the sacred text and composing a complete commentary on the Pauline epistles ca. 1055–1060. The same Wiliram who lamented the dearth of biblical scholarship in Germany notes,

I know a man in France by the name of Lanfranc, who used to be a very eminent dialectician; now he has turned to the learning of the church, and has taxed the wits of many by his subtle exegesis of the Psalter and the Pauline Epistles.[6]

Even Pope Nicholas II took note of Lanfranc's change of direction, albeit with a certain ambivalence:

We send you our beloved sons to cherish and instruct in dialectic and rhetoric . . . but if (as we have heard) you are taken up with the study of the bible, even so we enjoin you to teach them.[7]

---

of Bec (New York: Oxford University Press, 1978). See also her earlier articles, "Lanfranc's 'Commentary on the Pauline Epistles,'" *Journal of Theological Studies* n.s. 22 (1971): 86–112; and "Lanfranc's Notes on Patristic Texts," *Journal of Theological Studies* n.s. 23 (1971): 435–50. Also of interest are the comments of R. W. Southern on Lanfranc's role in Anselm's development in *Saint Anselm: A Portrait in a Landscape* (New York: Cambridge University Press, 1990), 39–65.

5. Artur Michael Landgraf, *Einführung in die Geschichte der theologischen Literatur der Frühscholastik* (Regensburg: Gregorius-Verlag, 1948), 13.

6. "*Unum in Francia comperi Lantfridum nomine, antea maxime valentem in dialectica. Nunc ad ecclesiastica contulit studia, et in Epistolis Pauli et in Psalteris multorum sua subtilitate exacuisse ingenia.*" Martène et Durand, *Vetera Scripta Ampl. Collect.* (Paris, 1724), i. 507 B–C. Quoted and translated in Margaret Gibson, "Lanfranc's 'Commentary,'" 86.

7. P. Jaffé, *Regesta Pontificum Romanorum*, 2nd ed., 2 vols., ed. G. Wattenbach,

In fact, Lanfranc had not really abandoned the liberal arts; rather, he had decided to apply them to what was for him a new subject: Holy Scripture. In this rhetorical and grammatical approach to the biblical text, Lanfranc echoes the practice of the Auxerre masters of the ninth century, but with him and his contemporaries, the practice is rediscovered and reinvigorated.[8] Indeed, such analytic strategies are fundamentally recast through their use in a new tool in reading technology, the glossed text.[9]

The original format of Lanfranc's commentary on the Pauline epistles arranged the page in three columns. The first column contains the Pauline text, wide-ruled and in a large hand. Lanfranc's brief comments are written in the interlinear space. The second, narrow column, contains the "key," as it were, to a set of notations made within the text and referring to the individual glosses in the third column, narrow-ruled in a much smaller hand.[10] The marginal glosses are an amalgam of patristic theological excerpts and Lanfranc's own longer notes. Lanfranc weaves all three of these ele-

S. Löwenfeld, F. Kaltenbrunner, P. Ewald (Leipzig: Veit, 1885, 1887), 4446. Cited in Gibson, *Lanfranc of Bec*, 39.

8. In fact, Margaret Gibson has shown that one of Lanfranc's predecessors, Hermann von Reichenau (d. 1054), composed a commentary on Paul in the same gloss format. This text survives in only one manuscript, MS St. Gall StiftsB. 64, which I have not consulted.

9. The method of glossing, that is, of supplying a biblical text with interlinear and marginal notations, certainly predates Lanfranc. Insular (Irish-influenced) manuscripts of the Bible from the eighth and ninth centuries (e.g., Zürich Staatsarchiv AG 19, no. XII [viii–ix cent.]: 2ff.) are glossed. What is distinctive about the gloss of Lanfranc and, especially, the later *Glossa Ordinaria*, is the way these texts are *designed* to include both the biblical text and the gloss. Whereas the glosses in these early manuscripts appear to have been inserted into an already prepared biblical text, the page in the eleventh- and twelfth-century glosses is prepared with two separate rulings: one for the biblical text and one for the glosses. It is this comprehensive plan for the *mise en page* that marks what Illich calls the "scholastic breakthrough." For a brief prehistory of the *Glossa Ordinaria*, see Guy Lobrichon, "Une nouveauté: les gloses de la Bible." *Le moyen age et la Bible*, eds. Pierre Riche and Guy Lobrichon (Paris: Beauchesne, 1984), 95–114.

10. Gibson, *Lanfranc of Bec*, 54ff.

ments into what one might call the first scholastic Pauline commentary.

The commentary is scholastic in the sense that it organizes so much exegetical material in a very small area. Each gloss is clearly set apart from the next, giving the reader a clear sense of the diversity of opinion within a particular exegetical tradition. Whereas in the great work of Haimo, diverse opinions are synthesized upon the page into a continuous running text, the gloss's obvious plurality supplies the reader with ample opportunity for disputation and distinction, two hallmarks of scholastic method. This new systematic approach to organizing information on the written page is what Ivan Illich has called "the dawn of scholastic reading."[11] For Illich, this is the very important moment in the history of Christian learning when, "after centuries of Christian reading, the page was suddenly transformed from a score for pious mumblers into an optically organized text for logical thinkers."[12] Illich unfairly diminishes pre-scholastic reading practices, but he is right to perceive a change in approach to the page; the glossed text does provide a new type of logical optical organization for biblical commentary, and this innovation made the glossed text a scholastic tool for several generations.[13]

11. Illich, 1.

12. Illich, 2.

13. That biblical glosses were produced and re-produced in monastic *scriptoria* makes them no less "scholastic" in this technical sense. Rather, it suggests if anything that our now-traditional distinctions between "monastic" and "scholastic" theology need careful nuance. I do not intend to denigrate in any way the profound contribution of Jean Leclerq, O.S.B., to the development of different "types" of theological inquiry (Jean Leclerq, O.S.B., *The Love of Learning and the Desire for God: A Study of Monastic Culture,* 3rd ed., trans. Catharine Misrahi [New York: Fordham University Press, 1982]). Rather, I want to call attention to Dom Leclerq's insistence that scholasticism is above all a *method* involving the introduction of logical and analytic tools such as the *quaestio* to theology. By inference, monastic theology, too, is a method, not a culture or a location. (Leclerq himself does not state this parallel explicitly and seems to tend toward the identification of monastic theology and monastic culture—the product of the "interior"

Lanfranc's Gloss on 2 Thessalonians

Lanfranc's commentary on 2 Thessalonians consists of his short interlinear glosses, patristic excerpts in the margins, and his own longer marginal glosses.[14] The interlinear glosses are usually brief phrases meant to clarify the structure and sense of Paul's text. For example, Lanfranc inserts a clause to make 2 Thessalonians 2:3 grammatically correct. The Latin verse reads:

Quoniam nisi venerit discessio primum [since unless the desertion will have come first]

Lanfranc inserts an independent clause after *Quoniam* to support the dependent clause introduced by *nisi:*

Quoniam non erit dies Domini, *nisi venerit discessio primum* [since *it will not be the Day of the Lord* unless the desertion will have come first][15]

This insertion both makes the sentence grammatically correct and fixes a certain meaning to Paul's teaching: The "falling away" and the advent of Antichrist will precede the Day of the Lord. Lanfranc uses these brief glosses throughout the text to "clean up" the grammar so the text reads smoothly with no possibility of confusion about the literal sense.

---

monastic schools.) Thus, properly speaking, monks can and do engage in scholastic theology or monastic theology, depending on the particular method used or the genre in which they choose to write. This rigorous distinction is all the more necessary when addressing the eleventh and twelfth centuries, when much of the "scholastic," "pre-scholastic," or, perhaps best, "early scholastic" [*frühscholastik*, as in A. Landgraf] theology is done by monks such as Lanfranc. See Landgraf, *Einführung in die Geschichte* .

14. I have used the edition produced by the Maurist Luc d'Archery in 1648, reprinted in Migne's PL 150.339–46, which Gibson finds reliable on the whole. (Gibson, "Lanfranc's 'Commentary,'" 95.) The Migne edition inserts the interlinear glosses into Paul's text, then gives the marginal glosses in a separate section below.

15. PL 150.342 (interlinear). NB, the interlinear glosses are not arranged in Migne's usual column form, so I will simply cite the approximate column and designate it interlinear, as above.

The longer theological glosses are mostly patristic, drawn from "Ambrose" and Augustine. The "Ambrose" Lanfranc cites is a compilation of Ambrosiaster's commentary on Romans through 2 Corinthians, Theodore of Mopsuestia's commentary on Galatians through Philemon, and John Chrysostom's Hebrews commentary.[16] His citations from Augustine are taken from Florus of Lyons's Augustinian *florilegium* on Paul. However, where Florus sees fit to cite the entire passage he thinks relevant to the scriptural text in question, Lanfranc reduces the citations to only that portion (usually one or two sentences) that he finds essential to comment on the verse.[17] The glosses from both patristic authorities demonstrate Lanfranc's penchant for pruning vigorously. Since the gloss is first and foremost a continuous edition of a scriptural text, Lanfranc pares the patristic material down so that all the material for a single verse or chapter becomes manageable and accessible on one page.

Into this assortment of patristic material, Lanfranc intersperses his own glosses, and these are often—but not always—marked with his own name. They follow the patristic comments on particular verses in an almost antiphonal fashion, suggesting that Lanfranc intends to let the authorities have their say and then offer his own opinion. Lanfranc's marginal glosses do not differ substantively from his interlinear glosses; both seem to address issues of grammar and questions of meaning. It seems that only length distinguishes the marginal gloss from the interlinear.[18] For Lanfranc, grammatical sense and theological meaning go hand in hand.

16. Gibson, "Lanfranc's 'Commentary,'" 101 n.2. Lanfranc apparently possesses a manuscript of the Ambrosiaster/Theodore composite that is independent of Rabanus, since Rabanus's source has Ambrosiaster on Galatians, while Lanfranc uses Theodore. In Lanfranc, Antiochene exegesis perseveres in the Latin West, a faint, anonymous, but enduring voice in the Pauline exegetical tradition.

17. Gibson, "Lanfranc's 'Commentary,'" 96.

18. That there is no generic distinction between marginal and interlinear glosses is not unique to Lanfranc; in fact, it seems to be a characteristic of the gloss format in general, as Beryl Smalley noted for the *Glossa Ordinaria*. Smalley, *Study of the Bible*, 53, 56.

Lanfranc begins his commentary with a summary of Theodore's *argumentum*, but he includes only two of the three purposes Theodore identifies in the letter. For Lanfranc, "Paul writes this letter first to praise them; then he instructs them not to think that the consummation of the ages is upon them and teaches them about Antichrist."[19] Lanfranc leaves out the third purpose, Paul's intention to correct those in the community that have gone astray. For Lanfranc, it seems, the letter is primarily about Antichrist and the end of time. He supports this conclusion with a comment of his own in which he connects this letter's composition to concerns arising from 1 Thessalonians' discussion of the resurrection:

> In the previous letter, he spoke about the day of judgment: *we who are remaining may not precede those who have fallen asleep.* Now, however, lest they think what is future to refer to their own time, he determines when that future event may come, because if he had not, either they may believe an error, or those who follow them might no longer expect the day of judgment.[20]

For Lanfranc, Paul composed this letter to keep apocalyptic enthusiasm at bay and, at the same time, to keep apocalyptic hope—properly understood—alive.

Lanfranc's glosses on the first chapter of the letter are relatively few. The interlinear comments are mostly grammatical, attempting to clarify the referents of relative pronouns or supplying participles and other verb forms that the text assumes are understood. Occasionally, he gives a cross-reference to another passage in Scripture; for example, on 2 Thessalonians 1:11, "that God may find you worthy of his calling and complete in power every good resolve and work of faith," Lanfranc paraphrases the deponent verb *dignaretur*

---

19. "*Scribit hanc epistolam primum collaudans eos; deinde instruit eos ne existement incumbere sibi consummationem temporum, et de Antichristo.*" PL 150.339C. Cf. Swete, 42.

20. "*In superiori Epistola dixit de die iudicii: Nos qui residui sumus, non praeveniemus eos qui dormierunt. Modo autem, ne isti suo tempore existiment hoc futurum, determinat quando sit futurum, quod nisi fecisset, vel falsus esse crederetur, vel dies iudicii a posterioribus amplius non expectaretur.*" PL 150.340C–341A.

with the active *dignos faciet*, "make you worthy," emphasizing God's gracious initiative. He then quotes Matthew 25:34 as evidence of the type of "calling" to which Paul refers: "Come, blessed of my Father."[21] Lanfranc seems to think of all these events—God's call, the fulfillment of "every good resolve and work of faith"—as eschatological events more than present realities.

The marginal glosses on the first chapter are brief. After quoting from Florus's Augustine on judgment and punishment—the just suffer for their purification and the damned suffer in their damnation—Lanfranc includes his own comment on the notion that the tribulations of the just are an example of the future punishment God will hand out to the reprobate:

for the one who judges so horribly, and yet justly, those who sin and already lament their sins, how justly he will judge those who never lament their sin and still do not cease sinning.[22]

By this interpretation, Lanfranc allows that the persecutions suffered by the Thessalonians are initiated justly by God as punishment for their former sins. The punishment of those who have repented from sin is a warning of the more serious punishment promised to those who do not repent, but both afflictions reflect God's just judgment. This interpretation is qualified only slightly by Lanfranc's brief concession of another possibility. Perhaps, he writes, "the works of men are an example, that is, the demonstration *(ostensio)* that God is just in giving good things to the good and bad things to the bad."[23] Here persecutions are demonstrations of human injustice, and, by contrast, God's justice. Lanfranc is traditional in his identification of the topic of the first chapter, and he summarizes that tradition with quotes from both Augustine and "Ambrose" /

21. "*Hac: Venite, benedicti patris mei.*" PL 150.341 (interlinear).
22. "*qui enim sic horribiliter, et tamen iuste, iudicat eos qui peccant, et prius peccata plangunt, quam iuste iudicabit eos qui nunquam plangunt, et tamen peccare non desinunt.*" PL 150.341B.
23. "*Vel, opera hominum sunt exemplum, id est, ostensio, quod Deus iustus sit, in dando bonis bona, malis mala.*" PL 150.341B.

Theodore. But his own comments, based upon a frank, literal interpretation of the Latin word *exemplum,* are a departure from the tradition's usual circumlocution. For Lanfranc, the grammatical sense can trump the theological tradition. This is not to say that either the tone or the end result of Lanfranc's commentary is iconoclastic. In fact, his exegesis of the second chapter is more or less traditional. Roughly half of the glosses are taken from Augustine and Theodore. He first quotes Augustine's comments from the *City of God* identifying the *refuga* of verse 3 with Antichrist. Then he offers his own gloss, by far his longest contribution to the commentary. Lanfranc begins again with a grammatical point: *discessio* is the antonym of *accessio:*

It is impossible for there to be a *discessio* where there has not already been an *accessio.* Thus it is necessary for the accession to be complete. For it is said, "All nations will be blessed in your seed," and "All nations will come to him."[24]

The point of departure is innovative: Lanfranc is the first in the exegetical tradition to use these opposites (or complements) to discuss the events of the end. But the point of doctrine is traditional: An *accessio* is an addition that makes something complete. By citing the Scriptures from Genesis and John, Lanfranc links this term to the worldwide spread of the Gospel. Since the early Church, Christians have asserted that Jesus' charge to "Make disciples of all nations," must be accomplished before the day of the Lord, and Lanfranc picks up this theme. He continues:

When this is complete, the *discessio* will begin, as it is written, "Charity will grow cold from the abundance of iniquity." When the *discessio* is complete, as if the beast were already prepared, it will be opportune for the one who will sit [in the temple] to appear, that is, for the Son of Perdition to be revealed.[25]

---

24. "*Impossibile est discessionem fieri ubi accessio prius facta non sit; necesse est ergo, inquit, impleri accessionem, de qua dictum est, 'In semine tuo benedicentur omnes gentes'; et: Venient omnes gentes ad eum.*" PL 150.342B.

25. "*Quo impleto incipiet discessio, de qua dicitur: Ex abundatia iniquitatis*

In this passage, he connects 2 Thessalonians to the two other major apocalyptic texts from the New Testament. With the synoptic "little apocalypse" Lanfranc argues that the end time will be marked by the increase of wickedness and the cooling of charity (Mt 24:12). This he connects with the arrival of the Beast from Revelation 13.[26] 2 Thessalonians thus presents Lanfranc with a comprehensive summary of the apocalyptic teaching given throughout the Bible.

For Lanfranc, the "growing cold" of charity is the definitive sign of the end.[27] Charity itself restrains Antichrist's coming; as it weakens, Antichrist draws near. "For what place would [Antichrist] have found in the time of the apostles, the martyrs, the confessors, or any time when charity does not grow cold?"[28] This is not to say that thus far the church has been free of iniquity. Lanfranc is careful to point out that "certain first-fruits of the desertion *(discessio)* appeared at the very beginning of the *accessio,* when some pretended that they were disciples of Christ."[29] Antichrist will gather those within the Church who practice iniquity, and thus the faithful should cling to their religion and remain in it until Antichrist is revealed. "But for me," says Lanfranc, "[I am] in a soul doomed to death, wherefore it would be well to know after how many years the *accessio,* and conse-

---

refrigescet charitas, quia discessione completa, quasi iam parato iumento, opportunum erit adesse sessorem, id est, revelari filium perditionis." PL 150.342C.

26. It is unclear to which "beast" Lanfranc refers, the first from the sea (Rv 13:1) or the second from the earth (Rv 13:11). In most Christian apocalyptic writing, the first beast is usually Antichrist, and the second beast is usually his prophet.

27. This was a favorite image of Jerome, too, although it does not appear that Lanfranc is directly dependent on any one Hieronymian text. For Jerome's use of the phrase, see, e.g., *Commentarii in Isaiam,* Sancti Hieronymi Presbyteri Opera, CCSL 73, ed. Marcus Adriaen (Turnhout: Brepols, 1963), 6.14; *Commentarii in prophetas minores,* Sancti Hieronymi Presbyteri Opera, CCSL 76–76A, ed. Marcus Adriaen (Turnhout: Brepols, 1969–70), *In Michaeam* 2:7.

28. *"Quem enim locum inventurus erat tempore apostolorum, martyrum, confessorum, vel non refrigeratae charitatis?"* PL 150.342C.

29. *"in ipsis principiis accessionis apparent quaedam primitiae discessionis, ut quidam se Christi discipulos simulent."* PL 150.343A.

quently the desertion, and so at last the Day of the Lord, will come."[30] Lanfranc expresses considerable anxiety about the end. He longs to know when the end will come, but seems resigned to his ignorance. Lanfranc's frank intimacy is a concise example of the "psychological imminence" we have found implicit throughout the tradition. His anxiety comes not from knowing when the end will come, but from not knowing.

This lengthy comment, inserted after verse 2, is actually a summary comment on the entire second chapter; the rest of the glosses are small comments on particular verses or words. The glosses drawn from Theodore and Augustine on the second chapter are brief summary excerpts from their texts. From Theodore, Lanfranc takes the notion that the desertion is the time when almost everyone deserts the holiness of life, an opinion sympathetic with his own view above. From Augustine, he cites the argument that Antichrist will pose "as the temple," meaning as the Church. Noteworthy by its absence is Augustine's clear preference for a spiritual interpretation of the body of Antichrist. Even in this passage, Lanfranc leaves out the notion that Antichrist is made up of the "evil and false ones" within the Church. The Augustinian glosses are edited in such a way that the substance of the spiritual interpretation disappears. What remain are opinions generally friendly to a future, events-oriented apocalyptic realist perspective.

When Lanfranc adds his own brief comments to these, they seem to offer supplements from the political tradition of interpretation, perhaps drawing on Haimo. For example, commenting on the "mystery of iniquity," Lanfranc notes in the interlinear gloss that the *discessio* is the "apostasy of the Roman Empire, or of the faith." In the marginal gloss, he comments that Antichrist has worked in Nero

---

30. *"mihi autem in anima moritura, quo valet rescire post quot annos prius esse fieri ascensionem* [sic], *consequenter descessionem* [sic], *et sic demum adesse diem Domini."* PL 150.343A. Although the Migne text reads *ascensionem*, I have interpreted it as *accessionem*, since this fits the context far better, while "ascension" makes little sense.

and the rest of his members. Soon thereafter, Lanfranc notes that
"'the one who now holds' designates the Roman Empire, in the destruction of which Antichrist will come." This very traditional comment shows nothing of Haimo's distinction between the end of the
empire and the end of the world, but Lanfranc continues with a passage that has notable similarity to the Haimo commentary, or perhaps even Adso's treatise on Antichrist: "For this is what he says:
This will remain only so long as the Roman emperor who holds this
world will hold it until he may be [taken away] from the midst."[31]
Whatever his source, Lanfranc clearly chooses to supplement the
spiritual interpretation of Augustine, the rather distinctive realist
comments of Theodore/"Ambrose," and even his own interpretation, with the common political Roman material. His matter-of-fact
statement of Rome's persistence in this otherwise Haimonean summary offers the suggestive possibility that we see in Lanfranc a rare
occasion in which Adso's treatise on Antichrist returns to influence
the commentary tradition.

If the long gloss that follows the second verse of the second
chapter reflects Lanfranc's own opinions on the coming of Antichrist, one wonders whether these brief comments on Rome show
his scholarly honesty in showing the plurality of authorities, or if, in
fact, these two options are not necessarily mutually inconsistent.
Might it be that the "cooling of charity" is coincident with the collapse of Rome? Lanfranc does not say so explicitly, but, as we will
see, his contemporary Bruno does precisely that. Whatever Lanfranc's opinion may be about the signs of the end, his commentary

31. "*Ut qui tenet Romanum designat imperium, quo destructo veniet Antichristus.
Hoc est enim quod dicit: tantummodo hoc restat ut Romanus imperator, qui tenet hunc
mundum, teneat donec de medio fiat.*" PL 150.344A. This gloss bears remarkable similarity to the language and content of Haimo's comment on the same passage: *Id
est hoc solummodo restat ut Nero, qui nunc tenet imperium totius orbis* (PL 117.781B).
Given the narrow textual evidence and given Lanfranc's own tendency to summarize others' comments in his own words, it is impossible to prove that Lanfranc
used Haimo's commentary, but the similarities are suggestive.

clearly affirms the apocalyptic realist perspective. Within this frame-work, Lanfranc has edited the Augustinian position carefully, so that it supports rather than contradicts his realist eschatology.

Lanfranc's comments on the third chapter are brief: As his intro-ductory statement indicates, he believes the letter to be concerned with apocalyptic themes, and the third chapter's more mundane topic does not hold his interest. For Lanfranc, Paul writes to the Thessalonians to teach them the definitive signs of the end. An-tichrist, a single historical figure, will come when the time is ripe, when charity has grown cold and iniquity abounds. What is distinc-tive about Lanfranc's interpretation is the sense of historical realism with a vague, unspecified interest in the political factors such as the fall of Rome and very little interest in the rebuilding of the temple in Jerusalem. His apocalyptic scenario is historical, but it is a "moral history" of the end times, inspired by a verse in the Gospels' "little apocalypse." This verse was a favorite apocalyptic trope of Jerome and Gregory,[32] but Lanfranc is the first to introduce it explicitly into the 2 Thessalonians commentary tradition.

In addition to this substantive innovation, Lanfranc's commen-tary testifies to a new form of biblical exegesis. While the gloss form dates at least from the Carolingian period, in Lanfranc it is further refined. Most of the interlinear glosses and many of the marginal glosses attributed to Lanfranc demonstrate the close textual work of a master of the *trivium* as he moves from grammatical clarity to doc-trinal speculation. Lanfranc adds to this intimate encounter with the text the theological authority of Augustine and "Ambrose" / Theo-dore and summary comments on the traditional role of Rome and her emperor in the eschatological events. While Carolingian au-thors had read their texts as carefully as Lanfranc and those who would follow him, they always read Scripture through the Fathers, arranging patristic opinion to achieve a particular reading of the text. Lanfranc, on the other hand, tries to understand the text

32. See n. 27 above for Jerome and Chapter 3 for Gregory.

through close grammatical analysis first and then to complete his interpretation with individual glosses summarizing the tradition.[33] It is this rediscovery of the direct encounter with the text and the formal distinction between this encounter and the supporting evidence of tradition that marks the first step toward scholastic interpretation.

Bruno the Carthusian

The Pauline commentary attributed to Bruno the Carthusian shows similar evidence of a direct encounter with the text, or what G. R. Evans has called "a fresh eye" for the material.[34] The work gives rather standard summaries of the tradition and uses a traditional format, but it also bears the marks of Bruno's own textual work and theological tendencies. Bruno gives his own original *argumentum* to each Pauline letter, identifying its purpose and method. He then proceeds in course of the commentary itself to give both a

33. See Lobrichon, "Une nouveauté: les gloses de la Bible," 105, for more on this point.

34. The authenticity of this commentary, which survives in whole or in part in twenty-two known manuscripts, has long been a subject of debate. Artur Michael Landgraf was among the first to dispute that it was an authentic work of Bruno's, citing what he thought were unreconcilable differences between it and Bruno's Psalms commentary; "Probleme des Schriftums Brunos des Kartäusers," *Collectanea Franciscana* 8 (1938): 542–90. Anselm Stoelen took up the challenge from Landgraf, carefully arguing point-for-point that, although certain interpretations were not identical in the two works, the differences were not irreconcilable. Anselm Stoelen, "Les commentaires scripturaires attribués à Bruno le Chartreux," *Recherches de théologie ancienne et médiévale* 25 (1958): 177–247. Having argued that the works were not necessarily incompatible either theologically or chronologically, Stoelen then intended to argue for the possibility of their consistent authorship. Unfortunately, Dom Stoelen died before he could complete this work, and no one (to my knowledge) has stepped in to continue the argument. I find the first half of his argument persuasive; even if Bruno is not the author of the work, it seems likely that it was written by one very near him. I will continue to refer to the author as "Bruno," and will introduce the historical circumstances of Bruno's life, believing that these are relevant even if only his influence and not his authorship lies behind the text.

clear sense of the traditional exegesis and his own—distinctively Gregorian—interpretation.

Bruno the Carthusian gained this title only late in life, when he abandoned his career to seek refuge in silent contemplation at Chartreux. We know very little about his birthplace and youth. We do know that he was an accomplished scholar at a young age, becoming director of studies at the Rheims school ca. 1056. He held this post for nearly twenty years until he was appointed chancellor of the Archdiocese of Rheims under Archbishop Manasses in 1075. Manasses was notorious for his resistance to the centralizing reforms of Pope Gregory VII. Bruno sided with the pope against Manasses, and in the bitter struggle that followed his bishop's defiance of the papal legate, Bruno was forced into exile from his archdiocese for roughly four years, 1076–1080. When he returned, Bruno may have lost the taste for Church disputes, since within a year he left to pursue a life of contemplation. By 1084, Bruno had established the Chartreux house at Grenoble with several other companions, and he lived in peaceful silence for six years. In 1090, Pope Urban II called Bruno away from his cloister to Rome to serve as the pope's advisor. When Bruno had fulfilled his obligation to the pope, he left the world again and established another house of contemplation in Calabria in 1091–92. Bruno spent the last decade of his life in Calabria, and he died in 1101.

The Pauline commentary has not been dated precisely, but given its style and tone, it is probably a school text, and thus may date from the earliest period in this long public life, from his years as director of studies at Rheims. Its significance as an example of early scholastic thought lies in its use of the *quaestio* in addressing theological issues in the letters, as Artur Landgraf has shown.[35] Beryl Smalley has also pointed to its importance as a predecessor to the Ordinary Gloss.[36] In their eyes, Bruno's exposition of Paul is an es-

35. Landgraf, *Einführung,* 40–41.

36. Smalley, "La *Glossa Ordinaria:* Quelques prédécesseurs d'Anselme de Laon," *Recherches de théologie ancienne et médiévale* 9 (1937): 365–400.

sential forerunner[37] of the twelfth-century achievement in theological method and biblical critical method.

Nevertheless, beyond the form, the 2 Thessalonians commentary suggests that a further contribution of Bruno's commentary is its striking originality of content. Bruno is far less inclined to cite patristic authorities explicitly or even to appropriate their ideas directly. Bruno, even more than Lanfranc, reads the text with Evans's "fresh eye," and only occasionally looks up from the text to see what others have said. The commentary—at least the commentary on 2 Thessalonians—is significant for the sense of Bruno's theological mind at work with the text that emerges from the commentary and makes it a significant contribution to the tradition.

Bruno on 2 Thessalonians: Textual Scholarship and Gregorian Eschatology

Bruno's commentary on 2 Thessalonians begins with his own prologue to the letter. Like Haimo and others before him, Bruno acknowledges the relationship between this letter and Paul's teaching in 1 Thessalonians about the resurrection. When the Thessalonians heard Paul's announcement that "we who are still living will be taken up to meet him in the air," they concluded that the Day of Judgment must be at hand. Bruno proceeds to identify the Apostle's rationale for writing in greater detail:

Paul decided to write to them, for if he did not clarify this ambiguity and they found that what they thought Paul had predicted did not occur even after Paul's days had passed, they may determine that Paul had lied in everything he had taught and thus fall off the path of truth that Paul had handed on to them.[38]

---

37. See Heiko Obermann, *Forerunners of the Reformation* (Philadelphia: Fortress Press, 1981), ch. 1, for a full discussion of the term "forerunner," a term that I find congenial to Landgraf's *frühscholastik* and Smalley's *predecesseurs*.

38. *"judicavit Paulus ideo iterum scribere eis, ne si non determinaretur haec ambiguitas, dum post dies Pauli invenirent non contigisse quod Paulum putabant sic praedixisse, et in hoc et in omnibus quae docuerat, arguerent Paulum de mendacio, et sic a via veritatis, quam illis tradiderat, recederent."* Bruno the Carthusian, *Expostio in Epistolas Pauli*, PL 153.413C.

Or, Bruno imagines with Paul, perhaps the devil could take advantage of the Thessalonians' credulity and appear in the air wearing a crown and claim to be Christ. Beyond this eschatological error, Paul also writes to correct the "curious and lazy" among the Thessalonians who had not heeded Paul's teaching and to praise the patience of those who had suffered persecution. Bruno summarizes:

These three things, persecution, the day of judgment, and the unrepentant are the *materia*. . . . And with this *intentio,* he [writes], that those who are suffering for Christ may persevere in their suffering, and that those who are afraid because they think that judgment is at hand may fear falsity, and that those who thus far have been unrepentant, even in shame, may find themselves cast out from communion with the others.[39]

Through rhetorical analysis, Bruno has identified the *materia,* or material of the letter, and the *intentio,* the purpose for writing. Bruno then proceeds with his exegesis of chapter 1.

For Bruno, Paul's intention in the first part of 2 Thessalonians is to "arm" *(armaverat)* those who are suffering persecution with patience. This he does first by praising their faith, which "has expanded beyond the tribulations" *(crescit super tribulationes).* These tribulations are an "example of the just judgment of God" (1:5), since

it is just for the saints to be tried so that they may be purified, and it is just for the wicked to have power over the just so that their wickedness may be complete.[40]

It is this explanation itself that "arms" the saints in Thessalonica to suffer with patience, since God "judges by the disposition and the end of the just" *(probat per affectus et finem utriusque justi et impii).* Even though they suffer "according to their intellect and will" *(etiam*

---

39. *"Haec tria, persecutiones, diem judicii, et illos incorrectos materiam habuit. . . . Ea utique intentione sic agit ut qui patiuntur pro Christo perseverantes sint in patiendo, et qui territi erant propinquitatem putantes judicii, non terreantur de falsitate, et qui adhuc incorrecti fuerant, saltem erubescendo, se a communione aliorum projectos resipiscant."* PL 153.414C.

40. *"Justum enim est sanctos tribulari, ut purificentur; impios potestatem habere in justos, ut impietatis eorum consummetur."* PL 153.415D.

secundum intellectum et voluntatem vestram patimini), the just must be armed with the knowledge of God's coming reward. For Bruno, it seems impossible to give fitting reasons *(idoneas causas)* for the suffering of the saints and the prosperity of the wicked. He paraphrases Psalm 72 from the Vulgate to this same effect: "I ponder so that I may understand why there is punishment here for the just and prosperity for the wicked, but to understand this is toil."[41] For Bruno, this difficulty points to a distinction between human judgment, which judges by appearances, and divine judgment, in which the just will truly be rewarded and the wicked will receive their punishment.

Bruno then notes a transition in Paul's argument from the nature of God's justice to the time of its arrival, "in the revelation of the Lord Jesus." Bruno interprets the details of the Second Coming in a curious mix of literal and nonliteral meanings. That Christ will come "from heaven" indicates that he will come in power. These words are spoken to the just, who rejoice in his power to overcome their persecutors. That he will come "in flame of fire" is spoken to the wicked, warning them of their being cast into the flames of punishment. This coming "in flame of fire" does not mean that Christ himself will be surrounded visibly with fire; rather, it is a figurative expression akin to when "some prince is said to come in fire and slaughter, since when he comes, many people are killed and many things are burned."[42] Likewise, the coming of the Lord signals the time when the flames of punishment will flare upon the wicked. Thus, most of the chapter is read as a figurative description of Christ's coming in judgment. And yet Bruno seems quite convinced that the fires of hell are real fire, and thus the wicked will really burn.

41. *"juxta illud quod ait David in eo psalmo Quam Bonus: Existimavi ut cognoscerem, quare hic poena justo, prosperitas tribuatur impio; sed hoc cognoscere labor est."* PL 153.416A.

42. *"In flamma ignis Christus dicitur venire, non quod flamma circa eum sit, sed quia eo adveniente consurget illa, sicut quilibet princeps dicitur venire in igne et occisione, quia eo adveniente et multi occiduntur et multa comburuntur."* PL 153.416D.

For Bruno, it seems, these words are consolation for the just and dire warning for the wicked, and thus Paul fulfills his first *intentio*.

Having discussed Paul's initial intention, Bruno now moves on to address the second: the fears of those who think that judgment is at hand. Paul urges the Thessalonians not to be shaken from their faith in any way, since the day of judgment will not come "unless first the *discessio* comes" (2:3). For the first time in this commentary, Bruno cites "Ambrosius" (here Ambrosiaster) explicitly on the nature of the *discessio*. But he does not quote Ambrosiaster directly; in fact, he expands Ambrosiaster's claim:

Ambrose calls this the *discessio*, since the Roman—that is, the Christian— Empire would endure and not be hindered, whithersoever it may be moved, whether to Constantinople or another place.[43]

This clearly extends beyond anything Ambrosiaster would have or could have said. For Ambrosiaster, the Roman Empire was at best an ambivalent force in the world, the home of Nero and Julian, and its downfall would signal the coming of Antichrist. But Bruno believes that the pseudo-Ambrose affirms the much later apocalyptic doctrine of the Christian Empire's translation *(translatio imperii)* and survival until the end. To this curious hyper-interpretation, Bruno opposes his own:

I say that this Christian Empire will be dissolved because there will be no kings who will punish heretics and destroy those who lay waste to the church, nor will the world be subject in the unity of the faith to the Roman pontiff, who holds dominion *(imperium)* spiritually. Thus the world will fall away from both Christian empires, both secular (such as kings), and spiritual (that is, the pope).[44]

43. "*Discessionem vocat Ambrosius, quoniam Romanum, id est Christianum imperium, quocunque mutetur, sive Constantinopoli sive alibi, nihil impedit solummodo Christianum duret imperium.*" PL 153.418D.

44. "*Quoniam, inquam, hoc Christianum imperium dissolvetur, quod nec reges erunt qui haereticos puniant, pervasores ecclesiarum destruant, nec Romano pontifici, qui spiritale imperium habet, mundus in unitate fidei subjectus erit, sed sic ab utroque Christiano imperio, et saeculari, sicut sunt reges, et spiritali, ut papa, mundus discedet.*" PL 153.418D.

Bruno brings to this text a very particular understanding of *imperi-um* in the world, the famed "two swords" theory of Pope Gelasius. The Christian "Empire" or "dominion" is not constituted by the sec- ular power of a single Christian Roman emperor, for Bruno is al- ways careful to refer to "kings," in the plural. The Christian *imperi-um* rests in the integration of the secular power of Christian kings with the spiritual authority of the pope (*pontifex* or *papa*, both in the singular). While Bruno gives no explicit rank or relationship of one to the other, it is clear that the secular power's role in the world is as protector of the Church, and thus the temporal power exists for the sake of the spiritual. This brief comment seems to partake of the theory developed by Cardinal Humbert of Silva Candida in the 1050s and later carried onto the throne of Peter by Hildebrand, Pope Gregory VII.[45] The subordination of the authority of the tem- poral to the spiritual is the hallmark of the Gregorian reform, with which Bruno had some sympathies.[46] Bruno posits with the tradi- tion that the *discessio* refers to the Roman *imperium*, but then he of- fers an innovative understanding of its twofold nature.

In the decline of this twofold *imperium*, Bruno envisions the ar- rival of the "first beast" of Revelation 13:

45. "Anyone then who wishes to compare the priestly and royal dignities in a useful and a blameless fashion may say that, in the existing church, the priesthood is analogous to the soul and the kingship to the body, for they cleave to one anoth- er and need one another and each in turn demand services and renders them one to another. It follows from this that, just as the soul excels the body and com- mands it, so too the priestly dignity excels the royal or, we may say, the heavenly dignity the earthly." Humbert of Candida Silva, *Libri III Adversus Simoniacos*, ed. F. Thanner, *MGH Libelli de Lite* I (Hanover: Impensis Bibliopolii Hahniani, 1891), 225. Excerpted and translated by Brian Tierney, *The Crisis of Church and State 1050–1300* (Toronto: University of Toronto Press, 1988), 41.

46. Judging from his bitter—and rather prolonged—controversy with Bishop Manasses in Rome, Bruno seems to have been quite committed to Pope Grego- ry's condemnation of simony. It is difficult to make an argument for any deeper sympathies than these, but the similarity shows at least further circumstantial evi- dence of the proximity in time and purpose of the Pauline commentary with Saint Bruno.

Then the first beast will be ready, the beast which Antichrist will mount. This beast is the assembly of the unfaithful who indeed are members of Antichrist and struggle together with so great a head for the destruction of the faith. And with this *discessio* accomplished, Antichrist will find his opportunity.[47]

The first beast is a spiritual body composed of the unfaithful. It is both the "body of Antichrist" and his horse. Bruno invokes the Gregorian sense of the spiritual body of Antichrist as those "unfaithful" who participate in Antichrist's work. But this spiritual body must be content to remain hidden for the present, for Antichrist's time has not yet come:

If he [Antichrist] would come into the world now, when the majority of people obey the Roman pontiff and when Christian kings thus far preserve the faith, he would have a beast to mount that was not ready, and he would not be able to proceed on his way. When there is such a *discessio*, the faith will survive on the throne of Peter, even if only in a few. For the saints are said to have obtained that prayer of Christ when he said to Peter, "I have prayed for you, Peter, that your faith may not fail."[48]

For Bruno, what one might call a *pax Gregoriana* holds off the coming of Antichrist. Should this balance be upset, the first beast may be in the ready, and Antichrist will come. Bruno is careful to note that even the Adversary will not overcome the faith of the pope, but the fate of the faithful beyond the See of Peter is not mentioned. Already, Bruno's first reading of the apocalyptic *discessio* (2:3) is a pro-

47. *"tunc primum paratum erit jumentum quod ascendet Antichristus, id est infideles, qui membra Antichristi certatim in destructione fidei cooperentur tali capiti, et facta hac discessione veniet Antichristus in sua opportunitate."* PL 153.419A. Note, this is a departure from the Tyconian interpretation of Rv 13, wherein the first beast is Antichrist proper, while the second beast is his spiritual body, his sinful "members." See, e.g., Haimo, *Expositio in Apocalypsin,* Liber IV, PL 117.1092D–1098C.

48. *"Sed si modo veniret mundo, obediente ex maiori parte Romano pontifici in unitate fidei, et regibus Christianis adhuc fidem tuentibus, imparatum haberet iumentum, quod ascenderet, et non suo modo proficere posset. Quando tamen futura est illa discessione, in sede beati Petri etsi in paucis, fides tamen perdurabit. Quod dicunt [sic] sancti obtinuisse illam orationem Christi, de qua Petro ait: 'Ego pro te rogavi, Petre, ut non deficiat fides tua.'"* PL 153.419A.

leptic commentary on "what restrains" in verse 7, and indeed on the whole chapter. Bruno makes clear that Antichrist's advent is staved off by the twofold *imperium* of pope and Christian kings.

Almost abruptly, Bruno moves on to another possible interpretation of the *discessio*. He concedes that others "are silent" *(taceant)* about the secular power and believe that the *discessio* refers only to believers "falling away" from the "unity of the faith." In this reading, doctrinal error alone prepares the way for "Antichrist, astride the beast who will ascend."[49] But he gives no further comment on this opinion, and, after his thorough consideration of the first reading, the latter seems shallow.

Bruno then rehearses the traditional exegesis of the "Man of Sin, the Son of Perdition." He is the Man of Sin just as Christ is the man of justice. He is the Son of Perdition since he is born for the destruction of his people just as Christ was born for the salvation of the just. Alluding to Haimo, Bruno notes that Antichrist will be extolled over the saints, who are called "gods," but not by their own design *(nuncupitave Deus dicitur)* and over God himself. He notes that the "temple" in verse 4 refers literally *(ad litteram)* to the temple in Jerusalem where Jesus taught, but he does not cite any spiritual or allegorical interpretation (a la Augustine) to balance it. He seems quite content to stick to the literal sense. Antichrist will appear in this temple claiming that he is the true God and that Christ was a deceiver and a magician.[50] Bruno then steps back from the apocalyptic scenario to put it in its proper perspective: Paul spoke of these things because they all must happen before the day of the Lord.[51]

---

49. *"Tunc veniet ascensor Antichristus strato iumento quod ascendat."* PL 153.419B.

50. *"asserens se esse verum deum, Christum autem fuisse deceptorem et magum."* PL 153.419C.

51. Commenting on v. 5, where Paul reminds the Thessalonians that he had told them all this before, Bruno notes that "it was Paul's custom initially to nourish the simplicity of the churches by teaching simple things, but, since they were accomplished, and since he wanted to leave, he first revealed to them the secrets of the mysteries of God." (*Mos enim erat Pauli in primis simplicitatem Ecclesiarum*

When Bruno moves on to discuss "what now restrains" Antichrist in 2:6, he simply reiterates his twofold *imperium* theory. "If he [Antichrist] would come while the unity of faith and the Christian empire endure, he would not be revealed in his own time."[52] Antichrist's opportunity comes only when Christian kings disappear and the faithful disobey the pope. For the present, Antichrist acts "through the members which precede this abominable head" *(per membra praecedentia hoc nefandum caput)*. Again, Bruno invokes this theme from Gregory the Great, but he does not explore it in any depth.

When Paul says that "what restrains" is "taken from the midst" (2:7), Bruno interprets this phrase in two ways. First, it may be an expression about the death of kings or popes, as when one says, "This dead person is taken from our midst—that is, removed from the community of humanity."[53] Or, Bruno offers, the phrase could refer to the overturning of morality and propriety in the time before Antichrist:

Just this restrains Antichrist, that who now holds the Christian empire and the unity of the faith may hold this for so long, until iniquity, which is now secret, may be taken from among the midst, that is from among the community, that just as now faith is in public *(in communi)* and iniquity in secret, so in the time of Antichrist faith may be in secret and iniquity in public, since his members will blush no more at acts of impurity than acts of purity, and those who have faith will be few.[54]

---

simplicibus fovere documentis; sed illis iam perfectis, eoque volente recedere, tunc primum revelabat illis occulta mysteriorum Dei. PL 153.419C). The signs of the end are hidden mysteries for the spiritually mature, and it is a sign of Paul's esteem for the Thessalonians' faith that he revealed these things to them so early. This brief comment seems to digress from the flow of Bruno's commentary, and it suggests that apocalyptic teachings are not for the simple believer, perhaps because they are too prone to misinterpretation.

52. *"Si durante unitate fidei et Christiano imperio, veniret, in suo non tempore revelaretur."* PL 153.419D.

53. *"Ab ea similitudine dictum est, qua dicimus: Hic homo mortuus factus est de medio, id est sublatus de communitate hominum."* PL 153.420A.

54. *"Tantummodo hoc moratur Antichristum ut qui nunc tenet Christianum imperium et unitatem fidei, teneat hoc tandiu, donec iniquitas, quae modo est sub mysterio, fiat*

The fall of the Christian kings and the unity of the faith will trigger a catastrophic reversal of morality and propriety. While the exegetical tradition has shared Bruno's conviction that evil will come to be glorified in the time of Antichrist, none have connected it so explicitly to the fall of the Christian *imperium*. Bruno's continued emphasis upon the proper ordering of temporal and spiritual power reiterates his commitment to the Gregorian position. The pope and the Christian kings keep Antichrist at bay.

After these finally fail and the world is turned upside down, Antichrist will appear, and Christ will kill him "with the breath of his mouth" (2:8). To understand Paul's meaning, Bruno turns to a patristic authority: "Blessed Ambrose says that Jesus will show himself to Antichrist, and, with a cry from Jesus, that evil one will be killed. But what he will cry out, we do not know."[55] Bruno here refers not to Ambrose or Ambrosiaster, but to Theodore of Mopsuestia, who says that "suddenly Christ will appear from heaven and, by just crying out, he will make [Antichrist] cease from his work."[56]

This passage shows that Bruno knows both Ambrosiaster and Theodore of Mopsuestia in some form. In reference to 2:3, he invokes the Ambrosiastrian understanding of the *discessio* by referring to "Ambrose," as I have discussed above. Here, in his only other explicit invocation of a patristic figure, his "Ambrose" can refer only to Theodore. For the first time in the exegetical tradition, elements of each "Ambrose" tradition are included within one commentary under the same name. The paucity of evidence of textual or linguistic dependence in Bruno's commentary precludes any strong argument about his use of sources. However, the latter passage is quoted by

---

de medio, id est de communitate, ut sicut modo fides in communi est, iniquitas in occulto, sic in tempore Antichristi fides sit in occulto, iniquitas in communi, quia membra eius non plus erubescent actum impietatis quam pietatis, et qui fidem habeant, paucissimi erunt." PL 153.420A.

55. *"Dicit beatus Ambrosius Iesum se ostensurum Antichristo, et clamante Iesu interficietur hic impius; sed quid clamabit, nescimus."* PL 153.420B.

56. *"et solummodo clamans cessare faciet ab opere, totum illum expendens. hoc enim dicit: spiritu oris, hoc est, voce,"* Swete, 57. See Chapter 2 in this volume.

Lanfranc in his commentary, and it is possible that Bruno takes the quote from there. It is at least plausible that he may possess a manuscript of the ubiquitous Ambrosiaster, whose political interpretive disposition he shares, and a copy of the recent Lanfranc commentary to supplement his reading. Whatever sources he uses, Bruno does not seem to consider the possibility of conflict or confusion, and simply moves on in the commentary. Bruno notes that "others" in the tradition have suggested that Michael the Archangel will kill Antichrist, but he dismisses these out of hand. "Certainly, Jesus will kill him, and then he will destroy him, since he is condemned in body and soul."[57]

According to Bruno, the letter's claim in 2:9 that Antichrist will come "by the work of Satan" is further evidence of his negative parody of Christ. For just as Christ came by the work of the Holy Spirit, so Antichrist will come by the work of the devil. His "lying signs and prodigies" are minor signs,[58] called "lying" either because they are illusory or because, though truly miraculous, they are designed to persuade people in a lie, that is, that Antichrist is God. Bruno simply cites the tradition's two possible answers and makes no effort to decide between them.[59] In all, Bruno seems far more concerned with the conditions of Antichrist's arrival than with his events and deeds once he has arrived.

In fact, the remainder of Bruno's treatment of chapter 2 gives a reliable but largely unremarkable summary of the traditional exegesis. Antichrist's works will seduce "those who are perishing," thus the unjust, but not the just. These unjust are perishing because they have rejected Christ (2:10). Bruno does not shrink from affirming the letter's claim that God sends Antichrist to the unjust for their damnation (2:11). The Thessalonians, however, will not see these

57. "*Dicunt alii quod Michael solo terrore suo interfecturus sit hunc Antichristum. Jesus quidem interficiet eum, et postea destruet eum damnatum et in corpore et in anima.*" PL 153.420B.

58. "*Signa minora prodigia vocat; maiora, miracula.*" PL 153.420C.

59. Neither does Augustine: CD 20.19, CCSL 47, 733.

days of Antichrist, since Paul tells them that they are "first-fruits" of salvation, and thus they have come at the beginning, not the end, of the Church.[60]

While Bruno's exegesis of the third chapter of the letter is surprisingly thorough, taking up two columns in Migne, he does little more than paraphrase the text. Paul first asks the Thessalonians to pray for the safety of his mission, "since not all have faith" (3:2). For Bruno, this means either that the mission field is still ripe and many people are still seeking the faith or that Paul faces great persecution from the "importune and evil men," among whom there is no one of faith.[61] Then Paul directs the Thessalonians to "remove themselves" from everyone who is walking on the wrong path (3:6). Through the rest of the directives in the chapter, Bruno simply clarifies Paul's statement through paraphrase.

Taken as a whole, Bruno's exegesis is another excellent example of eleventh-century exegetical innovation. While it is clear that Bruno is aware of the tradition that precedes him, and indeed twice quotes "Ambrose," he is less bound than his predecessors by the language and particular perspectives of that tradition. Bruno does not usually quote or even paraphrase his authoritative, traditional sources; instead, he uses the ideas in these sources to construct and support his original interpretation. Like Lanfranc, Bruno comes to the Pauline text with "fresh eyes." Unlike Lanfranc, Bruno makes no systematic attempt to distinguish his own contributions from those of the tradition. Instead, he incorporates them as "supporting evidence" for his interpretations.

Bruno gives his most distinctive contribution to the interpretation of *imperium* that lies behind the exegesis of the entire second chapter. For Bruno, the "unity of faith" in obedience to the spiritual authority of the pope, with the support and protection of the temporal power of Christian kings, preserves the present time from An-

60. PL 153.421A.
61. PL 153.422D.

tichrist's arrival. In this sense, the advent of Antichrist is dependent upon the ideal political condition of the late-eleventh century reformers. This twofold *imperium* invests the controversies over papal and imperial authority with apocalyptic significance, giving Bruno's exegesis a sense of actual imminence: should either the spiritual or temporal power fail, or should they be misaligned, Antichrist is sure to come. Coupled with this imminent apocalyptic realism is Bruno's conviction that the actual Antichrist is preceded by his "members," signified by the first beast in Revelation 13. The body of Antichrist, already present in the Church, will become prominent when the *imperium* fails.

Bruno's preference for a social/political interpretation of the end fits with his focus upon the historical figure of Antichrist. When in other texts he refers to Antichrist, the Adversary is usually understood as a persecutor of the faith. In his commentary on Psalm 9, for example, he portrays Antichrist as one "who will make himself God, but is simply a man filled with the devil, and who will cause you much suffering."[62] To this, in light of the tradition of interpretation of 2 Thessalonians, Bruno adds an understanding of the body of Antichrist, so that Bruno's exegesis of 2 Thessalonians is both imminent and immanent, both realist and spiritual. He, more than any in the tradition since Gregory the Great, integrates these two polar positions into a coherent interpretation of the present situation. Bruno's scenario is more optimistic than Gregory's—the current *imperium* still holds—but both share a sense of the significance of their contemporary history and politics in the final eschatological conflict.

Taken together, the commentaries of Lanfranc and Bruno suggest an apocalyptic intensity greater than that found in the Carolingian works. While we still see no evidence of predictive imminent millennialism, we find both figures focusing most intensely upon

---

62. *"Antichristus scilicet qui se Deum faciet, et homo simpliciter erit diabolo plenus, qui tuis multas inferet tribulationes"* Bruno, *Expositio in Psalmum IX*, PL 152.672C.

the sequence of historical events that will lead to Antichrist's arrival. Lanfranc sees the spiritual life as the engine of history: the full flowering of the gospel throughout the world, followed by the cooling of charity, will be the signposts of the end. He admits, reluctantly, that he does not know the day or hour, but the sense of imminence in his "soul doomed to death" is made perhaps all the more intense by his ignorance. If charity keeps the end at bay for Lanfranc, unity is the key for Bruno. Bruno shares a sense for historical change, but his eyes are upon the social and political dimensions of the "unity of faith." The proper arrangement of the Christian *imperium* under the pope is what restrains Antichrist. Here we see a theology of history that could undergird the apocalyptic rhetoric cast about during the Investiture controversy.[63] Indeed, both Lanfranc and Bruno show elements that are compatible with the ideals of reform that seemed to saturate the air of the later eleventh century. If the convictions of Leo IX and Hildebrand's reforming circle did not have millennial aspirations (I doubt they did), Bruno and Lanfranc's exegesis suggests that these ideals nonetheless found expression in the non-predictive apocalyptic eschatology of the 2 Thessalonians tradition.

The *Glossa Ordinaria* on Paul: Anselm of Laon

Bruno and Lanfranc, each in their own way, bear witness to the new fertility of biblical scholarship and to the enthusiasm for moral and institutional reform in the Church of the eleventh century. Such fertile projects were drawn together and harvested, in a sense, by the Schools of Laon and Auxerre. During the Carolingian era, Laon and Auxerre had assembled fine cathedral libraries possessing manuscripts of patristic texts and the works of "moderns" such as Haimo,

63. Gregory VII's rhetoric (e.g., his naming of the "antipope" Guibert as "Antichrist and Arch-heretic") does not, in itself, demonstrate an apocalyptic mindset, but most likely reflects the hyperbole of the bitter polemical arguments of the day. See Bernard McGinn, *Visions of the End* (New York, Columbia University Press, 1978), 94ff.

Rabanus, and Florus.[64] These libraries survived into the eleventh century, when they provided ample sustenance for the revived schools of Anselm of Laon and Gilbert the Universal at Auxerre. Under its master Anselm (properly *Ansellus,* d. 1117) and his brother Ralph (d. 1136?), the cathedral school at Laon produced both remarkable students and revolutionary tools at the dawn of scholasticism. Anselm taught William of Champeaux, Peter Abelard (whose interactions with Anselm are notorious), Gilbert of Poitiers, and Hugh, abbot of Reading, all of whom were influential masters in their own right.[65] Anselm's school in Laon also was instrumental in the production of one of the tools that made the work of such masters possible, the *Glossa Ordinaria.* The *Glossa Ordinaria* (GO) is a complete edition of the bible that excerpts and summarizes patristic and medieval exegesis in marginal and interlinear glosses. The editors of the GO were not great innovators; they adapted the gloss-format that had existed in some form since the ninth century and had recently been used to such profit by Lanfranc and Bruno. Nevertheless, the GO's singular achievement is in the presentation of so much material within a single series of volumes. This comprehensive scope made the GO a valuable standard for scholarly study of the bible for centuries.[66]

64. For Laon, see John J. Contreni, *The Cathedral School of Laon from 850 to 930: Its Manuscripts and Masters* (Münich: Münchener Beiträge zur Mediävistik—und Renaissance—Forschung, 1978). For Auxerre, see Musee d'Art et Histoire.

65. G. R. Evans, *The Language and Logic of the Bible: The Earlier Middle Ages* (New York: Cambridge University Press, 1984), 41.

66. Margaret Gibson and Karlfried Froehlich have traced the reception history of the Gloss from the twelfth century into the early modern period in the introduction to their facsimile edition of the first printed edition. Karlfried Froehlich and Margaret T. Gibson, *Biblia Latina cum Glossa Ordinaria,* facsimile of the Rusch *editio princeps* (Turnhout: Brepols, 1992). It is perhaps inappropriate to refer to the Gloss as the "textbook" on the Bible, since we have little evidence of cheaper, student editions of the book. One hesitates to try to introduce the *Glossa Ordinaria* in brief. So little of the date and place of compilation is known with confidence. Fastidious research continues under the aegis of Society for the Study of the Bible in the Middle Ages, an organization founded in 1994 at the 29th

But scholarly prowess was not the sole, narrow aim of the Laon and Auxerre masters. The inception of the Gloss project itself can be seen as part of the broader movement of reform in the mid eleventh century. As the Gregorian popes continued to try to purify and strengthen the institutions of the Church, the Laon scholars sought to provide an authoritative, comprehensive tool for the education of a reformed clergy. Their initial work focused upon the New Testament, and, in the words of Guy Lobrichon, the Laon glosses on the three Gospels[67] and the Apocalypse reflect an "evangelical," reform-minded disposition entirely consistent with the Gregorian revival.[68]

Anselm himself probably composed glosses on the Psalms and the Pauline epistles,[69] while the glosses on Matthew, Luke, John, and the Apocalypse are usually attributed to his brother Ralph. Gilbert (the Universal) of Auxerre is usually credited with glossing Lamentations, the Pentateuch, the major prophets, and perhaps the twelve minor prophets. Few of these attributions are firmly founded on critical evidence, and Margaret Gibson exhorts scholars of the GO

International Congress on Medieval Studies in Kalamazoo, Michigan. Since then, members of the society have held a frequent sessions at Kalamazoo on the *Glossa Ordinaria* under the scholarly leadership of E. Ann Matter, Mary Dove, and others, and they continue to unearth new material, so much that what is written now may soon be superseded. The *Glossa*, rescued from obscurity by Beryl Smalley nearly sixty years ago, has become one of the more fruitful fields of research in medieval studies. The most current work on the sources of the *Glossa Ordinaria* is E. Ann Matter, "The Church Fathers and the *Glossa Ordinaria*," in *The Reception of the Church Fathers in the West,* ed. Irena Backus, 2 vols. (Leiden: Brill, 1997), 83–111.

67. According to the testimony of Peter Comestor, neither Ralph nor Anselm completed a commentary on the Gospel of Mark.

68. Lobrichon, "Une nouveauté," 106.

69. The original work on this thesis was done by Beryl Smalley more than sixty years ago. Beryl Smalley, "Gilbertus Universalis, Bishop of London (1128–34), and the Problem of the *Glossa Ordinaria*," *Recherches de théologie ancienne et médiévale* 7 (1935): 235–62; 8 (1936): 24–60. Scholars have come to some consensus on this point. See also: Margaret T. Gibson, "The Glossed Bible," introduction to *Biblia Latina cum Glossa Ordinaria*, X; Evans, *Language and Logic of the Bible,* 42.

to exercise the virtue of prudence in such assertions about its earliest stages.

Gibson calls for an equal measure of faith for the study of the *Glossa*'s next phase, 1110/20–1140/50, since "we can see the point of arrival but absolutely no details of the route."[70] Since the composition and compilation of the GO stretched over two or three generations of scholars, textual variants are numerous, and progress toward a critical edition has only just begun in the last several years.[71] The text achieved some relative stability in the mid twelfth century, but even after this date, minor additions to the text continued even as late as the early thirteenth century.[72] For the first half of the twelfth century, the *Glossa Ordinaria* is best conceived as an extended work-in-progress that was standardized only when it was introduced and promoted in the Parisian schools by Peter Lombard and his follower Peter Comestor, who was chancellor of the cathedral school in Paris from 1168 to 1178. The size and the quality of surviving GO manuscripts suggest that the Gloss was never adopted as a "textbook" for students; rather, it became the standard library reference edition of the Bible found in every good library, whether secular or monastic.[73]

The Pauline *Glossa Ordinaria*[74] is usually known by its *incipit, Pro*

70. Gibson, "Glossed Bible," XI.

71. The first volume of the critical edition has been published in the CCCM series: *Glossa Ordinaria*, pt. 22, *Cantica Canticarum*, ed. Mary Dove, CCCM 170 (Turnhout: Brepols, 1997). For the problems surrounding the production of the critical edition, see Mark Zier, "The Manuscript Tradition of the *Glossa Ordinaria* for Daniel and Hints at a Method for a Critical Edition," *Scriptorium* 47:1 (1993): 3–25.

72. Lobrichon, 112. Evidence of such diversity has led Bertola to suspect that the Gloss exists in a multitude of independent recensions and did not "develop" as a single work. Thus the task of arriving at a single critical edition would be impossible. E. Bertola, "La *Glossa Ordinaria* biblica ed i suoi problemi," *Recherches de theologie ancienne et médiévale* 45 (1978): 34–78. Zier's article is an attempt to respond to this argument.

73. Gibson, "Glossed Bible," XI.

74. I have used the University of Chicago's Rosenberger f24–5, which appears

altercatione, and, as I noted, it is usually attributed to Anselm of Laon.[75] It follows a similar format to that of Lanfranc, with both marginal and interlinear glosses. There appears to be no substantive distinction between marginal and interlinear glosses: Long glosses are marginal, short glosses that clarify or paraphrase are interlinear, and glosses of moderate length are marginal in some manuscripts and interlinear in others.[76] The Pauline GO draws upon the breadth of patristic material, and it also contains (perhaps for the first time) explicit citation of Carolingian sources such as Haimo, and even more contemporary sources such as Lanfranc and Bruno. More ambitious than its predecessors, the GO attempts to summarize the Pauline exegetical tradition comprehensively, and in large measure, it succeeds. It is a masterwork of exegetical and theological research.

---

to be a Rusch *editio princeps* of 1479, like that produced in facsimile and edited by Karlfried Froehlich and Margaret T. Gibson. The Rusch *editio princeps* lays out the scriptural text in two center columns of uniform width and variable length. The interlinear font is one-half that of the scriptural text; the marginal font is approximately two-thirds that of the scriptural text. This edition usually begins each marginal gloss with an "C"-shaped rubric, but it seems likely that several smaller glosses have been combined into a single larger gloss. The interlinear glosses are each introduced by a vertical "s" rubric. Brief glosses of a word or two are usually positioned over the word or phrase to which they refer. Longer interlinear glosses begin at the left margin of the column and are further rubricated by a sequence of symbols corresponding to designated places in the text. These follow sequentially for each line: the first gloss is a "cross" or "dagger" mark; the second, a vertical line topped with a triangle of three dots; the third, rarely used, is a vertical arrow.

75. Lobrichon argues that the textual discrepancies between several *Pro altercatione* manuscripts make it impossible to classify them under this single title. "The superficial uniformity which has classified the Anselmian glosses under the title *Pro altercatione* is nothing but a decoy; it obscures the different states." He refers specifically to the differences found in the 2 Thessalonians gloss between Troyes, BM 512, and Paris, BN lat. 14409. I am concerned with the stable form of the gloss as it appears in the complete *Glossa Ordinaria* from the mid twelfth century on, so I have not addressed these specific differences.

76. Zier, 15.

2 Thessalonians in the Glossa Ordinaria

The *Glossa Ordinaria* on 2 Thessalonians is remarkable above all for the amount of material it condenses into approximately three pages (in the Rusch edition) of glossed text. Such a comprehensive scope in such limited space compels the editor to paraphrase and summarize particular exegetical points, rather than quote the text directly. The editor, like his contemporaries, strives for succinct thematic precision rather than textual accuracy. Neither is the editor fastidious in the citation of his sources. No interlinear glosses are ascribed to any author, and only a few of the marginal glosses cite their source. Augustine and Haimo are the only figures cited in the Rusch edition. Glosses taken from Augustine often, but not always, cite the particular work from which they come; Haimo is identified by name only. There appears to be no set rule or rationale for attribution, and I suspect that there is considerable diversity among the various manuscripts.

The 2 Thessalonians gloss begins with the standard Vulgate introduction noting that it addresses questions on the end of time and that Paul wrote the letter from Athens through Titus the deacon and Onesimus the acolyte. Two marginal glosses accompany this standard introduction. The first is taken from Ambrosiaster's commentary, noting that the letter is written to continue the discussion of the eschatological matters introduced in 1 Thessalonians, "although obscurely." Among the matters discussed, Ambrosiaster continues, are the destruction of Rome, the coming of Antichrist, and the correction of certain disruptive brethren.[77]

This introduction is followed by several more, from Theodore of Mopsuestia (perhaps through Rabanus Maurus), Haimo, and an anonymous source (perhaps Anselm himself). None of these sources is identified by name, and the inclusion of all of them at first

77. *Glossa Ordinaria* (MS University of Chicago Rosenberger f24–25), vol. 4, f. 174r, col 2. cf. Ambrosiaster, CSEL 81, 235.

seems redundant and cumbersome. Upon closer examination, one finds that each contributes a slightly different perspective on the substance and purpose of the letter. The gloss taken from Theodore focuses upon the first chapter. Faced with great persecution, Theodore says, the Thessalonians are encouraged to persevere in patience and trust in God's just judgment.[78] Next, Haimo's introduction focuses upon the second chapter as the solution to the community's apocalyptic anxiety.[79] The anonymous (Anselmian?) gloss then identifies Paul's specific "intentions" in writing, "to exhort the good people to patience and correct the troublemakers, and also to clear up what he had mentioned obscurely in the preceding epistle,"[80] and, to wrap up, it summarizes the overall order of argument:

First he greets them; then he gives thanks for their benefits. After this, he encourages them toward patience and constancy. Then he asserts that Antichrist will precede the return of Christ and he announces certain obscure signs of Antichrist's coming, treating the abolition of Roman rule and the slaying of Antichrist. At the end, he implores them to correct the meddlers among them.[81]

The sum effect of these four introductions is a thorough acquaintance with each of the letter's major themes and with most of the sources used in the letter's glosses. Particular topics raised by Ambrosiaster, Theodore, and Haimo are drawn together in Anselm's outline of the whole.

78. *"Orta enim apud eos graviori tribulatione: item monet eos ad patientiam, ostendens iustum dei iudicium ut boni gloriam consequantur, mali poenam."* f. 174r, col. 2.

79. *"Scribit etiam non instare diem domini sicut occasione prioris epistolae videbatur. Cum enim priorem epistolam legendo pervenissent ad illum locum ubi dici apostolus 'Mortui in adventu eius resurgent primi. Deinde nos qui vivimus, qui residui sumus, simul rapiemur cum illum,' etc., conturbati sunt, nimiumque perterriti putantes vicinum diem domini ne damnaretur eo quod tarde ad fidem venientes imperfecti essent."* f. 174r, col. 2.

80. *"Et est intentio apostoli bonos et quietos ad patientiam monere et inquietos corrigere et quod obscure in precedenti episola dixerat hic aliquatenus aperire."* f. 174r, col. 2.

81. *"Primo salutat, deinde gratias agit de bonis eorum. Postea monet ad patientiam et constantia. Inde asserit quod adventum Christi Antichristus praeveniet et aliqua adventus Antichristi signa licet obscura denuntiat, agens de abolitione romani regni et interfectione Antichristi. Circa finem vero ut curiosos corripiant obsecrat."* f. 174r, col. 2.

The glosses on the first chapter of 2 Thessalonians focus upon two major issues. The question of theodicy, provoked by Paul's discussion of the Thessalonians' suffering as an "example of the just judgment of God" (v. 5), occupies roughly half of the marginal gloss on chapter 1. The commentary on this section departs from the usual "patchwork" gloss-form, and it offers instead a single anonymous gloss, the longest of any on 2 Thessalonians. This longer excerpt seems to be a reflective meditation on verse 5, restating the verse, paraphrasing it, and complementing it with other related scriptural passages. According to this gloss, the community's suffering is an example of the just judgment of God because God "afflicts every son that he accepts" (*affligit omnem filium quem recepit,* cf. Heb. 12:6). Peter writes that God's judgment begins within his own house (1 Pt 4:17), so it is fitting that the Thessalonian Christians should experience God's judgment first. Such suffering will purify them for God's final judgment, while the suffering of evil people will only defile them more.[82] The gloss concludes on a note of humility, quoting Psalm 72: "I thought that I might know this, but it is a struggle for me until I enter the sanctuary of God and understand the end of these things."[83] Why the editor would choose to include this gloss, so uncharacteristic in its length and scriptural cross-references and almost homiletic in tone, is a mystery. But, with only a few more brief, clarifying glosses, he moves on to consider the second issue in chapter 1, the nature of Christ's coming in judgment.

When verse 8 claims that Christ will come "in flames of fire," glosses offer two possible interpretations. First, as we find in Bruno, a gloss asserts that this does not mean that he will be surrounded in flames, but rather that his coming will consume his enemies. Alternatively, Haimo suggests that fire will precede his coming, consum-

---

82. "*Si quis enim finem attendit, non iniustum dicet esse bonos purgare, malos sordescere, sicut utrique ex vita sua meruere.*" f. 174r, col 1.

83. "*Simile huic dicit David, Existimabam ut cognoscerem hoc, labor est ante me donec intrem in sanctuarium Dei, et intelligam in novissimis eorum.*" f. 174r, col. 1. Cf. Ps 72:16 (Vulgate).

ing in flames the same area swallowed by the waters of the flood. This fire will burn the land and the "thickness of the air" and purify the elect.[84] When Christ finally comes, he will be brilliant in the eyes of the faithful and terrible in the eyes of the unbelievers.[85] It is worth noting that at the end of verse 8, which speaks of Christ's judgment upon "those who do not know God and who do not obey the Gospel," the glossator tells us that the first phrase refers to "those who have not accepted the faith" and the second to "heretics and false Christians." This lemma appears to come directly from Haimo, but it excises his mention of "Jews" in the second case. This omission may simply have been for the sake of space; it also may reflect a different theology of Judaism.

The *Glossa Ordinaria* on 2 Thessalonians 1 uses a variety of sources, patristic and "modern," to give a thorough introduction to the whole letter. But it depends heavily upon a single unidentified source to offer an interpretation of the chapter's major issue—the question of innocent suffering. While this single source incorporates the insights of the tradition of commentary—and indeed expands them by referring to other Scripture, it is nonetheless unusual to find such a large synthetic gloss at the expense of other voices from the tradition. This broad synthesis proves to be the exception and not the rule, for when the editor proceeds to consider chapter 2, his command of the exegetical tradition becomes apparent.

The gloss on chapter 2 is constructed from familiar sources. The editor draws his material from Ambrosiaster, Augustine, Haimo, and Lanfranc in roughly equal measure, with a few points from Jerome and a few more that may come from Bruno's commentary.

---

84. "*Domini Ihesu venientis in flamma ignis non quod sit flamma circumdatus, sed per effectum quia inimicos exuret. Vel ideo dicit in flamma ignis quia ignis erit in mundo qui praecedet eum tantum spatium aeris occupans quantum occupavit aqua in diluvio, qui exuret terram et crassitudinem aeris et purgabit electos.*" f. 174r, col. 2. Cf. Bruno, PL 153.416D; Haimo, PL 117.778D.

85. "*Ipse enim clarus et mirabilis videbitur in credentibus. Severus autem apparebit in incredulous cum eos poenis aeternis coarctabit.*" f. 174r, col. 2.

In addition, there are several notes that do not seem to come from any traditional exegetical source and may be the editor's original comments. These comments seem to follow no other organizational principle than the consecutive order of verses; they do not appear to construct an argument through their particular organization, as I have demonstrated in the Carolingian commentaries and will argue for in Peter Lombard's work. The second chapter's glosses produce an index of the exegetical tradition, a reference work rather than a theological commentary in its own right.

With a quote from Ambrosiaster, the editor marks the transition from the first chapter's discussion of the present to the second's treatment of the Day of Judgment. There is a brief interlinear gloss pondering what "our gathering into him/it" could mean: "into Christ, as to the body of an eagle, or into identity, so that we who now tend toward division may live united in mind and body."[86] The concern seems to be theological rather than grammatical, since the text, *et nostrae congregationis in ipsum,* can hardly refer to anything but *Ihesu Christi* just before it. But the gloss offers no particular answer.

As Paul encourages the community not to be persuaded by any false spirit, the Gloss refers to 2 Corinthians 11:14, noting that the devil can appear as an angel of light. While the threat of deception in verses 1–4 has long been attributed to the devil (e.g., by Ambrosiaster—see Chapter 2 in this volume), this explicit cross-reference is an addition to the exegetical tradition. This addition, together with the gloss on chapter 1, suggests a editorial predilection for such scriptural cross-references and strengthens the impression of this work as a reference text.

When the glossator comes to address the Day of the Lord itself, he introduces the theological problem in the text with a paraphrase from Augustine's letter to Hesychius: "Why would he not want them to have their loins girt and a burning torch in hand, waiting for

---

86. *"Christum, ut ad corpus aquile vel in identitatem, ut mente et corpore vivamus qui modo in diversum tendimus."* f. 174r, col. 2.

the Lord to return from the wedding feast?"[87] To this question he adds Augustine's anti-apocalyptic answer, that everyone should prepare for his death as he would prepare for the Day of the Lord, since it is on the merits of his life that judgment will be given.[88] This text, cited at the beginning of this apocalyptic scriptural passage, would seem to set a cool tone for the exegesis that follows. However, the glossator follows this immediately with Ambrosiaster's depiction of Paul's motives in chapter 2: Paul gives clear signs of the end so that the devil may not deceive them into thinking that it is imminent. Without any effort to adjudicate between these two types of interpretation, the glossator already gives a sense of the two general interpretive options—the apocalyptic realist reading, represented by Ambrosiaster, or the spiritual, moral reading of Augustine.

What follows in the glossing of chapter 2 is a structured exchange of opinions across the centuries between the two interpretive options. Paul's mention of the *discessio* is interpreted first as his oblique discussion of the destruction of the Roman Empire. To this commonplace interpretation, the glossator adds the possibility that the Apostle refers to the collapse of the spiritual "Roman Empire" of the Church or the widespread abandoning of the faith.[89] It is worth noting that the glossator distinguishes between the fall of Roman ecclesial authority and the abandoning of the faith. Such a distinction may be due to the glossator's utilization of two independent sources. For example, the emphasis upon the collapse of Rome can be found in Bruno, while the emphasis upon the practice of the faith

87. "*Non quando [quin?] velit ut habeant succinctos lumbos et lucernas ardentes in manibus expectantes quando revertatur dominus a nuptiis.*" f. 175r, col. 1. Cf. Augustine, Ep. 199, PL 33.905.

88. "*In quo enim quemque invenerit suus novissimus dies, in hoc eum comprehendet mundi novissimus dies. Quoniam qualis quisque in die illo moritur, talis in die illo iudicabitur, et ideo vigilare debet omnis christianus ne imparatum eum inveniat Domini adventus.*" f. 175r, col. 1. Cf. Augustine, Ep. 199, PL 33.905.

89. "*Occulte loquitur de destructione imperii Romani—ne irritaret eos ad persecutorem ecclesiae. Vel hoc dicit de spirituali imperio romanae ecclesiae. Vel discessione a fide.*" f. 175r, col. 1.

in the end is typical of Lanfranc's exegesis. But neither Bruno nor Lanfranc opposes his interpretation to the other; for them, I would argue, each refers to the same reality. The collapse of Rome is the collapse of faith, since Rome is the spiritual protector of faith. Is the glossator introducing a theological distinction between the practice of the faith and the authority of the Roman church? Or does he simply include these two options as two ways of speaking about the same reality? On the basis of this scant evidence, it is impossible to solve this puzzle. But one can see how the glossator's inclusive editorial strategy could allow for such a distinction to be made by later interpreters.[90]

Such inclusivity is reflected throughout the gloss on 2 Thessalonians 2, as the commentary is exchanged between Augustine and various literal interpreters. The various literal readings above are followed by Augustine's alternative reading of the *discessio* as *refuga*, referring to Antichrist himself. With Haimo, the gloss identifies Antichrist as the "son of the devil," not by nature, but by imitation. From Augustine, an interlinear gloss declares that "Son of Perdition" includes Antichrist and his members. An interlinear gloss on *in templo* draws on Jerome and states that this refers either to the Church or to a rebuilt temple in Jerusalem. These realist readings are balanced by another rereading of Augustine (from Tyconius), giving the Latin *in templum* and suggesting that it refers to the body of Antichrist already present in the Church. But the Augustinian gloss is followed immediately by Haimo's summary biography of Antichrist:

Thus Antichrist will be born in Babylon, of the Tribe of Dan. . . . And when he comes to Jerusalem, he will circumcise himself, saying to the Jews, "I am the Christ, the one promised to you." Then all the Jews will

90. Thomas Aquinas, for one. See his lectures on 2 Thessalonians in *Opera omnia*, vol. 15, p. 578: *"discessio, quod multipliciter exponitur in Glossa. Et primo a fide, quia futurum erat ut fides a toto mundo reciperetur. . . . Vel discessio a Romano imperio cui totus mundu erat subditus. . . . Et ideo dicendum est, quod discessio a Romano Imperio debet intellegi non solum a temporali, sed a spirituali."*

flock to him and rebuild the temple destroyed by the Romans, and he will sit there and say that he is God.[91]

This is followed by a brief doctrinal statement on Antichrist, also from Haimo, that the fullness of evil dwells within Antichrist just as the fullness of divinity dwells in Christ. The devil, "the head of the evil and the king of all the sons of pride," lives in Antichrist.[92] The glossator is careful to include all the narrative and doctrinal detail accrued in the exegetical tradition, but never to the exclusion of the Augustinian alternative.

Indeed, the only material that seems to be deliberately excised from the text is any expression of exegetical preference. The interlinear gloss from Jerome cited above suggests that *in templo* might refer to either the Church or a rebuilt temple in Jerusalem, but it does not include Jerome's clear preference for the former.[93] Similarly, the glossator quotes more or less accurately Augustine's lengthy perorations upon the possible interpretations of *"quod detineat"* in verse 6, with one notable excision. Augustine rehearses the various interpretations of Nero as Antichrist, that he will be resurrected as Antichrist, or that he is not yet dead but will emerge from hiding as Antichrist in the end. He then dismisses these ideas out of hand: "For myself, I am astonished at the great presumption of those who venture such guesses."[94] He then proceeds to speak of a spiritual understanding of the verse, in which the evil people and impostors

91. *"Haimo: Nascetur autem Antichristus in Babilonie de tribu dan. . . . Et cum venerit Hierosolimam circumcidet se dicens iudaeis, 'Ego sum Christus vobis promissus.' Tunc confluent ad eum iudaei et reaedificabunt templum a romanis destructum sedebitque ibi dicens se esse deus."* f. 175r, col. 1.

92. *"Nam sicut in Christo omnis plenitudo divinitatis habitavit ita in Antichristo plenitudo malitiae et omnis iniquitas habitabit, quod in ipso erit caput omnium malorum et rex super omnes filios superbiae."* f. 175r, col 1. Cf. Haimo, *In Thess. Sec.,* PL 117.780.

93. Jerome, Ep. 121: *"et in templo Dei, vel Hierosolymis (ut quidam putant) vel in ecclesia (ut verius arbitramur) sederit."* See Chapter 2 in this volume.

94. *"Sed multum mihi mira est haec opinantium tanta presumptio."* CD 20.19, CCSL 47, 732. Bettenson, 933.

within the Church will depart and constitute a "great body" for Antichrist. The glossator follows Augustine's text as far as the statement about Nero's resurrection as Antichrist. He then omits the next several lines, excluding the possibility that Nero still lives and removing from the text Augustine's summary dismissal. Instead, he skips directly to the spiritual interpretation of the *mali et ficti in ecclesia*.[95] With this excision, the glossator presents a complete index of interpretive positions without any expression of preference or bias, either his own or that of a Father of the Church.

The exegetical exchange continues throughout the glosses on the second chapter. Augustine's lengthy citation ends with the moral exhortation for all the faithful to cling to their faith until the end. This is followed by a summary of Lanfranc's discussion of the *accessio* to the faith that precedes the *discessio* and the cooling of charity.[96] The "mystery of iniquity" is identified alternatively as the secret work of pseudo-Christians during the *accessio* (Lanfranc)[97] and as the devil's hidden work in the persecution of Roman emperors, foreshadowing Antichrist's murder of Enoch and Elijah (Haimo).[98]

95. The *City of God* reads as follows: "*ut hoc quod dixit: Iam enim mysterium iniquitatis operatur, Neronem voluerit intelligi, cuius iam facta velut Antichristi videbantur. Unde nonnulli ipsum resurrectum et futurum Antichristum suspicantur; alii vero nec occisum putant, sed subtractum potius, ut putaretur occisus, et vivum occultari in vigore ipsius aetatis, in qua fuit, cum crederetur extinctus, donec suo tempore reveletur et restituatur in regnum. Sed multum mihi mira est haec opinantium tanta praesumptio. Illud tamen.*" CD 20.19, CCSL 47, 731–32. The GO reads slightly differently: "*Et hoc quid dixit: Iam enim misterium operatur iniquitatis neronem voluerunt intelligi, cuius facta velut Antichristi videbantur. Unde non nulli vel vivum raptum occultari donec suo tempore reveletur vel occisum resurrecturum et futurum Antichristum suspicabantur. Quidam putant hoc dictum esse de malis et fictis qui sun in ecclesia.*" f. 175r, col. 1. Despite the paraphrase, the Gloss covers all the major elements from Augustine's text but one: Augustine's own opinion.

96. "*Suo tempore: Completa accessione ad romanum imperium et ad romanae ecclesiae obedientiam aderit discessio ab utroque imperio.*" f. 175r, col. 2. Cf. Lanfranc, PL 150.342B.

97. Lanfranc, PL 150.343A.

98. Haimo, PL 117.781A.

Verse 7's *donec de medio fiat* is glossed by Haimo's reference to the fall of Rome[99] and by Bruno's suggestion that people will commit sinful acts in public with no shame in the last days.[100] The glosses on the "lying signs" of Antichrist include both Haimo's comparison to Simon Magus's false resurrection[101] and Augustine's admitted uncertainty as to whether the signs are real or illusory.[102] The GO on 2 Thessalonians 2 portrays the breadth of theological opinion within the exegetical tradition succinctly and without any apparent bias or judgment.

The glosses on the third chapter of 2 Thessalonians draw on many of the same sources and offer them in similar contrapuntal order. The great majority of the glosses are taken from Augustine—most likely through the collection of Florus of Lyons. When the glossator comes to address the end of verse 2, "for not all have faith," he first offers the easiest readings of the text. He wonders if the verse means that all those who will accept the faith have not yet done so, and thus Paul's mission is not yet complete,[103] or perhaps that the troublesome people (*importunis,* v. 1) do not have faith, in contrast to the Thessalonians to whom Paul writes.[104] By this reading, the phrase serves as a transition to verse 3, "But God is faithful, and he will strengthen you and protect you from evil." Having given these rather straightforward readings, the glossator now introduces new sources to the exegetical tradition. From Augustine's letter to Vitalis, the gloss interprets Paul's comment to mean that "all are not intended to believe, even with your prayers—only those preordained for eternal life and predestined for the adoption as chil-

---

99. Haimo, PL 117.781B.

100. Bruno, PL 153.420A.

101. Haimo, PL 117.782A.

102. Augustine, CD 20.19, CCSL 47, 733.

103. *"Ideo dico liberemur: quia nondum accepterunt omnes fidem per me qui accepturi sunt."* f. 175v, col. 1.

104. *"Vel omnes qui importuni non habent fidem, sed vos qui habetis confirmabit deus, unde subdit fidelis, etc."* f. 175v, col. 1.

dren."[105] From Prosper's collection of Augustinian sentences, the gloss continues to expand upon the theme or predestination:

It should be known that the ability to have faith, like the ability to have love, is natural for man; but to [actually] have faith or love is the grace of the faithful. But when the will to believe is prepared in others by God, it is necessary to discern what comes from his mercy and what from his justice. For all his ways are mercy and truth [Ps 24, Vulgate] Thus both his mercy, by which he delivers without recompense, and his truth, by which he judges justly, can be discovered.[106]

Similarly, the glossator includes Florus's citation from Augustine's *On the Work of Monks* in comment upon verse 10, "we instructed you that if someone does not want to work, he should not eat." Augustine claims that, while some surely interpret this maxim as a reference to "spiritual works," it seems clear from this text and throughout Paul's letter that "he wishes the servants of God to do corporal work" to support themselves.[107] These quotes from Florus are the most significant, substantial comments upon chapter 3. The glossator does not include any of the lengthy quotes of Cassian found in Rabanus and offers only a few marginal notes from Ambrosiaster. The Augustinian material clearly represents for the glossator the heart of the matter.

---

105. "*nec vobis orantibus omnes sunt credituri sed tantum praeordinati in vitam aeternam, praedestinati in adoptionem filiorum.*" f. 175v, col. 1.

106. "*Et sciendum quia posse habere fidem sicut posse charitatem natura est hominum; habere autem fidem sicut charitatem, gratia est fidelium. Sed cum voluntas credendi aliis praeparatur a Deo, discernendum est quid veniat de misericordia eius et quid de iudicio. Universae viae dicuntur misericordia et veritas. Investigabiles igitur sunt, et misericordia, qua gratis liberat, et veritas, qua iuste iudicat.*" f. 175v, col. 1. Cf. Prosper of Aquitaine, *Liber sententiae ex opere Augustini*, PL 51.427–96.

107. "*Dicunt quidam de operibus spiritualibus hoc Aposolum praecepisse. Alioquin si de corporali opere hoc diceret, in quo vel agricolae vel opificies laborant, videretur sentire adversus Dominum qui in Evangelio ait: Nolite solliciti esse quid manducetis. [Mt 6. 31] Sed superflue conaturet sibi et caeteris caliginem obducere, ut quod utiliter charitas monet, non solum facere nolint, sed nec intelligere: cum multis aliis locis epistolarum suarum quid hinc sentiat Apostolus apertissime doceat. Vult enim servos Dei corporaliter operari, unde vivant, ut non compellantur egestate necessaria petere.*" f. 174v, col. 2–f. 175r, col. 1.

In sum, the *Glossa Ordinaria* on 2 Thessalonians provides the most thorough treatment of the letter in the commentary tradition thus far.[108] The glossator marshals many sources, both ancient and modern, to comment on the whole text. The interlinear glosses address all but ten of roughly one hundred twenty lines of scriptural text—far too much to present in this study. The marginal glosses on chapters 1 and 3 draw upon a few sources and quote them at great length to clarify a few of the theologically interesting ideas. In the interpretation of chapter 2, more disputed in the history of exegesis, the gloss portrays the double tradition of interpretation as a sort of exchange or conversation across the centuries. Like a judge, the glossator stands above the argument, excluding any judgment or opinion, even a judgment from Augustine or Jerome, that might be considered "special pleading." He allows only the various arguments to make a claim on the text. Absent from the 2 Thessalonians gloss are the reformist passions that we see in Lanfranc and Bruno, but the three share a passion for clarity and a fresh view of the text. The Ordinary Gloss on 2 Thessalonians has the character of an impartial record of theological debate, and thus, at the birth of the "theological science,"[109] it could function as the comprehensive reference index to the exegetical tradition.

108. It also represents perhaps the most thorough *summa* of teaching on Antichrist in the whole *Glossa Ordinaria*. The Gloss on Daniel seems to depend almost entirely upon Jerome, without any clear reference to the Carolingian sources. The synoptic "little apocalypses" either are almost entirely dependent upon Bede (Mark, Luke) or document the exchange between Paschasius Radbertus and Jerome/Origen, without some of the other patristic material in the Antichrist tradition (Matthew). The Apocalypse is interesting in its discussion of Antichrist, but again, the influence of Bede seems to predominate. (Although the "authoritative" text of the Apocalypse is in question, and such work would lead me too far afield from this study. See E. Ann Matter, "Church Fathers in the *Glossa Ordinaria*," 108.)

109. Marie-Dominique Chenu, *Nature, Man, and Society in the Twelfth Century*, selected, edited, and translated by Jerome Taylor and Lester Little (Chicago: University of Chicago Press, 1968), 270ff.

From *Glossa Ordinaria* to *Glossa Magnatura:* Peter Lombard

Soon after the ordinary gloss reached the point of its "first crystallization,"[110] a new generation of scholars took up its comments on Paul and the Psalms and made them the basis of their own expanded study. The two most notable expansions came from Gilbert of Poitiers (d. 1154), and Peter Lombard (d. 1160). Gilbert's gloss on Paul dates from ca. 1130, and in it he integrates the interlinear and marginal glosses from the Ordinary Gloss into a single text that runs continuously. Apparently, in its earliest form, this gloss was not produced with the complete scriptural text. Instead, certain scriptural catchwords are found throughout the text, just as commentaries had been composed throughout the tradition. Since copies of Gilbert's text are often found in collections with the *Glossa Ordinaria,* it seems reasonable to conclude that it was thought to supplement, not supplant, the work of Master Anselm.[111] Nonetheless, Anselm's work did come to be known as the *parva glosatura* in relation to Gilbert's *media glosatura,* both to be distinguished from the *magna glosatura* of Peter Lombard.

Peter Lombard's commentary on Paul was composed several years after that of Gilbert, written (and probably delivered as lectures) between 1139 and 1141.[112] In its first redaction, it is one of his earlier works, although it seems that the text in its present form is the result of further editing some time between 1155 and 1158. Herbert of Bosham, one of Peter's students, wrote that Peter began his commentary on Paul with the sole purpose in mind to "elucidate what was brief and obscure in the older glosses of Master Anselm of Laon."[113] Herbert continues to say that Peter prepared his work only

110. Lobrichon, "Une nouveauté," 109.
111. Christopher F. R. de Hamel, *Glossed Books of the Bible and the Origins of the Paris Booktrade* (Dover, N.H.: D. S. Brewer, 1984), 5–6.
112. Marcia Colish, *Peter Lombard,* 2 vols. (Leiden: Brill, 1994), 23.
113. *"ut antiquioris glosatoris magistri Anselmi laudunensis brevitatem elucidarent*

for his own personal use and that he became occupied with the de-
mands of his office as Bishop of Paris and died before his final revisions could be made. If this motive is credible, than Peter's commentary, too, was intended only as a supplement to the *Glossa
Ordinaria.*[114] De Hamel even finds it likely that the work was not
published until after Peter's death in 1160.[115] Once it was published,
however, it was quickly copied and passed throughout Europe. In
the third quarter of the twelfth century, the glosses of Gilbert and
Peter were the regular accompaniment of any edition of the glossed
Bible, and by 1175, it was not at all unusual to find a full glossed bible
comprising Peter Lombard's *magna glosatura* on Psalms and the
Pauline corpus and the Laon/Auxerre glosses on the rest of the
Bible.[116]

While both the *media glosatura* and the *magna glosatura* might be
examined to the benefit of this study, I have chosen to focus upon
the work of Peter Lombard as the next full step in the exegetical tradition. While Gilbert's expanded gloss was considered well-nigh
"miraculous" by his contemporaries,[117] it was supplanted quickly by
the "greater" work of the Lombard. It is in Peter's commentary on 2

---

obscuram." Herbert of Bosham, preface to the *Magna glosatura,* MS Trinity College B. 5. 4, cited in Colish, 23.

114. See Jacques-Guy Bougerol, "The Church Fathers and the Sentences of
Peter Lombard" in *The Church Fathers in the Latin West,* ed. Irena Backus (Leiden:
Brill, 1997), 113–64.

115. De Hamel, 8.

116. However, it is not accurate, I believe, to claim that the Lombard's gloss
replaced the Ordinary Gloss. If anything, Peter Lombard himself had a hand in in-
stitutionalizing the Gloss by his references to it in his *Sentences.* So, too, do his intellectual heirs (e.g., Peter Chanter and Stephen Langton, and even Thomas
Aquinas) begin their expositions on Pauline scripture by referring to the Gloss.
See Lobrichon, "Une nouveauté," 110.

117. *"opera mirabili labore mirabiliter composita."* See this text, Gilbert's funeral
sermon, as printed and commented upon by Jean Leclercq, O.S.B., "L'Eloge
funèbre de Gilbert de la Porée," *Archives d'histoire doctrinale et littéraire du moyen
âge* 19 (1952): 183–85.

Thessalonians, then, that the exegetical tradition I have traced comes to fruition.[118]

Peter Lombard on Paul

As the name suggests, Peter Lombard was born in the region of Novara in Lombardy, somewhere between 1095 and 1100. Beyond this detail, we know nothing of Peter's life until he is introduced by Bernard of Clairvaux in a letter to Gilduin, Prior of St. Victor in Paris, ca. 1134–36. Bernard tells Gilduin that Peter was recommended to him by Humbert, bishop of Lucca, and that Bernard himself has supported Peter financially while he studied in Rheims. The abbot then asks Gilduin to provide hospitality for Peter for a short time of study in Paris, until the Feast of the Nativity.[119] From this brief letter of introduction, we can conclude that Peter's academic credentials were of the highest order. At the cathedral school of Rheims was Alberic, later the notorious opponent of Abelard, but at this time one of the notable heirs to Anselm of Laon.[120] The school of Rheims was known for its emphasis upon traditional scriptural interpretation—an emphasis reflected in the thorough methodical exegesis in Peter's early work. Later, upon arrival at St. Victor, Peter may have studied with Hugh, although there is no evidence that

118. In addition to the brief tenure of Gilbert's work as an influential force on the history of exegesis, the fact that none of his work has been edited or published in any critical form contributes to his absence from this work. I have been able to consult only one manuscript of this work, Zwettl 58, f. 1–198 (12th century), and I find that this is insufficient textual basis for any critical evaluation. Theresa Gross-Diaz has done considerable work on Gilbert's Psalm commentary (*The Psalms Commentary of Gilbert of Poitiers: From Lectio Divina to the Lecture Room* (Leiden: Brill, 1996); there is still much to be done on his Pauline commentary. My thanks again to the Hill Monastic Manuscript Library at Saint John's University in Collegeville, Minnesota, for their assistance with the microfilm of this MS.

119. Bernard of Clairvaux, *Epistola* 410, in *Opera*, ed. J. Leclercq, C. H. Talbot, and H. M. Rochais (Rome: Editiones Cistercienes, 1957–77), 8, 391.

120. John R. Williams, "The Cathedral School of Rheims in the Time of Master Alberic, 1118–1136," *Traditio* 20 (1964): 93–114.

could confirm or deny such speculation.[121] Wherever he pursued his studies, the Lombard emerged as an acknowledged Parisian scholar and author by 1142. In 1145, he became a canon of Notre Dame, and he progressed quickly through the ranks of ecclesiastical office even as he taught and wrote.[122] He was elected bishop of Paris on the Feast of SS. Peter and Paul, 1159 and he died a year later. Little is known of his brief tenure as bishop, and his epitaph in St. Marcellus speaks of him only as the author of the *Four Books of Sentences* and the glosses on the Psalms and Paul.

As I have said above, the Pauline gloss, the *Collectanea in epistulas omnes Pauli,* is one of Peter's earliest works, but he continued to revise it in the later years of his life. Although the work is based largely upon the GO, Peter's main purpose—the clarification of Anselm's ambiguities—required him to return to Anselm's sources. Ignatius Brady's study of the *Collectanea* led him to conclude that Peter had before his eyes the GO, the *media glosatura* of Gilbert (although this source is never mentioned by name), the Augustinian compilation of Florus of Lyons,[123] Ambrosiaster, Haimo, Rabanus Maurus, Cassiodorus, and Peter Abelard's commentary on Romans.[124]

Like Abelard before him, Peter Lombard disregarded the traditional *argumenta*[125] to the Pauline epistles, preferring instead to com-

---

121. Marcia Colish pursues this question at some length, Colish, 19–20.

122. Ignatius Brady, O.F.M., Prolegomenon to *Sententiae in IV Libris Distinctae,* edited with an introduction by Ignatius Brady, vol. 1 (Rome: Grottaferrata Collegii S. Bonaventurae ad Claras Aquas, 1971–81), 18*–19*.

123. Brady notes that in places, Peter follows Florus in some textual errors, but he does not cite particular instances. Brady, Prolegomenon, 76*. The Augustinian material on 2 Thessalonians is accurate in both Florus and Peter.

124. Brady, Prolegomenon, 75*ff.

125. Brady points out that the traditional *argumenta* are not published in most of the extant MSS (Brady, Prolegomena, 73*). As further evidence, they themselves do not receive any direct comment from Peter. This is not to say that Peter's *accessus* are entirely original, for they sometimes draw directly from the introductory comments of earlier scholars such as Ambrosiaster and Haimo. See, e.g., my discussion of the introduction to 2 Thessalonians, pp. 10–14.

pose his own *accessus* with more precise attention to the circumstances in which Paul had written, to whom he wrote, and the structure of his argument. Marcia Colish has pointed out that, while Abelard and other contemporaries composed similar introductions for their works on Paul, they then abandoned them to explore their own particular theological interests within the text. Peter, on the other hand, usually allows these rhetorical limits to define his commentary. His purpose, more often than not, is to clarify the grammatical and rhetorical sense of the letter, nothing more.[126]

Peter's *accessus* to the Pauline corpus rehearses the traditional arguments about the relationship of the Pauline letters to the structure of the Bible, their purpose, number, and order. Included in this discussion is a surprisingly vehement defense of the Pauline authorship of Hebrews and an extended introduction to Romans, upon which Peter clearly places great emphasis. Then, as if running through a checklist of topics to be covered, Peter writes—in very dry, impersonal scholarly style:

Arguments have been given for the purpose, number and order of the letters, and whence and why the Apostle wrote to the Romans has been explained. What remains to be considered are the matter, the intent, and manner of argument. The general matter of all the letters is the teaching of the Gospel; the intention, to make one mindful of obeying the evangelical teaching. But beyond this we will enquire after the proper matter and intent of each letter.[127]

He then presents the particular matter, intent, and manner of argument for Romans. Peter continues to follow this procedure in the *accessus* to each letter: *locus, occasio, materia, intentio, modus tractandi.*

---

126. Colish, 195ff.

127. *"Assignatis rationibus operis, numeri et ordinis Epistolarum, explicato quoque unde et quare Apostolus Romanis scripsit, superest de materia et intentione et modo tractandi exsequi. Generalis omnium Epistolarum materia est doctrina Evangelii; intentio, monere ad obediendum evangelicae doctrinae. Praeter haec autem in singulis proprias intentiones et materias requiremus."* Peter Lombard, *Praefatio, Collectanea in omnes pauli apostoli epistolas,* PL 191.1302B.

When Peter turns from his introductions to the proper task of commentary, he departs from the glossed-text format. Like Gilbert of Poitiers before him, Peter opts instead for the continuous catena-form of commentary, using catch-words from the scriptural text to identify the lemma upon which he comments.[128] Why Gilbert and Peter would both choose to return to this format is not immediately clear. But such a format does afford Peter greater control over his sources, allowing him to impose a particular order upon glosses that were scattered around the page in the glossed-text format. In such a way, I will argue, Peter can construct a particular reading of a text through the ordering of his sources. Such attention to the potential structure of arguments may very well lie behind Peter's decision to compose a running commentary, since he shows himself to be con- scious of rhetoric in his analysis of Paul. But even if such arguments were not conscious reasons for Peter's choice of genre, I still contend that they are at least a net effect in his exegesis of 2 Thessalonians.

In fact, the commentary on 2 Thessalonians holds little interest if such an argument cannot be found. At first glance, the letter appears to offer little if any improvement to the *Glossa Ordinaria*. The Lom- bard's commentary recapitulates the entire text of the ordinary gloss, weaving the marginal and interlinear comments together with simple transitions of *"Vel ita"* or *"Quasi dicit,"* following no ob-

128. The original form of the Lombard's text is disputed. Marcia Colish ar- gues that the original format of Peter's commentary included "Paul's entire text, quoted in coherent subdivisions" (Colish, 193). These subdivisions would then be followed by a "running commentary" on each subdivision as a whole, and only then would Peter lemmatize the particular passages upon which he desired to comment. Such a format, says Colish, "makes the *Collectanea*, physically, the most usable work of Pauline exegesis of its period" (Colish, 193). Christopher de Hamel argues to the contrary (de Hamel, 21ff.). Based upon MSS Admont 36 and 52, which are the "earliest datable examples," de Hamel concludes that the first form of Peter's glosses was written continuously, with the scriptural catch-words underlined in black. He cites MSS Laon 103, Admont 233, and Lincoln 176 as fur- ther evidence. What Colish represents as the original format of the text is for de Hamel the "broken-up layout," which "forms the second stage in the layout of Peter Lombard glossed manuscripts."

vious pattern or rule. His only additions are expansions or corrections of the gloss's patristic sources. Based on an examination of the material alone, Peter Lombard's commentary on 2 Thessalonians appears only to make the text of the GO more precise and historically accurate. While this redaction is no small contribution to scholarship, it nonetheless seems on first reading to lack any original theological content.[129]

But such a conclusion is premature and comes from asking the wrong question of the Lombard's text. Those expecting to find "the birth of scholasticism" in Peter's writing and thus looking for signs of innovative theological method will be disappointed. Peter's commentary on 2 Thessalonians is, in fact, remarkably traditional. Like Haimo, Rabanus, and other Carolingians, Peter summarizes the tradition of interpretation by lining up authorities without any explicit attempt to adjudicate between them with a *quaestio*. Peter's theological position is expressed through his exegetical strategy, not his use of dialectic. For it is only in his arrangement, addition, and/or omission of traditional material that the Lombard's scholarly persona and theological inclinations emerge in the commentary on 2 Thessalonians.

Peter's *accessus* to the letter recapitulates the *Glossa* material from Theodore, Ambrosiaster, Haimo, and Anselm, but he rearranges the order in which they appear. He begins with Theodore, who discusses the most basic facts of historical context: that the letter is written to the Thessalonians at a time when the Greeks suffered persecution. The Theodoran gloss then summarizes the first chapter's purpose: Paul exhorts the community to have patience and promises that God's judgment is just. This gloss is followed by

129. I have made this argument in a paper delivered to the 1996 meeting of the American Society of Church History in Atlanta, January 4–6: "A Theology of Antichrist? Peter Lombard's Commentary on 2 Thessalonians in Context." The paper is unpublished, but it is available on microfilm through the Theological Research Exchange Network (TREN), P.O. Box 30183, Portland, OR 97230; (800) 334–8736 or http://www.tren.com.

one from Ambrosiaster, who relates this letter to 1 Thessalonians: what was said generally in the first is made as specific as Paul may dare in the second. This point is expanded by Haimo's citation of 1 Thessalonians 4:16–17, which he believes to be a source of confusion. Then the Anselmian analysis of the letter's *intentio* and *modus* summarizes the whole. Minor adjustments to order such as these fit the material from the Ordinary Gloss into Peter's strict formula: *locus, occasio, materia, intentio, modus.*

Peter's exposition of chapter 1, like the *accessus,* is primarily a recapitulation of the Gloss's material, arranged in a particular order. In considering verses 4–7, where Paul praises the Thessalonians for their patience as they suffer persecution "as an example of the just judgment of God, that [they] may be honored in the kingdom of God for which [they] suffer," Peter arranges the various glosses, interlinear and marginal, in a way that reflects the development of the text's grammatical sense, word by word. He first quotes the text only as far as *"quas sustinetis in exemplum iusti iudicii Dei,"* and the comments reflect upon the future punishment of the persecutors, of which the Thessalonians' suffering is but a model. "For if God punishes sins among the penitent so severely, what will he do to the hard of heart?" Peter continues with a gloss from Augustine's *Contra Faustum:*

And so he says that the trials of the just are an example of the just judgment of God so that it be understood that he who does not preserve the just from purgation so they might be perfected will not spare the wicked, the broken branches, from the fire. As Peter says, "If it begins with us, what will be the end of those who do not believe? And if it is difficult for the just to be saved, when will the sinner and the wicked yield?"[130]

While the gloss draws from this same source, the glossator abbreviates it and does not give the reference to 1 Peter. The Lombard has expanded the quote to reflect more accurately the text of Augustine's work.

130. *"Si enim tam severe punit Deus peccata in poenitentibus, quid faciet induratis? Ideo dicit pressuras iustorum exemplum esse iusti iudicii Dei, ut intelligatur quod non*

He proceeds to consider the next phrase: *sustinetis, [dico, ideo] ut digni habeamini*. Under this phrase, Peter gathers glosses that refer to not only to the punishment of the wicked, but also to the future reward of the victims as well. The phrase thus becomes an occasion to reflect upon God's justice in its final form, when the just will be exalted and the wicked will be destroyed, and the reflection takes shape from the comments of Ambrosiaster and Haimo and the longer, anonymous comment from the GO. And so Peter proceeds in like manner through chapter 1, organizing comments along the general outline of the grammatical structure of the verses. As each phrase is added, another dimension unfolds in the sense of the text. In this way, Peter imposes a logical structure upon the seemingly random dispersal of comments from the GO.

Peter's commentary on chapter 2 proceed in much the same way. As Paul exhorts the Thessalonians not to be deceived, Peter explains each potential deception in its course. Inserting a comment of Ambrosiaster (not in the GO), he summarizes these points and makes the transition to the *discessio* in verse 3: "[Paul] gives the time and the signs of the coming of the Lord, since the Lord will not come before the collapse of the Roman empire takes place and Antichrist appears. And this is what he says."[131] Considering the "desertion," Peter Lombard lines up the same series of possible interpretations as appears in the Gloss: "He speaks secretly of the departure of the nations from the Roman empire . . . *or* he says this about the spiritual empire of the Roman church *or* when they depart from faith."[132] Or, he adds, following Augustine, it could read "Unless first

---

parcet impiis tanquam sarmentis praecisis ad combustionem, qui non parcit iustis propter perficiendam purgationem. Unde Petrus ait: Si initium a nobis, quis finis erit eis qui non credent? Et si iustus vix salvabitur, peccator et impius ubi parebunt?" (1 Pt 4: 17–18). Peter Lombard, *In epistolam II ad thessalonicenses*, PL 192.313B.

131. "*Tempus et signa adventus Domini Apostolus rescribit, quia non prius veniet Dominus quam regni Romani defectio fiat, et appareat Antichristus. Et hoc est quod subdit.*" PL 192.316D. Cf. Ambrosiaster, CSEL 81, 239, ll. 17–19.

132. "*Occulte loquitur de destructione Romani imperii. . . . Vel hoc dicit de spirituali imperios Romanae Ecclesiae. Vel de discessione a fide.*" PL 192.317A.

the Exile" and refer to Antichrist himself, as the one who has fled from God most radically. This brings him naturally to discuss Antichrist himself, and Peter thus rehearses most of the standard doctrinal and biographical points on the Adversary: He is the "Man of Sin" because he is the "servant, author, and font" of sin. To say he is the "Son of Perdition" is to say he is the son of Satan, but by imitation, not by nature. He will oppose Christ in all things, and he will exalt himself over "everything which is called a God," which might refer either to the pagan gods or to the saints, who are called "gods." He will even try to exalt himself over the Trinity when he takes his place in the temple.

When Peter comes to this point about the temple, he acknowledges that this might refer either to the Church or to a rebuilt Jewish temple in Jerusalem. The latter possibility leads him into Haimo's biographical summary of Antichrist: born in the tribe of Dan, he will come to Jerusalem, circumcise himself, and gather all the Jews around him. But after this minor digression, and without any further commentary, he turns again to Augustine and wonders whether the temple ought to refer to the body of Antichrist.[133] Peter gives an inclusive summary of the apocalyptic realist interpretations (nothing is left out!), but this summary seems to be punctuated throughout with the words of Augustine. Augustine always has the last word.

When Peter comes to verses six and seven, concerning what or who holds Antichrist in check for the present and with the "mystery of iniquity already at work," he draws on a wider variety of sources and spends more time with each exegetical option. His attention heightens to such a point here that one wonders if this verse is for him the heart of the matter. He begins with the Gloss's attribution of the restraining power to the "great commission" and the endurance of the life of piety in the Church: When all have access to the faith, then the charity of the people will grow cold and An-

133. PL 192.317C.

tichrist will come. He then turns to Haimo's statement that the mystery of iniquity is the work of the devil hidden in the persecution of the martyrs by Nero and others like him:

For the devil already is working the mystery of iniquity. . . . Thus [Paul] calls the killing of the saints and persecution of the Christian faithful carried out by Nero and his captain "the mystery of iniquity." . . . Even then [in Paul's time], the devil was already secretly at work through Nero and the others, killing the martyrs, just as at that time he will work through Antichrist, killing Elijah, Enoch, and many others. . . . And Nero and the rest are shadows of the future, of Antichrist, just as Abel and David were figures of Christ.[134]

This lengthy quote from Haimo extends far beyond the Gloss's brief summary of the point, again demonstrating Peter's penchant for precision and thoroughness.

This lengthy gloss is then complemented, or perhaps opposed, by an equally lengthy quote from Augustine. The citation begins with Augustine confessing his ignorance as to the proper meaning of the text and surveying the options. He expresses his disdain for those who associate this passage with the Roman imperial power and with the variety of speculations about the return of Nero. Augustine places them all in the same category and dismisses them: "For myself, I am astonished at the great presumption of those who venture such guesses."[135] The scrupulous glossator had removed this sentence from his quote, but Peter restores the text in its entirety. In addition, the gloss had placed this passage first among the marginal glosses on verses 6–7, but Peter has moved it to the end. Why?

---

134. "Nam diabolus iam operatur mysterium iniquitatis. . . . Mysterium ergo iniquitatis appellat interfectionem sanctorum et persecutionem quam inferebant Nero et princeps eius fidelibus Christi, quorum iam factum quasi Antichristi videbatur. . . . iam tunc diabolus occulte per Neronem et alios operabatur occidendo martyres, sicut tunc aperte operaturus est per Antichristum interficiendo Eliam et Enoch aliosque plurimos. . . . Et sunt Nero et alii umbra futuri scilicet Antichristi, sicut Abel et David fuerunt figura Christi." PL 192.318C.

135. "Sed multum mira mihi est haec opiniatum tanta praesumptio." PL 192.319A; cf. Augustine, CD 20.19, CCSL 47, 732; and Chapter 3 in this volume.

The net effect of this arrangement places Augustine in a dialectical relationship with the more literal opinions of Haimo and Ambrosiaster. With a rhetorical flourish similar to Augustine's own, Peter thus qualifies the citation of Haimo by placing Augustine as a
sort of commentary upon him. With Haimo's comments lined up
immediately before Augustine's, Haimo is implicated along with the
other "presumptuous" speculators on Nero and Rome. While we
never hear Peter in his own voice, his arrangement of the material
allows Augustine to speak for him to discourage such apocalyptic realism.

Having disposed of the apocalyptic realist position in such a way,
Peter then gives a thoroughgoing spiritual reading of the mystery of
iniquity, again drawing on the GO and on Augustine. Evil within the
Church, now lying secret, will remain so "until it is led out of hiding, when a person will not be anymore ashamed to commit adul-
tery or . . . any such thing as they are to walk or speak."[136] Or, similarly, the mystery of iniquity is the hidden number, not of vices, but
of the evil and false Christians themselves who remain in the church
until they constitute a great people for Antichrist. With this in mind,
the Lombard echoes Augustine's warning: "Let those who now hold
faith cling to it, and persevere in it firmly."[137] It seems clear that this
is the message and interpretation that Peter prefers.

The remainder of the commentary upon chapter 2 proceeds in
much the same way. Peter presents a thorough summary of the traditional facts and hypotheses of Antichrist's story, mostly from
Haimo: The devil will possess Antichrist completely, but not like
madmen, who are not responsible for their actions.[138] He will be
killed by Christ upon his return, but the means of his execution are

136. "donec iniquitas quae modo est mystica fiat de medio, id est aliquid de commu-
nibus, ut non erubescat homo adulterari . . . et alia huiusmodi facere, sicut nec ambulare,
neque loqui." PL 192.319B.

137. "Tantum hoc superest agendum, ut quit tenet nunc fidem teneat, id est firmiter
in ea perseveret, donec mysterium inquitatis de medio fiat." PL 192.319C.

138. PL 192.320C; cf. Haimo, PL 117.781D.

unknown. Antichrist may be killed by the power of the Holy Spirit or by the power of Christ's spoken word, or, perhaps, by Michael the Archangel.[139] Peter tells us of Antichrist's attempted ascension on the Mount of Olives and of the delay between his death and Christ's return. He includes Haimo's comparison of Antichrist's works to the illusions of Simon Magus and Augustine's more agnostic admission that they could be called "lying signs" either because they are illusions or because, though real, they lead people toward the devil, the father of lies.[140] Peter Lombard assembles all of these opinions directly from the GO, without expansion or correction, and without any apparent attempt to dispose of one or the other opinion in the dialectical fashion I have demonstrated above. Perhaps he cannot, since the tradition seems to offer no "spiritual reading" of these verses. Peter must be content in this case only to summarize the traditions he has received.

For the remainder of chapter 2 and all of chapter 3 that follows, Peter Lombard seems content to do just that: to summarize the traditions presented in the GO. Chapter 3's purpose is not disputed throughout the tradition. Indeed, as I have shown, many scholars have all but ignored the third chapter in their exegesis. Those who do comment seem to be in considerable agreement on the meaning of Paul's instructions in this passage. On verse 2, "for not all have faith," Peter echoes the GO. Either it means that all who will receive the Gospel have not yet done so, or, as with Augustine, it refers to those whose fate is preordained and predestined for destruction. Peter again seems to express no preference.

On Paul's specific instructions concerning the "troublemakers" (curiosos), Peter rehearses the tradition. With Ambrosiaster, he comments on verse 8, "nor did we eat anyone's bread for free, but working day and night in labor and toil, lest we burden any of you," that Paul teaches not only by his words, but by his deeds and actions, too.

---

139. PL 192.320B cf. Haimo, PL 117.781C.
140. PL 192.320B cf. Haimo, PL 117.781C.

On the prohibition of verse 10, "if someone does not want to work, he should not eat," Peter, like the gloss, turns to Augustine's *On the Work of Monks,* finding the assurance that Paul refers here literally to work of the body, by which Christians should provide for their own needs. In his era, before the outbreak of mendicant movements, Peter Lombard is content to leave it at that.[141]

Peter Lombard's commentary on 2 Thessalonians does not in itself seem to be a tremendous improvement upon the content of the Ordinary Gloss. Upon the merits of this little letter alone, one cannot see why so many turned to this *magna glosatura* over the so-called *parva glosatura* and *media glosatura.* And yet, Peter's comments on chapter 2 of the letter demonstrate the advantages of the continuous-gloss structure for the construction of a theological opinion. Peter, whose apparent distaste for apocalyptic speculation would later lead him to leave any mention of Antichrist out of his systematic theology in the *Sentences,*[142] is compelled to address the topic in 2 Thessalonians as part of his commentary on the Pauline corpus. But he does so in a way that controls and limits most of the Antichrist speculation by its enclosure within a more palatable Augustinian spiritual interpretation. Peter's commentary thus carries on the Carolingian tradition of careful, strategic reading across the breadth of the exegetical tradition in order to present, at least implicitly, his Augustinian point of view.

But despite Peter's implicit argument against Antichrist, his commentary, together with the Gloss, testifies to the survival of several

141. Though it is beyond the scope of this study, it would be interesting to see what Franciscan exegetes did with 2 Th 3. Paul's advice and Augustine's concomitant interpretation of Mt 6 would seem to be a stumbling block to Franciscan readers.

142. See Colish, 714. For her, Peter's exclusion of Antichrist from the *Sentences* reflects his opinion that "it is not a subject upon which responsible theological research can be done. It is not a field in which certitude is available. Thus it should not be allowed to obstruct the logical and theological passage of the structure from the ethical and sacramental lives of Christians to their posthumous outcomes." Ibid.

strands of tradition concerning Antichrist and the end of time. Indeed, it is testimony to the fact that these several strands can, and do, coexist within a single commentary. Throughout this study of apocalyptic exegesis, such coexistence has proven to be the hallmark of early medieval work. The opinions of the earlier Fathers seem to fall on one side or the other, either more in favor of a literal reading of the apocalyptic events with Ambrosiaster, Pelagius, Theodore, and even Jerome, or for the spiritual reading of the passage in the manner of Tyconius and Augustine. If in the "last Father," Gregory, we find also the first medieval exegete of 2 Thessalonians, it is in part due to Gregory's incorporation of *both* opinions with almost equal emphasis in his thought.[143] In one way or the other, such ambivalence or inclusivity is a quality found in each of the exegetes I have studied. Whether through the frank and fastidious inclusion of both traditions, as in Rabanus, or through the interesting disparity between Haimo's interpretations of 2 Thessalonians and the Apocalypse, medieval exegetes have preserved both apocalyptic realism and Tyconian spiritual interpretation—with different emphases, of course. Such a policy of inclusion is no less true for the scholastic exegesis of Peter Lombard; though he may not like the topic, still, he preserves the exegetical traditions on both sides.

But after Peter's commentary, and perhaps because it becomes established as the authoritative summary of the tradition, the exegetical strategy for interpreting this letter seems to change. On the one hand, a monastic author such as Hervaeus of Bourg-Dieu combines the traditional twofold exegesis of the letter with further attention to the moral meaning for the contemporary reader.[144] On the other hand, scholastic authors such as Robert of Melun and an anonymous Victorine commentator prefer to interrogate the text

143. Augustine includes both in the *City of God*, but, as I have argued, the structure of the book and his other comments on matters apocalyptic help to discern his preferred reading.

144. Hervaeus of Bourg-Dieu, *In Epistolam II ad Thessalonicenses*, PL 181.1385–1404.

and the tradition with a few pointed theological questions in an explicit attempt to negotiate between interpretations.[145] Peter Lombard's commentary stands at the point of origin for both traditions. The *Collectanea in epistolas omnes Pauli* is both the capstone of the exegetical tradition I have been tracing, the classic summary of seven centuries of interpretation, and the foundation stone for a new, scholastic style of exegesis that no longer feels the need to recapitulate that tradition. Peter Lombard's commentary on 2 Thessalonians represents the culmination of the integrative exegetical style found in Gregory and honed in the Carolingian period, which brings the twin traditions of apocalyptic realism and Tyconian spiritualism into some balance. Explicit dialectic would replace this reverent and subtle—perhaps at times too subtle—method, and the firebrand ideas of Joachim of Fiore would kindle the flame of controversy in the beams of the apocalyptic tradition. Peter's commentary, reserved in style and inclusive in content, precedes all these developments. Indeed, it is the classic work upon which these novelties are based or from which they depart.

145. Robert of Melun, *Oeuvres de Robert de Melun*, ed. Raymond M. Martin, O.P., vol. 2: *Quaestiones de epistolis Pauli* (Lovain: Spicilegium Sacrum Louvainiense, 1938); [Ps] Hugh of St. Victor, *Quaestiones in Epistolam II ad Thessalonicences*, PL 175.589–94.

CHAPTER 6

CONCLUSION

It should be no surprise to any student of early medieval literature, and especially of early medieval exegesis, that the fruit of medieval thinking was a synthesis of earlier patristic authorities. What I
have studied across eight centuries is the emergence of an early medieval exegetical tradition. Early medieval exegetes constructed a
reading of 2 Thessalonians that united and synthesized opposed positions, and thus arrived at a complex new understanding of the
presence and absence, the immanence and imminence, of the apocalyptic Adversary. But such a synthesis was not simply the product of
some medieval deference to authority or predisposition to harmonizing apparent opposites. If these traits are truly to be found in the
intellectual life of the Middle Ages, they do not suffice to explain
away the synthesis of presence and anticipation in the 2 Thessalonians commentary tradition. The synthetic readings I have identified
represent efforts to discern the sense and structure of Christian eschatology, which is always rooted in the past (in the life and identity
of Jesus), but projected toward the future (toward the consummation of time and history in the end). In other words, these synthetic
readings give shape to medieval Christian life and history as suspended between the resurrection of Christ and the heavenly
Jerusalem. In so doing, they preserve the dynamic tension of the
New Testament's apocalyptic symbols and develop Pauline eschatology in greater detail.

The Early Medieval Synthesis:
Summarizing the Chronological Argument

The roots of the exegetical tradition around 2 Thessalonians are sunk in the soil of conflict. In the late fourth and early fifth centuries, the commentaries of Ambrosiaster, Pelagius, and Theodore of Mopsuestia, together with Jerome's letter to Algasia, express what I have taken to be the "mainline eschatology" of the ancient Christian Church. Though there are some differences of opinion upon the details of the end, these four texts share the general conviction that the "rebellion" will be a distinct historical event in the future and that Antichrist will be a concrete individual acting in history.

But this general consensus faced a formidable adversary. Augustine of Hippo accuses those who maintain such a realist apocalyptic eschatology of "presumption." To pretend to know clearly the details of the events of the end is to reach beyond the grasp of human knowledge. One can know only the essential facts of the coming of Antichrist and the end. With Tyconius, Augustine offers an alternative reading of eschatology that posits that the importance of texts such as 2 Thessalonians lay in their immanent spiritual meaning, as an assessment of the divided body of the present Church in which there are many antichrists. While dogmatic summaries of the essential events of revealed eschatology are permitted, they are clearly subordinated to the immanent moral understanding of eventual judgment.

By the fifth century, then, it is clear that opinion upon matters eschatological is divided. The majority of early Christian exegetes of 2 Thessalonians believe that the letter offers a historical account of the end of time and the coming Antichrist. Consequently, they endeavor in their commentaries to understand the particular historical details to which the letter seems to refer. Against these figures stands Augustine. While he shared the support of thinkers such as Jerome in opposing a millennialist reading of the Apocalypse, and while he, too, will agree to the most general outline of "eschatological events," including the rise and the fall of Antichrist, he seems to stand alone (with only the heterodox Tyconius) in his consistent resistance to any detailed realist eschatology. Nevertheless, because of his position as the preeminent Doctor of the Western Church, his opinion would hold formidable authority for the centuries that followed.

Early medieval exegetes quarry the patristic writings—commentaries, letters, sermons, and treatises—for any reference to 2 Thessalonians or the figures and doctrines to which it refers. These comments form the building blocks, the bricks and mortar, from which early medieval exegetes construct their own commentaries, and, in so doing, construct the symbol of Antichrist himself. These opinions—of Ambrosiaster, Pelagius, Jerome, Augustine, Theodore, and even Gregory—together form what Pierre Hadot has called the "topics" of an exegetical tradition, the "formulae, images, and metaphors that forcibly impose themselves on the writer . . . in such a way that the use of these prefabricated models seems indispensable to them in order to be able to express their own thoughts."[1] The figure of Antichrist that emerges—both the single historical figure awaited by Ambrosiaster and the community of wickedness hidden within the Church found in Tyconius, Augustine, and Gregory—is complex and suspended through time.

The greater part of early medieval interpretive effort is devoted to that future figure of Antichrist; the Tyconian reading receives its most vivid portrayal in Gregory and thereafter is consistent in its admonition to believers that they should avoid evil lest they be part of the body of Antichrist. Medieval exegetes mostly comb the patristic tradition to arrive at an understanding of the signs of the end and Antichrist. To this primary reading, most fuse elements of the Augustinian interpretation, but always as yet another meaning of the text, not in opposition to the rest. Augustine's seemingly reluctant

---

1. Hadot, *Philosophy as a Way of Life*, 66–67.

admission that the Scriptures *may* refer to a sequence of historical events in the end is seized by early medieval exegesis as a point of harmony that dulls his polemical edge.

For example, Gregory the Great's exegetical work includes several thematic improvisations upon the Tyconian/Augustinian image of the body of Antichrist. But Gregory incorporates this spiritual reading into an apocalyptic fugue, a contrapuntal play of presence and anticipation that announces the imminence of Antichrist's arrival through the signs of his immanence. The flourishing of the body of Antichrist within the Church can only provide further testimony to the approach of its head in the last days. Gregory, the "last of the Latin Fathers" points the way to early medieval eschatological exegesis, insofar as he integrates the Tyconian/Augustinian imagery into a predominantly realistic apocalyptic account.

Two and a half centuries later, Carolingian exegesis of 2 Thessalonians carries an echo of Gregory's apocalyptic fugue, holding together Antichrist's two bodies—the social body of the present and the individual body to come. Using their distinctive exegetical methods, wherein commentary consists of layering patristic excerpts to construct a new synthetic whole, Carolingian exegetes such as Rabanus Maurus and Sedulius Scotus continue to incorporate the Augustinian position into a realist reading of the text drawn from Theodore and Pelagius, respectively. Florus of Lyons makes no attempt to integrate particular patristic opinions in any way, since he prefers to produce independent summaries of the opinions of Augustine, Jerome, and Gregory. Nevertheless, Florus appears willing to summarize both the apocalyptic realism of Jerome and the anti-apocalyptic reading of Augustine, without any apparent sense of opposition between them. For all of these thinkers, it is not at all problematic to place the two positions side-by-side.

Haimo of Auxerre presents perhaps the most interesting exception to this tendency among the Carolingians, since he makes no attempt in his 2 Thessalonians commentary to include an Augustinian perspective. Instead, he offers only realist apocalypticism in his

Pauline commentary, saving the Augustinian/Tyconian interpretation for his commentary on the Apocalypse. Haimo's departure from the general integrative approach to 2 Thessalonians in fact reflects a further development in the early medieval synthetic approach to apocalyptic matters. Haimo accepts the "peaceful coexistence" of the apocalyptic realist and Latin spiritual traditions of interpretation, but distinguishes between them on the basis of genre. The spiritual interpretation is appropriate to the visionary text of the Apocalypse, while the apocalyptic realist interpretation fits the more practical catechetical purposes of Paul. In Haimo, then, we find harmony between the traditions, but in a different key. In all cases, what is distinctive about the Carolingian commentaries is the simultaneity of presence and anticipation, together with a deep reluctance to predict the end. This combination of elements, I have argued, is not simply a consequence of their methods of harmonizing the Fathers. Rather, it both fosters and reflects a nonpredictive psychological imminence characteristic of early medieval apocalypticism, which feeds the early medieval imagination with apocalyptic imagery and rhetoric. The 2 Thessalonians tradition testifies to the persistent presence of apocalypticism that may or may not have intensified around key dates or events, but never disappears from the cultural imagination even when imminent "prophecies pass away" (1 Cor 13:8).

In the midst of the renewal and reform movements of the eleventh century, scholarship on 2 Thessalonians takes on a new face in the schools of France. These early scholastic commentaries pay close attention to the "rhetorical situation" of Paul's letter: to whom he wrote, why he wrote, the form of his argument. Consequently, their commentaries, like Haimo's, prefer the apocalyptic realist reading of the text: Paul wrote to the Thessalonian community to give the signs of the end. Thus, even when Lanfranc cites Augustine, he edits the text in such a way that the Father's statements seem to support, rather than contradict, the traditional realist account.

With the *Glossa Ordinaria* and Peter Lombard's commentary in the early twelfth century, this early medieval consensus begins to dissolve. Through a more thorough retrieval of the Augustinian sources, these two commentaries suggest that patristic interpretations of the text may not be so harmoniously integrated. The glossator simply presents the two theological positions in a dialectical fashion, without attempting to resolve the argument or harmonize the sources. Peter Lombard, on the other hand, advocates the Augustinian position, thereby upsetting the balance found in earlier sources between presence and expectation. To a certain extent, what Peter has done is to retrieve from Augustine the tension and opposition between readings that the early medieval tradition had united. In Peter Lombard's commentary on 2 Thessalonians, we see both the last evidence of the early medieval commentary tradition and the first evidence of its demise. While Peter's work retains the *form* of the early medieval commentary—a running text, inclusive of a variety of patristic and medieval opinions upon it—the argument of his reading is deliberately opposed to the consensus of opinion throughout the early medieval tradition. Peter's commentary, though formally consistent with the early medieval exegetical tradition, effectively subverts that tradition with a strategic retrieval and re-deployment of the opinions of Saint Augustine.

This is not to say that Peter Lombard ends realist apocalyptic speculation. In fact, even before the Joachimist "revival" of apocalyptic speculation, one finds ample evidence of twelfth-century interest in apocalyptic matters. For example, there are at least forty surviving manuscripts of Adso's treatise on Antichrist, under various pseudonyms, from the twelfth century, showing some considerable interest in the apocalyptic Adversary. What we find in Peter Lombard's commentary is rather the end of a general consensus on the basic sense of the text and, perhaps, then, the end of the psychological imminence that balances presence and expectation of Antichrist. After Peter, writers choose whether to accept the traditional realist reading or to reject it as Peter had. What we see with Peter Lombard, then, is the beginnings of a divide between what Marcia

Colish has called "monastic" and "scholastic" eschatology.[2] For Colish, "monastic" eschatology "anxiously seeks to answer questions arising from the worries of people concerned with what is going to happen to their own souls . . . during the coming last days." It "also reflects a tendency to politicize the idea of Antichrist . . . sometimes connecting this theme with the tradition of Nero as Antichrist."[3] "Scholastic" theologians, on the other hand, "have no hortatory or visionary concerns, and they take a dim view of apocalyptic speculation."[4] If these categories are understood as heuristic rather than denotative, with the understanding that there are "scholastic" monks and "monastic" school-trained friars,[5] she is certainly right to identify a parting of the ways, a division that we can recognize in Peter Lombard. But it is important to note that the monastic writers are not just those "who write in light of popular belief."[6] They draw on a long and well-developed tradition of thought, one to which the 2 Thessalonians commentaries bear witness. It is the scholastic writers (and only some of them) who recover the minority position of Augustine or disregard apocalyptic symbols altogether. "Scholastic" eschatology, at least as represented by Peter Lombard and those dependent upon him, represents real innovation in the tradition of eschatological reflection.

The Persistence of Apocalypticism: Implications for the History of Theology

Early medieval exegesis of 2 Thessalonians challenges still-prevalent assumptions about the history of medieval theological eschatology. Traditionally, the history of apocalyptic eschatology in the early Middle Ages has followed the contours of a tragic "decline-and-fall"

---

2. Colish, 698–701. 3. Colish, 698.

4. Colish, 699.

5. Peter Olivi being perhaps the most striking example of a scholastic visionary. See David Burr, esp. chs. 1–3.

6. Colish, 698.

plot line. While the early Fathers of the Church had a vivid sense of the imminence of the Lord's coming, the tides of time gradually eroded these apocalyptic convictions. With Augustine, the story goes, apocalyptic speculation receives a thorough dressing-down as an area of serious theological reflection. After Augustine, apocalyptic texts are consistently interpreted in a spiritual fashion, as an allegory of the Church in the present time. Thus Stephen D. O'Leary's engaging study of the rhetoric of apocalyptic argument still presumes that the "allegorical understanding of prophecy developed out of necessity in the centuries after the Apocalypse was produced."[7] O'Leary's argument continues:

With the passage of time and the conversion of the empire to Christianity, however, the text [the Apocalypse] became more and more difficult to interpret as a set of historical predictions: the prophesied End had failed to materialize, and the former Antichrist now convened ecclesiastical councils and used his troops to suppress heresy. . . . Under these circumstances, the drama of the End came to appear as an allegorical representation of the Church's struggle against its enemies in all ages.[8]

The allegorical understanding of Augustine is taken to be the natural and inevitable response to the frustrated expectations of the early Church. After Augustine, Christian theology abandoned apocalyptic realism for allegory, and, its seems, lost its apocalyptic edge. As the story often goes, the aversion to apocalyptic speculation and this allegorical tradition of interpretation dominated Christian eschatology until Joachim of Fiore's prophetic, historical interpreta-

---

7. O'Leary, 72.

8. O'Leary, 202. My intent is not to disparage in any way O'Leary's contribution to scholarship on apocalypticism. Rather, I have chosen to use his work as my example because its powerful argument about the internal logic of apocalyptic rhetoric presumes that this univocal, unidirectional development in the history of eschatology is self-evident, when it need not. My argument, in my view, could only help O'Leary's in the long run, since it argues for the persistence of both what O'Leary calls the "tragic" (realist) reading and what he calls the "comic" (spiritual) interpretation of Augustine throughout the tradition of theological reflection.

tion of the Apocalypse revived the enthusiasm of the early Church in the twelfth century.

This reading of the early Middle Ages, or at least of early medieval high culture, as essentially post-apocalyptic, has been challenged by scholars such as Richard Landes and Johannes Fried. They have recovered hints and clues of apocalyptic movements at certain key times in medieval history. Like them, to paraphrase Mark Twain, I believe the death of apocalypticism in the Middle Ages has been greatly exaggerated. The force of Augustine's spiritual and ecclesial reading of the Apocalypse, while significant, simply cannot overcome the realism of the medieval apocalyptic imagination. For Landes and Fried, this suggests a hidden history of apocalyptic enthusiasms, one subdued or erased by more conservative clerical elites. But the 2 Thessalonians tradition suggests that apocalyptic realism is both more pervasive and less subversive than any particular imminent millennialism, whether of A.M. 6000, A.D. 1000, A.D. 1033, or some other. The apocalyptic imagination is a constant cultural fact in the Middle Ages, and its essential vocabulary is preserved and explicated in the 2 Thessalonians tradition. But if apocalyptic hope and anxiety broke out in Rabanus Maurus's Fulda or in Lanfranc's Bec, no particular traces of this outbreak show up in their commentaries. The most we can theorize, I think, is an apparent change of temperature in medieval apocalyptic thought in the years after 1000, connected intimately to the Gregorian reform movement and reflected in the commentaries of Lanfranc and Bruno.

But even these readings are shaped as much by the "restless traditionality" of the commentaries that precede them, and so the terms of discussion remain rather constant throughout the early medieval period. The 2 Thessalonians tradition offers a reading of apocalypticism that is neither millennialist prophesying nor ahistorical allegorizing. The reading that emerges preserves a sense of God's presence and activity in history while at the same time protecting that sense from erratic predictive fantasies. Antichrist always threatens from the future as the embodiment of the human rejection of the Gospel, and is always slain in Christ's triumphant return. Through the ongoing development of the doctrinal portrait of Antichrist, the dramatic character of the apocalyptic imagination preserves the Christian "sense of an ending" that invests human life "in the middest" with meaning and direction.[9] In so doing, the 2 Thessalonians tradition explicates a tradition of Christian eschatology that can be found throughout the New Testament.

New Testament scholars since Cullmann and Jeremias have long discussed the nature of the Kingdom of God in the parables of Jesus as "eschatology in the process of realization" or "proleptic eschatology." In the preaching of Jesus, the Kingdom of God is both "already" and "not yet."[10] This mutuality of the "already" and the "not yet" is constitutive of the classical Christian understanding of time and history. What some scholars have worried about with regard to apocalyptic literature as a genre is a perceived tendency to relieve the tension in favor of the future. That is, in the traditional account, apocalyptic texts find it difficult to discern signs of the Kingdom already at work in the world; instead, they view this age as wholly wicked and await the catastrophic intervention of the Kingdom of God as the age to come. However, such bold-faced dualistic apocalyptic eschatology does not really appear in the New Testament, since faith in Christ seems to obviate the radical pessimism of some earlier apocalyptic traditions.[11] Our initial discussion of 2 Thessalonians, where the already/not yet dynamic is seen in the presence and anticipation of both the "restrainer" and the "iniquity" that it/he restrains, is one case among several. Canonical Christian apocalyptic eschatology retains the tension between the already and the not yet.

9. Frank Kermode, *Sense of an Ending.*

10. Oscar Cullmann, *Christ and Time;* Joachim Jeremias, *The Parables of Jesus,* 2nd rev. ed. (New York: Charles Scribner and Sons, 1972); Norman Perrin, *The Kingdom of God in the Teaching of Jesus* (Philadelphia: Westminster Press, 1963).

11. James D. G. Dunn, *Unity and Diversity in the New Testament,* 2nd ed. (Valley Forge: Trinity Press International, 1990), ch. 13.

The 2 Thessalonians tradition explicates this tension further. The realist reading preserves the "not yet" of Christian anticipation. The elements of the Latin spiritual reading wove the sense of God's presence in history into the fabrics of the individual Christian's moral life and the life of the Church. Taken as a whole, the synthetic medieval reading represents a sober reflection upon the useful theological elements of the doctrines of Antichrist and the end. In effect, the early medieval tradition sketches the limits and possibilities of what one might call "orthodox" apocalyptic expectation. It may be—though I can only suggest it as something worth further inquiry—that the dissolution of this synthesis is more catalyst than response to the appearance of more radical apocalypticisms in the later Middle Ages. Apocalypticism is persistent; attempts—whether medieval or modern—to erase it from "respectable" Christianity may simply lead to its springing up in more radical and volatile forms outside the mainstream. Regardless, such tensive apocalypticism is a consistent feature of early medieval exegesis of 2 Thessalonians.

In the end, scholars such as Jaroslav Pelikan are right, but only partly so, to speak of "the apocalyptic vision and its transformation" in the early Church as "nothing less than the decisive shift from the categories of cosmic drama to those of being, from the Revelation of St. John to the creed of the Council of Nicea."[12] But neither is it the case that the withdrawal from imminent expectation is an elite conservative conspiracy of silence against popular imminent millennialism. Indeed, the cosmic drama of the Parousia was less and less the focus of Christology, sacramental theology, and other areas of theological speculation. But if the drama was no longer center stage, the set was never struck. The apocalyptic structure of history, the expectation of the Adversary, and the "psychological imminence" of the end became the backdrop against which these other theological elements were rehearsed. Apocalypticism was a persist-

---

12. Pelikan, vol. 1: *The Emergence of the Catholic Tradition (100–600)*, 123–32.

ent element of the medieval imagination, made all the more persist-ent by its release from predictive imminence or millennialism. For the first millennium of Christianity, early medieval theologians con-tinued to "live in the shadow of the Second Coming"[13] and to pon-der what that Second Coming might entail.

So Antichrist was alive and well in the early Middle Ages, both as the immanent presence of evil and as the coming evil one. In the 2 Thessalonians tradition, apocalyptic realism provides the most fer-tile ground for speculation, debate, and development, but it is al-ways balanced or supplemented in some way by the Augustinian spiritual interpretation. It is at the fault line between the two fields—in the encounter between apocalyptic realism and spiritual exegesis—that a distinctive early medieval apocalypticism is born. The double sense of Antichrist's presence in the midst of the Church and his historical persona still to come produces just the sort of non-predictive, psychological imminence that helps create the distinctive medieval ethos of *"Christianitas,"* or "Christendom."[14] The 2 Thessalonians tradition documents the development and longevity of this ethos in microcosm. Through the words of Paul, exegetes across the first millennium of the Christian Church con-structed a theological portrait of Antichrist, and they remained con-vinced, with the Apostle, that the apocalyptic Adversary was still to come, and yet, paradoxically, already at work in their midst.

13. I take the phrase from McGinn, "End of the World," 67. He, in turn, has adopted the phrase from Timothy Weber's book about American millenarian thought, *Living in the Shadow of the Second Coming: American Premillennialism 1875–1982* (Chicago: University of Chicago Press, 1987).

14. See Ch. 1, n. 41.

BIBLIOGRAPHY

Commentaries on 2 Thessalonians

Ambrosiaster. *Commentarius in epistulas Paulinas.* CSEL 81, part 3. Ed. Henry Joseph Vogels. Vienna: Hoelder-Pichler-Tempsky, 1969.

Atto of Vercelli. Patrologia Latina 134.655–664.

Biblia Latina cum Glossa Ordinaria. Facsimile Reprint of the Editio Princeps. Adolph Rusch of Strassburg 1480/1. Introduction by Karlfried Froehlich and Margaret T. Gibson. Turnhout: Brepols, 1992.

   MS University of Chicago Rosenburger f. 24–5. Vol. 4.

Bruno the Carthusian. Patrologia Latina 153.413–424.

Florus of Lyons. Patrologia Latina 121.545–549.

Gilbert of Poitiers. MS Cistercienser 58 (XII), f. 1–198.

Haimo of Auxerre [Haimo of Halberstadt]. Patrologia Latina 117.765–784.

   MS Bonn 288 (Koblenz, Jesuiten) f. 173–183.

   MS Bonn 289 (Eberhardsklausen) f. 221–230.

   MS Schlägl 194 (120), f. 113–122.

Hervaeus of Bourg-Dieu. Patrologia Latina 181.1385–1404.

[Ps.] Hugh of St. Victor. Patrologia Latina 175.589–594.

John Chrysostom. *Homilies on Thessalonians.* Ed. Philip Schaff. Nicene and Post-Nicene Fathers, 1st series, vol. 13. Grand Rapids: Eerdmans, 1965.

Lanfranc. Patrologia Latina 150.339–346.

Pelagius. *Pelagius's Exposition of the Thirteen Epistles of Saint Paul.* Texts and Studies 9. Edited with introduction by Alexander Souter. Cambridge: Cambridge University Press, 1922.

Peter Lombard. Patrologia Latina 192.311–326.

(Ps.) Primasius. Patrologia Latina 68.639–650.

Rabanus Maurus. Patrologia Latina 112.565–580.

Robert of Melun. *Oeuvres de Robert de Melun.* Ed. Raymond M. Martin, O.P. Vol. 2: *Quaestiones de epistolis Pauli.* Louvain: Spicilegium Sacrum Louvainiense, 1938.

Sedulius Scotus. *Collectanea in epistolam secundam ad Thessalonicenses.* Patrologia Latina 103.221–224.

Theodore of Mopsuestia. *Theodori episcopi in epistolas beati Pauli commentarii*. Ed. H. B. Swete. Vol. 2. Cambridge: Cambridge University Press, 1880–82.

Thietland of Einsiedeln. *In Epistolam II ad Thessalonicenses*, MS Einsiedeln 38:184ᵛ.

Other Primary Texts

"Acts of the Holy Apostles Peter and Paul." *Ante-Nicene Fathers* 8. Ed. Cyril Richardson, 477–486. Grand Rapids: Eerdmans, 1981.

"Acts of Peter." *New Testament Apocrypha*. Vol. 2. Ed. Wilhelm Schneemelcher, 271–321. Louisville: Westminster–John Knox Press, 1991.

Adso Dervensis. *De ortu et tempore Antichristi*. Ed. Daniel Verhelst. CCCM 45. Turnhout: Brepols, 1976.

Annales Fuldenses, ad an. 848. MGH: Scriptores rerum Germanicarum 1:365.

Augustine of Hippo, Saint. *De civitate Dei*. Ed. Bernard Dombart and Alphonsus Kalb. CCSL 47–48. Turnhout: Brepols, 1955. English translation *The City of God*. Trans. Henry Bettenson. New York: Penguin, 1972.

———. *Contra Faustum*. Patrologia Latina 42.207–518.

———. *De doctrina christiana*. Trans. D. W. Robertson Jr. New York: Macmillan, 1964.

———. *Epistolae*. Patrologia Latina 33. English translation in *Letters of Saint Augustine*. Fathers of the Church. Washington, D.C.: Catholic University Press, 1964.

———. *De gratia et libero arbitrio*. Patrologia Latina.

———. *Homiliae in epistola 1 Johannis*. Patrologia Latina 34.1999. English translation by John Burnaby. *Augustine: Later Works*. Library of Christian Classics. Philadelphia: Westminster–John Knox Press, 1955.

———. *Retractionum libri duo*. Ed. Pius Knöll. CSEL 36. Vienna: Hoelder, Pichler, Tempsky, 1902.

Bernard of Clairvaux. *Epistolae. Opera Bernardi*, vol. 8. Ed. J. Leclercq, C. H. Talbot, and H. M. Rochais. Rome: Editiones Cistercienes, 1957–1977.

Biblia Latina cum Glossa Ordinaria. Facsimile Reprint of the Editio Princeps. Adolph Rusch of Strassburg 1480/1. Introduction by Karlfried Froehlich and Margaret T. Gibson. Turnhout: Brepols, 1992.

MS University of Chicago Rosenburger f24–5. 4 vols.

Cassiodorus. *De institutione divinarum litterarum*. Patrologia Latina 70.1105–1150.

Eclogae tractatorum in Psalterium (Wendepunkte 6B). Corpus Christianorum, Scriptores Celtingae. Ed. Carol Ann Sheppard. Turnhout: Brepols, forthcoming.

Eusebius of Caesarea. *Ecclesiasticae historiae*. Patrologia Graece 20.9–904.

———. *Oratio de laudibus Constantini*. Patrologia Graece 20.1315–1438.

Gennadius. *De viris inlustribus*. Ed. Philip Schaff. Nicene and Post-Nicene Fathers, 2nd series, vol. 3. Grand Rapids: Eerdmans, 1952.

Glossa Ordinaria. Part 22. CCCM 170. Ed. Mary Dove. Turnhout: Brepols, 1997.

Gregory the Great. *Homiliae in euangeliis*. Patrologia Latina 76.

———. *Moralia in Iob*. CCSL 143–143B. Ed. Marcus Adriaen. Turnhout: Brepols, 1979–1985.

———. *Regula pastoralis*. 2 vols. Ed. Bruno Junic. Paris: Éditions du Cerf, 1992.

Haimo of Auxerre. *Expositio in Apocalypsin*. Patrilogia Latina 117.937–1220.

Humbert of Candida Silva. *Libri III adversus simoniacos*. MGH: Libelli de Lite I. Ed. F. Thanner. Hanover, 1891.

Irenaeus of Lyons. *Adversus haereses*. Ed. W. W. Harvey. Cambridge: Cambridge University Press, 1857.

Isidore of Seville. *Etymologiarum*. Patrologia Latina 82.73–728.

John Cassian. *De coenobiorum Institutis* X. PL 49. 375–383.

Jerome. *Commentarius in Danielem*. Sancti Hieronymi Presbyteri Opera, CCSL 75A. Ed. F. Glorie. Turnhout: Brepols, 1964.

———. *Commentarii in Isaiam*. Sancti Hieronymi Presbyteri Opera, CCSL 73. Ed. Marcus Adriaen. Turnhout: Brepols, 1963.

———. *Commentarii in prophetas minores*. Sancti Hieronymi Presbyteri Opera, CCSL 76–76A. Ed. Marcus Adriaen. Turnhout: Brepols, 1969–1970.

———. *Epistulae*. CSEL 66. Ed. I. Hillberg. Vienna: Hoelder-Pichler-Tempsky, 1961.

Maximus of Turin. *Homily 85*. Patrologia Latina 57.445–450.

Pseudo-Methodius. "Revelations." In *Sibyllinische Texte und Forschungen*, ed. Ernst Sackur, 59–96. Halle: Niemeyer, 1898.

Muretach. *In Donati artem maiorem*, CCCM 40. Ed. Louis Holtz. Turnhout: Brepols, 1977.

Nouveau Recueil des inscriptions Chrétiennes de la Gaule. Ed. E. LeBlant. Collections de documents inédits sur l'histoire de France, no. 248. Paris, 1892.

Origen of Alexandria. *On First Principles*. Trans. G. W. Butterworth. New York: Peter Smith, 1973.

Peter Lombard. *Sententiae in IV libris distinctae*. 3rd ed. Edited with introduction by Ignatius Brady. Rome: Grottaferrata Collegii Sanctae Bonaventurae ad Claras Aquas, 1971–1981.

Rabanus Maurus. *Allegoriam in universam sacra scripturam*. Patrologia Latina 112.849–1088.

———. *Commentaria in libros Machabaeorum*. Patrologia Latina 109.1125–1256.

———. *De institutione clericorum*. Patrologia Latina 107.293–420.

———. *De universo*. Patrologia Latina 111.9–614.

———. *Ennarrationum in Epistolas Beati Pauli*, Praefatio. Patrologia Latina 111.1275–1276.

———. *Expositio in Mattheum*. CCCM 174–174A. Ed. Bengt Löfstedt. Turnout: Brepols, 2000.

———. *Expostio super Jeremiam prophetam*. Patrologia Latina 111.793–1272.

————. *Hymnus in Pentecosten (Veni Creator Spiritus)*. Analecta Hymnica Medii Aevi 50. Ed. Guido Maria Dreves, S.J. Leipzig: Reisland, 1905.

————. *Martyrologium, Liber de computo*. CCCM 44. Ed. J. McCullough and W. M. Stevens. Turnhout: Brepols, 1979.

Remigius of Auxerre. *Expositio super Genesim*. CCCM 136. Ed. Burton Van Name Edwards. Turnhout: Brepols, 1999.

Sulpicius Severus. *Dialogues*. Ed. C. Holm. CSEL I.

————. *Chronicles*. Patrologia Latina 20.95–160.

Tertullian. *Apologeticus adversus gentes pro Christianis*. Patrologia Latina 1.257–536.

————. *Contra Marcionem*. 2 vols. Edited and translated by Earnest Evans. Oxford: Clarendon Press, 1972.

————. *De spectaculis*. Patrologia Latina 1.627–662.

Theodore of Mopsuestia. *Catechetical Commentary on the Nicene Creed*. Ed. A. Mingana. Woodbrook Studies 5 (Cambridge: Heffer and Sons, 1933).

Thomas Aquinas. *In secundam epistolam ad Thessalonicenses*. In *Opera omnia,* ed. Commissio Leonina, vol. 15. Paris: Philosophique J. Vrin, 1989.

Tyconius. *Liber regularum*. Texts and Studies 3. Ed. F. C. Burkitt. Cambridge: Cambridge University Press, 1894. Text reprinted with English translation in *The Book of Rules. Text and Translation*. Ed. and trans. William S. Babcock. Atlanta: Scholars Press, 1989.

Secondary Works

Alexander, Paul J. "The Diffusion of Byzantine Apocalypses in the Medieval West and the Beginnings of Joachimism." *Prophecy and Millenarianism: Essays in Honor of Marjorie Reeves*. Ed. Ann Miller, 53–106. Essex: Longmans, 1980.

Arias Reyero, Maximino. *Thomas von Aquin als Exeget: Die Prinzipien seiner Schriftsdeutung und seine Lehre von den Schriftsinnen*. Einsiedeln: Johannesverlag, 1971.

Babcock, William S. "Augustine and Tyconius: A Study in the Latin Appropriation of Paul." *Studia Patristica* 17 (1982): Part 3, 1209–15.

————, ed. *Paul and the Legacies of Paul*. Dallas: Southern Methodist University Press, 1990.

Backus, Irena, ed. *The Reception of the Church Fathers in the West*. 2 vols. Leiden: Brill, 1997.

Barraclough, Geoffrey. *The Medieval Papacy*. New York: W. W. Norton, 1979.

Barré, H. "Haimon d'Auxerre." *Dictionnaire de Spiritualité* 7 (Paris, 1969): 91–97.

Bertola, E. "I commentario paolino di Haimo de Halberstadt o di Auxerre e gli inizi del metodo scolastico." *Pier Lombardo* 5 (1961): 29–54.

————. "I precedenti storici del metodo del Sic et Non di Abelardo." *Rivista di filosofia neoscolastica* 53 (1961): 255–80.

————. "La Glossa Ordinaria biblica ed i suori problemi." *Recherches des theologie ancienne et medievale* 45 (1978): 34–78.

Bischoff, Bernard. "Wendespunkte in der Geschichte der lateinischen Exegese im Frühmittelalter." *Sacris Erudiri* 6 (1954): 119–89.

Blumenthal, Ute Renate, ed. *Carolingian Essays*. Washington, D.C.: Catholic University of America Press, 1984.

Bonner, Gerald. *Augustine and Modern Research on Pelagius*. Villanova: Villanova University Press, 1972.

———. "How Pelagian Was Pelagius?" *Texte und Untersuchungen* 94 (1968): 350–58.

———. "Saint Bede in the Tradition of Western Apocalyptic Commentary." In *Bede and His World: Jarrow Lectures 1958–1993*, 153–83. Brookfield, Vt.: Variorum, 1994.

Bougerol, Jacques-Guy. "The Church Fathers and the Sentences of Peter Lombard." In *The Church Fathers in the Latin West*, 2 vols., ed. Irena Backus, 113–64. Leiden: Brill, 1997.

Bouquet, M. *Recueil des Historiens des Gaules et de la France 9*. Ed. L. Delisle. Paris, 1869–1880.

Bowersock, Glenn. *Julian the Apostate*. Cambridge: Harvard University Press, 1978.

Bredero, Adriaan. "The Announcement of the Coming of the Antichrist and the Medieval Concept of Time." In *Prophecy and Eschatology*, ed. Michael Wilks, 3–14. *Studies in Church History*, Subsidia 10. London: Blackwell Publishers, 1994.

Bright, Pamela. *The Book of Rules of Tyconius: Its Purpose and Inner Logic*. Notre Dame, Ind.: University of Notre Dame Press, 1988.

Brinkmann, Hennig. *Mittelalterliche Hermeneutik*. Tübingen: Niemeyer, 1980.

Brown, Peter. *Augustine of Hippo*. Berkeley and Los Angeles: University of California Press, 1969.

Brown, Raymond E. *1, 2, 3 John*. Anchor Bible Commentary. New York: Doubleday, 1982.

Brünholzl, F. *Geschichte dew lateinishen Literatur des Mittelalters*. 2 vols. Münich: Wilhelm Fink Verlag, 1975.

Bull, Malcolm, ed. *Apocalypse Theory and the Ends of the World*. London: Blackwell Publishers, 1995.

Burr, David. *Olivi's Peaceable Kingdom: A Reading of the Apocalypse Commentary*. Philadelphia: University of Pennsylvania Press, 1993.

The Cambridge History of the Bible. 3 vols. Cambridge: Cambridge University Press, 1963–1970.

Campenhausen, Ernst von. *The Formation of the Christian Bible*. Philadelphia: Fortress Press, 1972.

Cantelli, Silvia. *Angelomo e la scuola esegetica di Luxeuil*. 2 vols. Spoleto: Centro italiano di studi sull'alto Medievo, 1990.

Carozzi, Claude. *Apocalypse et salut dans le christianisme ancien et médiéval*. In *Collection Historique*. Paris: Aubier, 1999.

Cartwright, Steven R., and Kevin L. Hughes, eds. *Second Thessalonians: Two Early Medieval Apocalyptic Commentaries.* Kalamazoo: Medieval Institute Publications, 2001.

Cavadini, John C., ed. *Gregory the Great: A Symposium.* Notre Dame: University of Notre Dame Press, 1985.

———. *The Last Christology of the West.* Philadelphia: University of Pennsylvania Press, 1993.

———. "School of Antioch." In *Harper Collins Encyclopedia of Catholicism,* ed. Richard McBrien, 67–68. New York: Harper Collins, 1995.

———. "The Sources and Theology of Alcuin's Treatise *De Fide.*" *Traditio* 46 (1991): 123–46.

Charlesworth, J. H., ed. *Old Testament Pseudepigrapha.* Garden City: Doubleday, 1983.

Charlier, C. "La compilation augustiniennes de Florus sur l'Apôtre: Source et authenticité." *Revue Bénédictine* 57 (1947): 132–86.

Châtillion, Jean. "La Bibles dans les écoles du XIIe siècle." In *Le Moyen Age et la Bible,* eds. Pierre Riche and Guy Lobrichon. Paris: Beauchesne, 1984.

Chenu, Marie-Dominique. *Nature, Man, and Society in the Twelfth Century.* Selected, edited, and translated by Jerome Taylor and Lester Little. Chicago: University of Chicago Press, 1968.

Cohn, Norman. *The Pursuit of the Millennium: Revolutionary Millenarians and Mystical Anarchists of the Middle Ages.* Rev. ed. New York: Oxford University Press, 1980.

Colish, Marcia. *Peter Lombard.* 2 vols. Leiden: Brill, 1994.

Collins, John J. *The Apocalyptic Imagination.* New York: Crossroad, 1989.

———. "Sibylline Oracles." In *Old Testament Pseudepigraphia,* vol. 1, ed. J. H. Charlesworth 317–72. Garden City: Doubleday, 1983.

———. *The Sybilline Oracles of Egyptian Judaism.* Missoula: Scholars Press, 1974.

Constable, Giles. *The Reformation of the Twelfth Century.* Cambridge: Cambridge University Press, 1996.

Contreni, John J. "The Biblical Glosses of Haimo of Auxerre and John Scotus Eriugena." *Speculum* 51 (1976): 411–34.

———. "Carolingian Biblical Culture." In *Iohannes Scottus Eriugena: The Bible and Hermeneutics,* ed. Gerd van Riel, Carlos Steel, and James McEvoy. Leuven: Leuven University Press, 1996.

———. "Carolingian Biblical Studies." In *Carolingian Essays,* ed. Ute-Renate Blumenthal, 71–98. Washington, D.C.: Catholic University of America Press, 1983.

———. "The Carolingian School. Letters from the Classroom." In *Giovanni scoto nel suo tempo,* ed. E. Menesto and Claudio Leonardi. Spoleto: Centro Italiano di studi sull'alto Medioevo, 1989.

———. *The Cathedral School of Laon from 850 to 930: Its Manuscripts and Masters.*

Munich: Münchener Beiträge zur Mediävistik—und Renaissance—Forschung, 1978.

———. "Haimo of Auxerre, Abbot of Sasceium (Cessy-les-Bois) and a New Sermon on I John V, 4–10." *Revue Bénédictine* 85 (1975): 303–20.

Cox, Patricia. "Origen and the Witch of Endor: Toward an Iconoclastic Typology." *Anglican Theological Review* 66 (1984): 137–47.

Cullmann, Oscar. *Christ and Time: The Primitive Christian Conception of Time and History.* Philadelphia: Westminster Press, 1964.

Daley, Brian E. "Apocalypticism in Early Christian Theology." In *Encyclopedia of Apocalypticism,* ed. John S. Collins, Bernard McGinn, and Stephen J. Stein, 3–47. New York: Continuum Press, 1998.

———. *The Hope of the Early Church: A Handbook of Patristic Eschatology.* New York: Cambridge University Press, 1991.

Daniélou, Jean. *A History of Early Christian Doctrine.* 3 vols. London: Darnton, Longman, and Todd, 1964–1977.

———. *From Shadows to Reality: Studies in the Biblical Typology of the Fathers.* Trans. W. Hibbard. Westminster, Md.: Newman Press, 1960.

———. *The Lord of History: Reflections on the Inner Meaning of History.* Chicago: Henry Regnery, 1958.

———. *Origen.* Trans. Walter Mitchell. New York: Sheed and Ward, 1955.

———. "Patristic Theology." In *Historical Theology,* eds. Jean Daniélou, R. Coustin, and E. Kent. New York: Pelican, 1969.

DeBruyn, Theodore. *Pelagius's Commentary on St. Paul's Epistle to the Romans.* Oxford: Clarendon Press, 1993.

De Hamel, Christopher F. R. *Glossed Books of the Bible and the Origins of the Paris Booktrade.* Dover, N.H.: D. S. Brewer, 1984.

Döbschutz, Ernst von. *Die Thessalonischer-Briefe.* Göttingen: Vandenhoeck und Ruprecht, 1974.

Donfried, Karl, and I. Howard Marshall. *The Theology of the Shorter Pauline Letters.* Cambridge: Cambridge University Press, 1993.

Dunbar, David G. "The Eschatology of Hippolytus of Rome." Ph.D. dissertation, Drew University, 1979.

———. "Hippolytus of Rome and the Eschatological Exegesis of the Early Church." *Westminster Theological Quarterly* 45 (1983): 322–39.

Dunn, James D. G. *Unity and Diversity in the New Testament.* 2nd ed. Valley Forge: Trinity Press International, 1990.

Emmerson, Richard K. "Antichrist in Late Medieval Illuminated Books: The Continuity of the Augustinian Tradition." Paper presented at "History, Apocalypse, and the Secular Imagination," a symposium on the *City of God,* University of British Columbia, September 18–20, 1997.

———. *Antichrist in the Middle Ages.* Seattle: University of Washington Press, 1981.

Emmerson, Richard K., and Bernard McGinn, eds. *The Apocalypse in the Middle Ages.* Ithaca, N.Y.: Cornell University Press, 1992.

The Encyclopedia of Apocalypticism. 3 vols. Ed. John J. Collins, Bernard McGinn, and Stephen J Stein. New York: Continuum Press, 1998.

Evans, G. R. *The Language and Logic of the Bible: The Early Middle Ages.* New York: Cambridge University Press, 1984.

Festinger, L. *A Theory of Cognitive Dissonance.* Stanford: Stanford University Press, 1957.

Fishbane, Michael. *Biblical Interpretation in Ancient Israel.* New York: Oxford University Press, 1985.

Fontaine, Jacques, Robert Gillet, and Stan Pellistrandi, eds. *Grégoire le Grand.* Paris: Éditions du Centre National de la Recherche Scientifique, 1986.

Fowl, Stephen E., ed. *The Theological Interpretation of Scripture: Classic and Contemporary Readings.* Cambridge, Mass.: Blackwell, 1997.

Fraade, Steven. *From Tradition to Commentary: Torah and Its Interpretation in the Midrash Sifre to Deuteronomy.* Albany: SUNY Press, 1991.

Fransen, Paul-Irénée. "Description de la Collection Grégorienne de Florus de Lyons sur l'Apôtre." *Revue Bénédictine* 98 (1988): 278–317.

———. "Description de la Collection Hiéronymienne de Florus de Lyons sur l'Apôtre." *Revue Bénédictine* 94 (1984): 195–228.

Frasetto, Michael, ed. *The Year 1000: Religious and Social Response to the Turning of the First Millennium.* New York: Palgrave Macmillan, 2002.

Frede, Hermann Josef, ed. *Ein neuer Paulustext und Kommentar.* 2 vols. *Vetus Latina: die Reste der altlateinischen Bibel* 7–8. Freiburg: Herder, 1973–1974.

———. *Epistolae ad Thessalonicenses, Timotheum, Titum, Philemonem, Hebraeos.* 9 fascicles. *Vetus Latina: die Reste der altlateinishcen Bibel* 25. Freiburg: Herder, 1975–1981.

Fredriksen, Paula. "Apocalypse and Redemption: From John of Patmos to Augustine of Hippo." *Vigiliae Christianae* 45:2 (1991): 151–83.

———. *Augustine's Early Interpretation of Paul.* Ann Arbor: University of Michigan Press, 1979.

———."Tyconius and Augustine on the Apocalypse." In *The Apocalypse in the Middle Ages,* ed. Richard K. Emmerson and Bernard McGinn. Ithaca: Cornell University Press, 1992, 20–37.

———. "Tyconius and the End of the World." *Revue des études Augustiniennes* 28 (1982): 59–75.

———. "Vile Bodies: Paul and Augustine on the Resurrection of the Flesh." In *Biblical Hermeneutics in Historical Perspective: Essays in Honor of Karlfried Froehlich,* eds. Paul Rorem and Mark S. Burrows. Grand Rapids: Eerdmans, 1991.

Frend, W. H. C. *The Rise of Christianity.* Philadelphia: Fortress Press, 1984.

Fried, Johannes. "L'attesa della fine dei tempi alla svolta del millennio." In *L'attesa della fine dei tempi nel Medioevo,* ed. Ovidio Capitani and Jürgen Miethke, 1–16. Bologna: Società editrice il Mulino, 1988.

———. "Recognizing Millennialism in the Middle Ages." Center for Millennial Studies. http: / / www.mille.org / scholarship / papers / fried.middleages.html.

Froehlich, Karlfried. "The Medieval Exegesis of Biblical Texts: Understanding an Understanding." Unpublished, 1994.

———. "Saint Peter, Papal Primacy, and the Exegetical Tradition, 1150–1300." In *The Religious Role of the Papacy: Ideals and Realities 1150–1300,* ed. Christopher J. Ryan, 3–44. Papers in Medieval Studies 8. Toronto: Pontifical Institute of Medieval Studies, 1989.

———. "Which Paul? Observations on the Image of the Apostle in the History of Biblical Exegesis." In *New Perspectives on Historical Theology in Honor of John Meyendorff,* ed. Bradley Nassif, 279–99. Grand Rapids: Eerdmans, 1996.

———, ed. *Biblical Interpretation in the Early Church.* Philadelphia: Fortress Press, 1985.

Geerlings, Wilhelm. "Hiob und Paulus: Theodizee und Paulinismus in der lateinischen Theologie am Ausgang des vierten Jahrhunderts." *Jahrbuch für Antike un Christentum* 24 (1981): 56–66.

Gibson, Margaret T. *The Bible in the Latin West.* Notre Dame: University of Notre Dame Press, 1993.

———. *Lanfranc of Bec.* Oxford: Clarendon Press, 1978.

———. "Lanfranc's Commentary on the Pauline Epistles." *Journal of Theological Studies* n.s. 22 (1971): 86–112.

———. "Lanfranc's Notes on Patristic Texts." *Journal of Theological Studies* n.s. 22 (1971): 435–50.

———. "The Twelfth-Century Glossed Bible." *Studia Patristica* 23 (1990): 232–44.

Gil, Juan. "Los terrores del año 800." In *Actas del Simposio para el estudio de los codices del "Comentario al Apocalipsis" de Beato de Liebana.* Madrid: Joyas Bibliográficas, 1978.

Goetz, Werner. *Translatio imperii: Ein Beitrag zur Geschichte des Geschichtsdenken und der politischen Theorien im Mittelalter und in der frühen Neuzeit.* Tübingen: J. C. B. Mohr, 1958.

Gorday, Peter. "Paulus Origenionus: The Economic Interpretation of Paul." In *Paul and the Legacies of Paul,* ed. William S. Babcock, 141–63. Dallas: Southern Methodist University Press, 1990.

———. *Principles of Patristic Exegesis: Romans 9–11 in Origen, John Chrysostom, and Augustine.* New York: Edwin Mellen Press, 1983.

Gorman, Michael. "A Critique of Bischoff's Theory of Irish Exegesis: The Commentary on Genesis in Münich Clm 6302 (Wendepunkte 2)." *Journal of Medieval Latin* 7 (1997): 178–233.

Gouguenheim, Sylvain. *Les fausses terreurs de l'an mil: Attente de la fin des temps ou approfondissement de la foi?* Paris: Picard, 1999.

Grant, Robert M. *Irenaeus of Lyons.* London: Routledge, 1997.

Grant, Robert M., with David Tracy. *A Short History of the Interpretation of the Bible.* 2nd ed. Philadelphia: Fortress Press, 1984.

Green, Garrett, ed. *Scriptural Authority and Narrative Interpretation.* Philadelphia: Fortress Press, 1987.

Greer, Rowan. *The Captain of Our Salvation.* Tübingen: J. C. B. Mohr/Paul Siebeck, 1973.

———. *Theodore of Mopsuestia: Exegete and Theologian.* Westminster, Md.: Faith Press, 1961.

Griffiths, Paul J. *Religious Reading: The Place of Reading in the Practice of Religion.* New York: Oxford University Press, 1999.

Gross, J. "Die Schlüsselgewalt nach Haimo von Auxerre." *Zeitschrift für Religions- und Geistesgeschichte* 9 (1957): 30–41.

———. "Ur- und Erbsünde bei Haimo von Auxerre." *Zeitschrift für Religions- und Geistesgeschichte* 11 (1959): 14–31.

Gross-Diaz, Theresa. *The Psalms Commentary of Gilbert of Poitiers: From Lectio Divina to the Lecture Room.* Leiden: Brill, 1996.

Gunton, Colin. *The Actuality of the Atonement.* Grand Rapids: Eerdmans, 1989.

Hadot, Pierre. *Philosophy as a Way of Life.* Ed. Arnold I. Davidson. Trans. Michael Chase. Cambridge, Mass.: Blackwell, 1995.

———. *Qu'est-ce que la philosophie antique?* Paris: Gallimard, 1995.

———. "Théologie, exégèse, révélation, écriture, dans la philosophie grecque." In *Les règles de l'interprétation,* ed. Michel Tardieu. Paris: Cerf, 1987.

Hanson, R. P. C. *Allegory and Event.* London: SCM Press, 1957.

Harnack, Adolf von. *Lehrbuch der Dogmengeschichte.* 4th ed. 4 vols. Tübingen, 1909.

Head, Thomas, and Richard A. Landes, eds. *The Peace of God: Social Violence and Religious Response in France around the Year 1000.* Ithaca: Cornell University Press, 1992.

Hellmann, S. *Sedulius Scotus.* Quellen und Untersuchungen zur lateinischen Philologie des Mittelalters 1, ed. Ludwig Traube. Münich: C. H. Beck, 1906.

Henry, Waast Barthélemy. *Histoire de l'Abbaye de Saint-Germain d'Auxerre.* Auxerre: Gallot, 1853.

Higgelbacher, Othmar. "Beziehung zwischen Ambrosiaster un Maximus von Turin? Ein Gegenüberstellung." *Freiburger Zeitschrift für Philosophie und Theologie* 41 (1994): 5–44.

Hill, Charles E. "Antichrist from the Tribe of Dan." *Journal of Theological Studies* 46 (1995): 99–117.

———. *Regnum Caelorum: Patterns of Future Hope in Early Christianity.* Oxford: Oxford University Press, 1992. Rev. ed: *Regnum Caelorum: Patterns of Millennial Thought in Early Christianity.* Grand Rapids: Eerdmans, 2001.

Holland, Glen. *The Tradition That You Received from Us: 2 Thessalonians in the Pauline Tradition.* Hermeneutische Untersuchungen zur Theologie. Tübingen: J. C. B. Mohr/Paul Siebeck, 1988.

Holtz, Louis. "Muretach et l'influence de la culture irlandaise à Auxerre." In *L'É-cole Carolingienne d'Auxerre: de Muretach à Remi 830–90*, ed. Dominique Iogna-Prat, Colette Jeudy, Guy Lobrichon, 146–56. Paris: Beauchesne, 1991.

Hughes, Frank Witt. "Early Christian Rhetoric and 2 Thessalonians." *Journal for the Study of the New Testament*, Supp. Series 30 (1989).

Hughes, Kevin L. "Augustine and the Adversary: Strategies of Synthesis in the Early Medieval Exegesis." *Augustinian Studies* 30:2 (1999): 221–33.

———. "Eschatological Union: The Mystical Dimension of History in Joachim of Fiore, Bonaventure, and Peter Olivi." *Collectanea Franciscana* 72:1 (2002): 105–43.

———. "The 'Fourfold Sense': De Lubac, Blondel, and Contemporary Theology." *Heythrop Journal* 42:4 (October 2001): 451–62.

Illich, Ivan. *In the Vineyard of the Text: A Commentary to Hugh's* Didascalion. Chicago: University of Chicago Press, 1993.

Iogna-Prat, Dominique. "L'œrvre d'Haymon d'Auxerre: État de la question." In *L'École carolingienne d'Auxerre: de Muretach à Remi 830–908*, eds. Dominique Iogna-Prat, Colette Jeudy, and Guy Lobrichon, 157–79. Paris: Beauchesne, 1991.

Iogna-Prat, Dominique, Colette Jeudy, and Guy Lobrichon, eds. *L'École carolingienne d'Auxerre: de Muretach à Remi, 830–908*. Paris: Beauchesne, 1991.

Jeremias, Joachim. *The Parables of Jesus*. 2nd rev. ed. New York: Charles Scribner and Sons, 1972.

Jewett, Robert. *The Thessalonian Correspondence: Pauline Rhetoric and Millenarian Piety*. Philadelphia: Fortress, 1986.

Jordan, Mark D., and Kent Emery Jr., ed. *Ad Litteram: Authoritative Texts and Their Medieval Readers*. Notre Dame: University of Notre Dame Press, 1992.

Kannengiesser, Charles, and Pamela Bright. *A Conflict of Christian Hermeneutics in Roman Africa: Tyconius and Augustine*. Protocol of the 58th Colloquy, Center for Hermeneutical Studies in Hellenistic and Modern Culture,16 October 1988. Berkeley, Calif.: Center for Hermeneutical Studies, 1989.

Kelly, J. N. D. *Jerome: His Life, Writings, and Controversies*. New York: Harper and Row, 1975.

Kermode, Frank. *The Genesis of Secrecy: On the Interpretation of Narrative*. Cambridge, Mass.: Harvard University Press, 1979.

———. *The Sense of an Ending: Studies in the Theory of Fiction*. New York: Oxford University Press, 1966.

Konrad, Robert. *De ortu et tempore Antichristi: Antichristvorstellung und Geschichts-bild des Abtes Adso von Montier-en-Der*. Kallmunz: Michael Lassleben, 1964.

Krey, Philip D. "Nicholas of Lyra: Apocalypse Commentary as Historiography." Ph.D. dissertation, University of Chicago, 1990.

Kugel, James L., and Rowan A. Greer. *Early Biblical Interpretation*. Philadelphia: Westminster Press, 1986.

Ladner, Gerhart B. *God, Cosmos, and Humankind: The World of Early Christian Symbolism.* Berkeley: University of California Press, 1995.

———. "Medieval and Modern Understandings of Symbolism: A Comparison." In *Images and Ideas in the Middle Ages: Selected Studies in History and Art,* 239–282. Rome: Edizione de Storia e Letteratura, 1983.

Laistner, M. L. W. "Antiochene Exegesis in Western Europe during the Middle Ages." *Harvard Theological Review* 40 (1947): 19–31.

Landes, Richard A. "The Fear of an Apocalyptic Year 1000: Augustinian Historiography, Medieval and Modern." *Speculum* 75:1 (January 2000): 97–145.

———. "Lest the Millennium Be Fulfilled: Apocalyptic Expectations and the Pattern of Western Chronography, 100–800 CE." In *The Use and Abuse of Eschatology in the Middle Ages,* ed. Werner Verbeke, Daniel Verhelst, and Andries Welkenhuysen, 137–211. Medievalia Lovaniensia, Series 1, Studia 15. Leuven: Leuven University Press, 1988.

———. "*Millenarismus absconditus:* L'historiographe augustinienne et le millenarisme du Haut Moyen Age jusqu'en l'an Mil." *Le Moyen Age* 98:3–4 (1992): 355–77; 99:1 (1993): 1–26.

———. "On Owls, Roosters, and Apocalyptic Time: A Historical Method for Reading a Refractory Documentation." *Union Seminary Quarterly* 49 (1996): 165–85.

———. *Relics, Apocalypse, and the Deceits of History: Ademar of Chabannes, 989–1034.* Cambridge: Harvard University Press, 1995.

Landes, Richard A., David Van Meter, and Andrew Gow, eds. *The Apocalyptic Year 1000.* New York: Oxford University Press, 2003.

Landgraf, Artur Michael. *Einführung in die Geschichte der theologischen Literatur der Frühscholastik.* Regensburg: Gregorius-Verlag, 1948.

———. "Probleme des Schriftums Brunos des Kartäusers." *Collectanea Franciscana* 8 (1938): 542–90.

Leclerq, Jean. "L'Eloge funèbre de Gilbert de la Porée." *Archives d'histoire doctrinale et littéraire du moyen âge* 19 (1952): 183–85.

———. *The Love of Learning and the Desire for God. A Study of Monastic Culture.* Trans. Catharine Misrahi. New York: Fordham University Press, 1982.

Lerner, Robert E. "The Refreshment of the Saints: The Time after Antichrist as a Station for Earthly Progress in Medieval Thought." *Traditio* 32 (1976): 97–144.

Lim, Richard. "Politics of Interpretation in Basil of Caesarea's Hexaemeron." *Vigiliae Christianae* 44 (1990): 351–70.

Lindbeck, George. "The Story-Shaped Church: Critical Exegesis and Theological Interpretation." In *The Theological Interpretation of Scripture: Classic and Contemporary Readings,* ed. Stephen E. Fowl, 39–52. London: Blackwell, 1997.

Lindemann, Andreas. "Paul in the Writings of the Apostolic Fathers." In *Paul and the Legacies of Paul,* ed. William S. Babcock, 25–45. Dallas: Southern University Press, 1990.

Lobrichon, Guy. "Une nouveauté: les gloses de la Bible." In *Le moyen age et la Bible,* ed. Pierre Riche and Guy Lobrichon, 95–114. Paris: Beauchesne, 1984.

Lobrichon, Guy, and Pierre Riché, eds. *Le Moyen Age et la Bible.* Paris: Beauchesne, 1984.

Louth, Andrew. *Discerning the Mystery: An Essay on the Nature of Theology.* New York: Oxford University Press, 1983.

Lovejoy, Arthur O. *The Great Chain of Being: A Study in the History of an Idea.* Cambridge: Harvard University Press, 1950.

Lubac, Henri de. *Catholicisme: les aspects sociaux du dogme.* Paris: Cerf, 1947.

———. *Corpus Mysticum.* 2nd ed. Paris: Aubier, 1949.

———. *Exégèse Medievale: Les quatre sens de l'Écriture.* 4 vols. Paris: Aubier, 1959–1962.

———. *Histoire et Esprit, l'intelligence de l'Écriture d'apres Origène.* Paris: Aubier, 1950.

Madigan, Kevin. "Ancient and High Medieval Interpretations of Jesus in Gethsemane: Some Reflections on Tradition and Continuity in Christian Thought." *Harvard Theological Review* 88:1 (1995): 157–73.

———. "Peter Olivi's *Lectura super Mattheum* in Medieval Exegetical Perspective." Ph.D. dissertation, University of Chicago, 1992.

Malherbe, Abraham J. *The Letters to the Thessalonians: A New Translation with Introduction and Commentary.* Anchor Bible 32B. New York: Doubleday, 2000.

Marenbon, John. *From the Circle of Alcuin to the School of Auxerre: Logic, Theology, and Philosophy in the Early Middle Ages.* Cambridge: Cambridge University Press, 1981.

Margerie, Bertrand de. *Introduction à l'histoire d'exegese.* 4 vols. Paris: Cerf, 1980–1990.

Markus, Robert A. *Saeculum: History and Society in the Theology of Saint Augustine.* Rev. ed. Cambridge: Cambridge University Press, 1988.

Marrou, Henri-Irenée. *A History of Education in Antiquity.* Trans. George Lamb. New York: Sheed and Ward, 1956.

Matter, E. Ann. "The Apocalypse in Early Medieval Exegesis." In *The Apocalypse in the Middle Ages,* ed. Richard K. Emmerson and Bernard McGinn, 38–50. Ithaca: Cornell University Press, 1992.

———. "The Church Fathers and the *Glossa Ordinaria.*" In *The Reception of the Church Fathers in the West,* 2 vols., ed. Irena Backus, 83–111. Leiden: Brill, 1997.

———. "Exegesis and Christian Education: The Carolingian Model." In *Schools of Thought in the Christian Tradition,* ed. Patrick Henry, 90–105. Philadelphia: Fortress Press, 1984.

———. *The Voice of My Beloved: The Song of Songs in Western Medieval Christianity.* Philadelphia: University of Pennsylvania Press, 1990.

McBrien, Richard, ed. *Harper Collins Encyclopedia of Catholicism.* New York: Harper Collins, 1995.

McDonald, Dennis Ronald. *The Legend and the Apostle: The Battle for Paul in Story and Canon.* Philadelphia: Westminster Press, 1983.

McGinn, Bernard. *Antichrist: Two Thousand Years of the Human Fascination with Evil.* 2nd ed. New York: Columbia University Press, 1999.

———. *Apocalyptic Spirituality.* Mahwah: Paulist Press, 1979.

———. *The Calabrian Abbot: Joachim of Fiore in the History of Western Thought.* New York: Macmillan, 1983.

———. "'The End of the World and the Beginning of Christendom." In *Apocalypse Theory and the Ends of the World,* ed. Malcolm Bull, 58–89. Oxford: Blackwell, 1995.

———. "John's Apocalypse and the Apocalyptic Mentality." In *The Apocalypse in the Middle Ages,* ed. Richard K. Emmerson and Bernard McGinn, 3–19. Ithaca, N.Y.: Cornell University Press, 1992.

———. *Visions of the End.* New York: Columbia University Press, 1978.

McGrath, Alistair E. *Iustitia Dei: A History of the Doctrine of Justification.* 2nd ed. New York: Cambridge University Press, 1998.

McIntyre, John. *The Shape of Soteriology.* Edinburgh: T and T Clark, 1992.

McKitterick, Rosamond. *The Frankish Kingdoms under the Carolingians, 751–987.* New York: Longman, 1983.

McNally, Robert A. *The Bible in the Early Middle Ages.* Westminster, Md.: Woodstock Papers: Occasional Essays for Theology, 1959.

McNamara, Martin. "The Irish Tradition of Biblical Exegesis, A.D. 550–800." In *Iohannes Scotus Eriugena: The Bible and Hermeneutics,* ed. Gerd van Reel, Carlos Steel, and James McEvoy, 25–54. Leuven: Leuven University Press, 1996.

———, ed. *Biblical Studies: The Medieval Irish Contribution.* Proceedings of the Irish Biblical Association 1. Dublin: Dominican Publications, 1976.

Merkt, Andreas. "Wer war der Ambrosiaster? Zum Autor einer Quelle des Augustinus-Fragen auf eine neue Antwort." *Wissenschaft und Weisheit* 59 (1996): 19–33.

Michelet, Jules. *Histoire de France.* Rev. ed. 19 vols. Paris: C. Marpon and E. Flammarion, 1879–84.

Minnis, A. J., Brian Scott, and David Wallace, eds. *Medieval Literary Theory and Criticism, ca. 1100–ca. 1375: The Commentary Tradition.* Oxford: Oxford University Press, 1988.

Musée d'Art et d'Histoire. *Saint-Germain d'Auxerre: Intellectuels et Artistes dans l'Europe Carolingienne IXe–XIe Siécles.* Auxerre: Musée d'Art et d'Histoire, 1990.

Nassif, Bradley. "Spiritual Exegesis in the School of Antioch." In *New Perspectives on Historical Theology,* ed. Bradley Nassif, 343–377. Grand Rapids: Eerdmans, 1996.

———, ed. *New Perspective on Historical Theology in Memory of John Meyendorff.* Grand Rapids: Eerdmans, 1996.

Newman, John Henry. *An Essay on the Development of Christian Doctrine.* Ed. Charles Frederick Harrold. New York: Longmans, Green, 1949.

Norris, Richard A., Jr. *The Christological Controversy*. Philadelphia: Fortress Press, 1980.

———. *Manhood and Christ: A Study of the Christology of Theodore of Mopsuestia*. Oxford: Clarendon Press, 1963.

Oakes, Edward T. *Pattern of Redemption: The Theology of Hans Urs von Balthasar*. New York: Continuum Press, 1994.

Obermann, Heiko. *Forerunners of the Reformation*. Philadelphia: Fortress Press, 1981.

O'Connell, John P. *The Eschatology of Saint Jerome*. Mundelein, Ill.: Saint Mary of the Lake Seminary, 1948.

O'Leary, Stephen D. *Arguing the Apocalypse: A Theory of Millennial Rhetoric*. New York: Oxford University Press, 1994.

Ortigues, Edmond. "Haimon d'Auxerre, théoricien des trois ordres." In *L'École Carolingienne d'Auxerre: de Muretach a Remi, 830–908*, eds. Dominque Iogna-Prat et al., 181–227. Paris: Beauchesne, 1991.

Otten, Willemien. "The Texture of Tradition: The Role of the Church Fathers in Carolingian Theology." In *The Church Fathers in the Latin West*, 2 vols., ed. Irena Backus, 3–50. Leiden: Brill, 1997.

Oury, Guy. "Essai sur la Spiritualité d'Herve de Bourg-Dieu." *Revue d'Ascetique et de Mystique* 43 (1967): 369–92.

Pagels, Elaine. *The Gnostic Paul: Gnostic Exegesis of the Pauline Letters*. Philadelphia: Trinity Press International, 1975.

Panofsky, Erwin. *Gothic Architecture and Scholasticism: An Enquiry into the Analogy of the Arts, Philosophy, and Religion in the Middle Ages*. New York: Meridian Books, 1957.

Pelikan, Jaroslav. *The Christian Tradition*. 5 vols. Chicago: University of Chicago Press, 1971–1988.

Perrin, Norman. *The Kingdom of God in the Teaching of Jesus*. Philadelphia: Westminster Press, 1963.

Picard, Jean-Michel. "L'exegese irlandaise de Epitres de saint Paul: Les gloses latines et gaeliques de Wurzburg." Unpublished paper delivered at the conference *L'étude de la Bible d'Isidore à Rémi d'Auxerre (600–900)*, Paris, June 1998.

Pincherle, Alberto. *La formazione teologica di sant' Agostino*. Rome: Edizion Italiane, 1947.

Pollmann, Karla. "Moulding the Present: Apocalyptic as Hermeneutics in *City of God*." In *History, Apocalypse, and the Secular Imagination: New Essays on Augustine's City of God 21–22*, ed. Allan Fitzgerald, Mark Vessey, and Karla Pollmann. Bowling Green, Ohio: Philosophy Documentation Center, 1999.

Quadri, Riccardo. "Aimone di Auxerre alla luce dei 'Collectanea' di Heiric di Auxerre." *Italia Medioevale e Umanistica* 6 (1963): 1–48.

Rangheri, Maurizio. "La 'Epistola ad Gerbergam reginam de ortu et tempore Antichristi' di Adsone di Montier-en-Der e le sui fonti." *Studi Medievali*, 3rd series 14, part 2 (1973): 677–732.

Ratzinger, Joseph. "Beobachtungen zum Kirchebegriff des Tyconius im 'Liber regularum.'" *Revue des etudes augustiniennes* 12 (1956): 173–85.

Rauh, Horst-Dieter. *Das Bild des Antichrist im Mittelalter: Von Tyconius zum Deutschen Symbolismus.* Münster: Verlag Aschendorff, 1973.

Ravier, André. *Saint Bruno the Carthusian.* Trans. Bruno Becker, O.S.B. San Francisco: Ignatius Press, 1995.

Rees, B. R. *Pelagius: A Reluctant Heretic.* Suffolk: Boydell Press, 1988.

Ricoeur, Paul. *The Symbolism of Evil.* Trans. Emerson Buchanan. Boston: Beacon Press, 1969.

Riel, Gerd van, Carlos Steel, and James McEvoy, eds. *Iohannes Scottus Eriugena: The Bible and Hermeneutics.* Leuven: Leuven University Press, 1996.

Rigáux, Beda. *Les Epitres de Saint Paul aux Thessaloniciens.* Paris: Éditions du Cerf, 1954.

Riggenbach, Eduard. *Die älteste lateinischen Kommentare zum Hebräerbrief.* Leipzig: A. Deichert, 1907.

Sanders, E. P. *Paul.* Oxford: Oxford University Press, 1991.

Sanders, James A. *From Sacred Story to Sacred Text.* Philadelphia: Fortress Press, 1987.

———. *Torah and Canon.* Philadelphia: Fortress Press, 1972.

Savon, Hervé. "L'Antéchrist chez les oeuvres de Grégoire le Grand." In *Grégoire le Grand,* ed. Jacques Fontaine et al., 389–405. Paris: Éditions du Centre National de la Recherche Scientifique, 1986.

Schreiner, Susan E. *Where Shall Wisdom Be Found? Calvin's Exegesis of Job from Medieval and Modern Perspectives.* Chicago: University of Chicago Press, 1994.

Shils, Edward. *Tradition.* Chicago: University of Chicago Press, 1981.

Simonetti, Manlio. *Biblical Interpretation in the Early Church.* Trans. John A. Hughes. Edinburgh: T and T Clark, 1994.

———. *Lettera e/o Allegoria.* Rome: Institutum Patristicum Augustinianum, 1985.

Simson, Otto von. *The Gothic Cathedral.* 3rd ed. Princeton, N.J.: Princeton University Press, 1988.

Smalley, Beryl. "Les Commentaires de l'epoque romane: glose ordinaire es gloses périmées." *Cahiers de Civilisation médiévale* 4 (1961): 15–22.

———. "Gilbertus Universalis, Bishop of London (1128–34), and the Problem of the *Glossa Ordinaria*." *Recherches de théologie ancienne et médiévale* 7 (1935): 235–62; 8 (1936): 24–60.

———. "La *Glossa Ordinaria*: Quelques prédécesseurs d'Anselme de Laon." *Recherches de théologie ancienne et médiévale* 9 (1937): 365–400.

———. *Studies in Medieval Thought and Learning from Abelard to Wyclif.* London: Hambledon Press, 1981.

———. *The Study of the Bible in the Middle Ages.* Notre Dame: University of Notre Dame Press, 1964.

Smith, Jonathan Z. *Imagining Religion: From Babylon to Jonestown.* Chicago: University of Chicago Press, 1982.

————. *Map Is Not Territory: Studies in the History of Religions.* Chicago: University of Chicago Press, 1993.

Smith, Wilfred Cantwell. *What Is Scripture? A Comparative Approach.* Minneapolis: Fortress, 1993.

Soskice, Janet Martin. *Metaphor and Religious Language.* London: Oxford University Press, 1985.

Souter, Alexander. *The Earliest Latin Commentaries on Saint Paul.* Cambridge: Cambridge University Press, 1927.

————. *A Study of Ambrosiaster.* Texts and Studies. Cambridge: Cambridge University Press, 1905.

Southern, R. W. *The Making of the Middle Ages.* New Haven: Yale University Press, 1953.

————. *Saint Anselm: A Portrait in a Landscape.* New York: Cambridge University Press, 1990.

Sprandel, Rolf. *Altersschicksal und Altersmoral: die Geschichte der Einstellungen zum Alten nach der Pariser Bibelexeges des 12.–16. Jahrhunderts.* Stuttgart: A. Hiersmann, 1981.

Stancliffe, Clare. "Early 'Irish' Biblical Exegesis." *Studia Patristica* 12 (1975): 361–70.

Stegmueller, Friedrich. *Repertorium Biblicum Medii Aevi.* 11 vols. Madrid: Consejo Superior, 1950–1988.

Steiner, George. *Real Presences.* Chicago: University of Chicago Press, 1989.

Steinhauser, Kenneth. *The Apocalypse Commentary of Tyconius.* Frankfurt am Main: Peter Lang, 1987.

Stock, Brian. *After Augustine: The Meditative Reader and the Text.* Philadelphia: University of Pennsylvania Press, 2001.

————. *Augustine the Reader: Meditation, Self-Knowledge, and the Ethics of Interpretation.* Cambridge, Mass.: Belknap Press, 1996.

————. *Listening for the Text: On the Uses of the Past.* Baltimore: Johns Hopkins University, 1990.

Stoelen, Anselm. "Les commentaires scripturaires attribués à Bruno le Chartreux." *Recherches de théologie ancienne et médiévale* 25 (1958): 177–247.

Stortz, Martha Ellen. "Exegesis, Orthodoxy, and Ethics: Interpretations of Romans in the Pelagian Controversy." Ph.D. dissertation, University of Chicago, 1984.

Straw, Carole. *Gregory the Great: Perfection in Imperfection.* Berkeley: University of California Press, 1988.

Studer, Basil. "Die patristische Exegese, eine Aktualizierung der Heiligen Schrift." *Revue des études augustiniennes* 42 (1996): 71–95.

Tanner, Kathryn E. "Theology and the Plain Sense." In *Scriptural Authority and Narrative Interpretation,* ed. Garrett Green, 59–78. Philadelphia: Fortress Press, 1987.

Teselle, Eugene. "The Cross as Ransom." *Journal of Early Christian Studies* 4 (1996): 147–70.

Tierney, Brian. *The Crisis of Church and State 1050–1300.* Reprint ed. Toronto: University of Toronto Press, 1988.

Torrance, T. F. *Divine Meaning: Studies in Patristic Hermeneutics.* Edinburgh: T and T Clark, 1994.

Trigg, Joseph W. *Biblical Interpretation.* Wilmington, Del.: Michael Glazier, 1988.

———. *Origen: The Bible and Philosophy in the Third-Century Church.* Atlanta: John Knox Press, 1983.

Verbeke, Werner, Daniel Verhelst, and Andries Welkenhuysen, eds. *The Use and Abuse of Eschatology in the Middle Ages.* Medievalia Lovaniensia, Series 1, Studia 15. Leuven: Leuven University Press, 1988.

Verhelst, Daniel. "Adso of Montier-en-Der and the Fear of the Year 1000," trans. An van Rompaey and Richard Landes. In *The Apocalyptic Year 1000,* ed. Richard A. Landes, David Van Meter, and Andrew Gow. New York: Oxford University Press, 2003.

———. "La préhistoire des conceptions d'Adson concernant l'Antichrist." *Recherches de théologie ancienne et médiévale* 40 (1973): 52–103.

Vessey, Mark, Karla Pollmann, and Allan D. Fitzgerald, O.S.A. *History, Apocalypse, and the Secular Imagination: New Essays on Augustine's* City of God. Bowling Green: Philosophy Documentation Center, 1999.

Weber, Timothy. *Living in the Shadow of the Second Coming: American Premillennialism 1875–1982.* Chicago: University of Chicago Press, 1987.

Wenger, Luke. "Hrabanus Maurus, Fulda, and Carolingian Spirituality." Ph.D. dissertation, Harvard University, 1973.

Wielockx, R. "Autour de la Glossa Ordinaria." *Recherches de théologie ancienne et médiévale* 49 (1982): 222–28.

Wiles, Maurice. *The Divine Apostle.* New York: Cambridge University Press, 1967.

Wilken, Robert L. *The Christians as the Romans Saw Them.* New Haven: Yale University Press, 1984.

———. *John Chrysostom and the Jews: Rhetoric and Reality in the Late Fourth Century.* Berkeley: University of California Press, 1983.

———. *Remembering the Christian Past.* Grand Rapids: Eerdmans, 1996.

———. *This Land Called Holy.* New Haven: Yale University Press, 1994.

Williams, John R. "The Cathedral School of Rheims in the Time of Master Alberic, 1118–1136." *Traditio* 20 (1964): 93–114.

Williams, Rowan. "The Literal Sense of Scripture." *Modern Theology* 7 (1991): 121–34.

———, ed. *The Evolution of Orthodoxy: Essays in Honor of Henry Chadwick.* New York: Cambridge University Press, 1989.

Wilmart, A. "L'exemplaire lyonnais de l'exposition de Florus sur les épîtres et ses dernier feuillets." *Revue Bénédictine* 42 (1930): 73–76.

—. "Sommaire de l'exposition de Florus sur les épîtres." *Revue Bénédictine* 38 (1926): 16–52.

Wrede, Wilhelm. *Die Echtheit der zweiten Thessalonischer-briefs untersucht.* Texte und Untersuchungen zur Geschichte der altchristlichen Literatur, neue Folge 9/2. Leipzig: Hinrichs, 1903.

Young, Frances. "The Rhetorical Schools and Their Influence on Patristic Exegesis." In *The Evolution of Orthodoxy: Essays in Honor of Henry Chadwick,* ed. Rowan Williams. New York: Cambridge University Press, 1989.

—. *Virtuoso Theology: The Bible and Interpretation.* Cleveland, Ohio: Pilgrim Press, 1993.

Zier, Mark. "The Manuscript Tradition of the *Glossa Ordinaria* for Daniel and Hints at a Method for a Critical Edition." *Scriptorium* 47:1 (1993): 3–25.

Zimdars-Swartz, Sandra. "A Confluence of Imagery: Exegesis and Christology according to Gregory the Great." In *Grégoire le Grand,* ed. Jacques Fontaine, Robert Gillet, and Stan Pellistrandi, 327–36. Paris: Éditions du Centre National de la Recherche Scientifique, 1986.

INDEX

Abelard, Peter, 149, 207, 225–27

Accessio. See Discessio (Falling Away)

Adam, 14–15, 30, 100

Adamology, 14

Adso, abbot of Montier-en-Der, 167–77, 190, 244

Against Heresies (Irenaeus), 29

Alcuin of York, 121–23, 126, 149

Allegorical sense of Scripture, 21, 51–52, 68, 83, 119, 133, 163, 201, 246; *See also* Biblical interpretation, Spiritual exegesis

Ambrose, xx, 37–38, 54, 79

Ambrosiaster, xx, 23–24, 28, 34, 37–50; on Antichrist, 44; eschatology of, 40–41, 49; exegetical method of, 39; on the devil, 39, 44–46, 49; and Jerome, 38; on moral responsibility of the damned, 48; on paganism, 42, 46–47, 49; possible identity of, 38; on predestination, 47; on Roman Empire, 49–50; theodicy in, 42

Anselm of Laon, 206–22, 223

Antichrist: attempted ascension of, 8, 78, 203, 235; born of the tribe of Dan, 58, 155, 171, 217, 232; damnation/destruction of, 13, 61, 98–99, 109, 159, 164, 202–3, 235; as devil incarnate, 6, 43, 109; as false Christ, 7, 63, 80; as human evil personified, 6, 8, 9, 14, 138, 177; Last World Emperor and,

127, 169, 172–73; Nero and, 7, 24, 45, 49, 69, 77, 104, 141, 143–44, 158, 189, 218–19, 233, 245; as perverted imitation of Christ, 46; possessed by the devil, 18, 70, 160–61, 234; realist account of, 23–24, 28–81; and Simon Magus, 161, 220, 235; as son of the devil, 154, 217, 232; as symbol, 6, 8–9, 13, 14, 112, 241, 245; spiritual account of, xxi, 24, 82–114, 234; *See also* Beast

Antichristology, 10–14, 19, 30, 58, 131, 139, 161

Antioch, school of, 50–53, 64, 66

Antiochus IV, 137

apocalypse as genre, 3

Apocalypse of John, 77, 101, 151, 174, 208, 237, 240, 243, 246–47; Haimo's commentary on, 163–64

Apocalyptic eschatology, 2–6; determinism and free will in, 4; Last World Emperor in, 169, 172–73; "mainline" consensus on, 31, 41, 63–64, 73, 240; and millennialism/millenarianism/chiliasm, 3–4; realist account of, 23–24; spiritual account of, 24; understanding evil through, 4, 6–9, 250

Apocalyptic realism, 23–24, 28–81

Apocalypticism, 2, 4–5, 19–21, 27, 116, 167, 173, 176, 178–79, 242–43; persistence of, 245–50

scholarship, 180, 207; on cooling of charity, 188–90; on *discessio/accessio,* 187–88; as glossator, 181–82, 183, 191, 210; and scholasticism, 179

Last Judgment, 34, 42, 68, 87, 100–102, 105, 107, 119, 142, 151, 153–54, 156, 160, 163, 185, 194, 196, 213–14, 215, 230, 241

Last World Emperor, 127, 169, 172–73

Lawrence, D. H., 9

Lerner, Robert E., 160

Letter on the Origin and Time of Antichrist (Adso). *See* Adso

Little Apocalypse, 12–13, 68, 71, 73, 76, 87, 119, 133, 188, 192

Louis the German, 126, 146

Louis the Pious, 126, 127, 146

Lovejoy, A. O., 15

Lying signs, 46, 61, 105, 203, 220, 235

Madigan, Kevin, xii

Magog, 175–76

Malherbe, Abraham, 11–12

Man of Sin, 7, 9, 12–14, 18, 24, 28, 32, 58, 70, 76, 77, 81, 82, 88–91, 93, 118, 154, 163, 174, 200, 232

Marius Victorinus, 34

Martin of Tours, 34

Martyrs, 158, 188, 233

Matter, E. Ann, xii

Maximus of Turin, 34

McGinn, Bernard, 4, 7–8, 9, 14

Messiah, 41, 134, 155

Millenarianism, 3, 5, 29, 74, 83, 97, 107, 138, 175

Millennialism, 2–3, 5, 12, 16–17, 19, 32, 74, 101, 127, 175, 205, 207, 241, 247, 249–50

Moralia in Job (Gregory the Great). *See* Gregory I, Pope

Mount of Olives, 8, 78, 81, 157, 159, 169, 235

Muretach of Auxerre, 148–49, 153

Mystery of iniquity, 13, 44–46, 49, 60, 71, 77, 79, 90–91, 98, 103–4, 134, 143, 158, 174, 189, 219, 232–34

Nero, 60, 69, 234; as restrainer, 103; as resurrected, 103; as type or member of Antichrist, 7, 24, 45, 49, 77, 142–44, 158, 189–90, 197, 218–19, 233, 245

Nicholas II, Pope, 181

O'Leary, Stephen D., 246

Operation of error, 47–48, 61–62, 162

Origen of Alexandria, 34, 36–37, 66, 75, 83, 123, 128

Otto the Saxon, 171–72

Papacy: apocalyptic role of, 198–200, 202, 204, 206; and Gregorian reform, 193, 208; as Rome, 197, 217

Paul of Tarsus: on Adamology, 14; and Antichrist, 2, 13, 30; as author, 10–11; authority of, 20; and eschatology, 12–13, 14, 48, 94, 239; and Job, 35; as model theologian, 19; on Rome, 104, 134, 144, 152, 163, 217; and scholasticism, 180, 182, 210, 223; spiritual exegesis of, 19–21, 81, 83, 113; Tyconius's use of, 86–87, 94

Pelagius, xx, 24, 28, 64–73, 82, 117–20, 121, 123, 125, 137, 142–44, 161, 237, 240, 241–42; and Ambrosiaster, 38; on Antichrist, 69–71, 73–74, 80; commentary on Pauline epistles, 23, 35, 66; and eschatology, 68; on the ceremonial Law, 70–71; exegetical method, 67, 73;

straining force," 76, 90, 118, 120; translation of, 17, 144, 153, 155, 168, 197

Rufinus, xx

Satan, 6, 7; Antichrist as incarnate, 46; Antichrist as son of, 14, 46, 70, 232; Christian life as struggle with, 53; binding/loosing of, 101; Body of, 87; and mystery of iniquity, 60; and pagan gods, 45; in salvation history, 45, 49; work of, 61, 135, 160, 203; See also Antichrist, Devil, Evil, Mystery of Iniquity

Scheppard, Carol Ann, 121

Scriptures. See Bible

Second Beast. See Beast

Second Coming. See Last Judgment

Second Epistle to the Thessalonians, 2, 10–14; authorship of, 10–11; commentary on, 2, 10, 17, 22–23; as doctrinal locus for Antichrist, 7, 10, 14, 19, 28; eschatology of, 10, 12, 14, 248; and First Thessalonians, 10, 12, 44; and Little Apocalypse, 13; and Pauline eschatology, 13; and tradition, 18, 19, 23–27, 35, 247, 249–50

Sedulius Scotus, 125, 141–44, 165, 166, 243; biblical commentary of, 141–42; exegetical method, 142; humanism of, 142; on the mystery of iniquity, 143; on Nero, 144; and Pelagius, 142–44; on Roman empire, 144; use of other sources, 142

Severus, Sulpicius, 34

Sibylline Oracles, 70, 103

Simon Magus, 161, 220, 235

Smalley, Beryl, 148, 193

Son of Man, 14, 88, 89–90

Son of Perdition, 12–14, 24, 58, 70, 82, 93, 154, 163, 187, 200, 217, 232

Spiritual exegesis, 20–21, 82–114, 250; Tyconian vs. Alexandrian, 85–86, 107–8; See also Allegorical sense of Scripture; biblical commentary; Paul of Tarsus

Stortz, Martha Ellen, 47

Temple: as figure of Body of Antichrist, 90, 102–3; as figure of Church, 59, 77, 89–90, 91, 93, 120, 133, 155, 170, 189, 218, 232; rebuilt by Antichrist, 24, 31, 33, 41, 44, 58, 70, 73, 103, 155, 170, 191, 200, 218, 232

Tertullian, 29, 31–32, 35, 38, 74

Theodore of Mopsuestia, 23, 24, 28, 34, 50–64, 71, 73, 82, 121, 123, 125, 165, 184–85, 187, 189, 190, 202, 211, 212, 229, 237, 240, 241, 242; on Antichrist, 80; career, 51; condemnation, 53–54; Christology, 52, 57; commentary on Pauline epistles, 54–55, 80; eschatology, 53, 63–64, 80; exegetical method, 51, 55–57; on Holy Spirit, 59; in Rabanus Maurus, 129–36; on "restraining force," 59, 61; on theoria, 52–53

Thietland of Einsiedeln, 173–76

Thiota of Fulda, 127–28

Trigg, Joseph W., 39

Tyconius, xx, xxi, 24, 28, 111, 113, 117, 121, 143, 151, 159, 218, 237, 241; on "body of Antichrist," 87, 113; Book of Rules, 84, 85, 89, 118, 120; on Church, 90–91, 107; and Donatist church, 83; eschatology of, 87, 88, 92; exegetical method,

*Constructing Antichrist: Paul, Biblical Commentary, and the Development of
Doctrine in the Early Middle Ages* was designed and composed in Dante with
Trajan display type by Kachergis Book Design of Pittsboro, North Carolina.
It was printed on sixty-pound Natures Natural and bound
by Thomson-Shore, Inc. of Dexter, Michigan.